MAILER IS LOOSE
AND
MAILER IS SWINGING

and his targets, to mention a few, are:

LBJ

JACQUELINE KENNEDY

CONTRACEPTION

MODERN ARCHITECTURE

THE WOMANIZATION OF AMERICA

CENSORSHIP

THE RIGHT WING

THE LEFT WING

THE MIDDLE-OF-THE-ROADERS

VIETNAM

He is in turn indignant, moving, loving, witty, and forever stimulating.

HE IS NORMAN MAILER!

THE IDOL
and the
OCTOPUS

POLITICAL WRITINGS BY
NORMAN MAILER
ON THE KENNEDY AND JOHNSON
ADMINISTRATIONS

A DELL BOOK

Published by
DELL PUBLISHING CO., INC.
750 Third Avenue
New York, N.Y. 10017

Dell ® TM 681510, Dell Publishing Co., Inc.

Manufactured in the United States of America

First Printing—June, 1968

Acknowledgment is made to the following magazines and publishers in whose pages these essays first appeared.

The Dial Press, Inc.: for "Farewell to Vietnam" and "The Argument of an Elector" from CANNIBALS AND CHRISTIANS by Norman Mailer.

Esquire: for "Superman Comes to the Supermarket," "The Fifth Presidential Paper—The Existential Heroine," "The Big Bite—March, 1963," "The Big Bite—April, 1963" and "In the Red Light: A History of the Republican Convention in 1964."

New York Herald Tribune: for "The Leading Man: A Review of *J.F.K.: The Man and the Myth*" and *"My Hope For America: A Review of A Book by Lyndon B. Johnson."*

Partisan Review: for "A Happy Solution To Vietnam," from "A *Partisan Review* Symposium on Vietnam."

Playboy: for "A Debate with William F. Buckley—The Real Meaning of the Right Wing in America."

G. P. Putnam's Sons: for "Presidential Poems" and "On Masturbation and Procreation," reprinted by permission of G. P. Putnam's Sons from THE PRESIDENTIAL PAPERS by Norman Mailer.

The Realist: for "A Speech at Berkeley on Vietnam Day" (originally published as "Norman Mailer on LBJ").

The Village Voice: for "A Vote for Bobby K" and "Lindsay and the City," reprinted with permission of *The Village Voice.*

Contents

Foreword

This book divides itself neatly into three parts: the
first is about the Kennedy administration, the last con-
cerns some of the events of the Johnson administration,
and between the First and Third Parts, which are more
or less formally written, appears a Second Part, a ghost,
an echo, a hint of an approach to what might be a new
political stance. (The author is sufficiently possessed by
titles to dignify this stance with a term—existential
politics.) This Second Part is a miscellany of existential politics, a truncated little handbook, a potpourri
of clippings, editings, and sniffings taken in large part
from the short introductions to his book *The Presidential Papers* and from an interview with Paul Krassner in *The Realist*. The styles are varied, the points
are sometimes all too brief, yet the author, or let us
say, The Compiler, obviously thought the project sufficiently deserving to be done. Put together, these little
pieces in the center add up to a set of superficial position papers, similar in kind to the position papers of
serious political candidates. With one difference.
Feeble, fragmentary, superficial, dated—written in 1962
and 1963, they never refer to China—these position
papers in the Second Part are nonetheless superior to
the position papers of nearly all candidates; for two
reasons: they offer no statistics, they present a few new
ideas. Besides, they are indispensable for our collec-
tion, since they illumine those concepts which live beneath the writings in the First Part and the Third
Part. Of these flanking parts, not too much apology
need be given. The two long pieces on the Democratic
Convention of 1960 and the Republican Convention of
1964 are thought by some to be close to the writer's
best work, and he would not necessarily disagree. Of
course, the piece on Jackie Kennedy was painful to
many when written and is doubtless more painful to-

day. It has a middle section which is needlessly long and close to comic in its intensity, for it sails under a full head of sermon; moreover, the criticism of Mrs. Kennedy's hour on television can now sit only in discomfort with the other memory of that later appearance on the cold Monday of America's tragic funeral.

Still, the piece can hardly not be reprinted. Indeed, it is your writer's duty. For *An Evening with Jackie Kennedy* reflects by the light of its grain what was best and most unique in the Kennedy period—that sense of intimacy with the government which encouraged one to take liberties. Nothing can seem more unhappy in retrospect than a liberty which expires in its own fumbling of taste, and yet . . . and yet . . . what optimism we must all have felt then if we could write in such a way, what secret confidence there must have been in the private good will of one's leaders, in their final good will. Yes, that was a happy period for America—there are times when you may wonder if we will be ever so happy as a nation again.

A note on the title. It was once to be used for *The Deer Park.* The Idol was to represent Charles Francis Eitel, the artist; the Octopus was Herman Teppis, the producer, the man of power. Here I use it to characterize two administrations, The Idol and The Octopus.

N. M.

FIRST PART

Kennedy Administration

Superman Comes to the Supermarket

FOR ONCE let us try to think about a political convention without losing ourselves in housing projects of fact and issue. Politics has its virtues, all too many of them—it would not rank with baseball as a topic of conversation if it did not satisfy a great many things—but one can suspect that its secret appeal is close to nicotine. Smoking cigarettes insulates one from one's life, one does not feel as much, often happily so, and politics quarantines one from history; most of the people who nourish themselves in the political life are in the game not to make history but to be diverted from the history which is being made.

If that Democratic Convention which has now receded behind the brow of the Summer of 1960 is only half-remembered in the excitements of moving toward the election, it may be exactly the time to consider it again, because the mountain of facts which concealed its features last July has been blown away in the winds of High Television, and the man-in-the-street (that peculiar political term which refers to the quixotic voter who will pull the lever for some reason so salient as: "I had a brown-nose lieutenant once with Nixon's looks," or "that Kennedy must have false teeth"), the not so easily estimated man-in-the-street has forgotten most of what happened and could no more tell you who Kennedy was fighting against than you or I could place a bet on who was leading the American League in batting during the month of June.

So to try to talk about what happened is easier now than in the days of the convention, one does not have to put everything in—an act of writing which calls for a bulldozer rather than a pen—one can try to make one's little point and dress it with a ribbon or two of metaphor. All to the good. Because mysteries are irritated by facts, and the 1960 Democratic Convention began as one mystery and ended as another.

Since mystery is an emotion which is repugnant to a political animal (why else lead a life of bad banquet dinners, cigar smoke, camp chairs, foul breath, and excruciatingly dull jargon if not to avoid the echoes of what is not known), the psychic separation between what was happening on the floor, in the caucus rooms, in the headquarters, and what was happening in parallel to the history of the nation was mystery enough to down the proceedings in gloom. It was on the one hand a dull convention, one of the less interesting by general agreement, relieved by local bits of color, given two half hours of excitement by two demonstrations for Stevenson, buoyed up by the class of the Kennedy machine, turned by the surprise of Johnson's nomination as vice-president, but, all the same, dull, depressed in its over-all tone, the big fiestas subdued, the gossip flat, no real air of excitement, just moments—or as they say in bullfighting—details. Yet it was also, one could argue—and one may argue this yet—it was also one of the most important conventions in America's history, it could prove conceivably to be the most important. The man it nominated was unlike any politician who had ever run for President in the history of the land, and if elected he would come to power in a year when America was in danger of drifting into a profound decline.

A Descriptive of the Delegates: Sons and Daughters of the Republic in a Legitimate Panic; Small-time Practitioners of Small-town Political Judo in the Big Town and the Big Time

Depression obviously has its several roots: it is the doubtful protection which comes from not recognizing failure, it is the psychic burden of exhaustion, and it is also, and very often, that discipline of the will or the ego which enables one to continue working when one's unadmitted emotion is panic. And panic it was I think which sat as the largest single sentiment in the breast of the collective delegates as they came to convene in Los Angeles. Delegates are not the noblest sons and daughters of the Republic; a man of taste, arrived from Mars, would take one look at a convention floor and leave forever, convinced he had seen one of the drearier squats of Hell. If one still smells the faint living echo of a carnival wine, the pepper of a bullfight, the rag, drag, and panoply of a jousting tourney, it is all swallowed and regurgitated by the senses into the fouler cud of a death gas one must rid oneself of—a cigar-smoking, stale-aired, slack-jawed, butt-littered, foul, bleak, hard-working, bureaucratic death gas of language and faces ("Yes, those *faces*," says the man from Mars: lawyers, judges, ward heelers, *mafiosos*, Southern goons and grandees, grand old ladies, trade unionists and finks), of pompous words and long pauses which lay like a leaden pain over fever, the fever that one is in, over, or is it that one is just behind history? A legitimate panic for a delegate. America is a nation of experts without roots; we are always creating tacticians who are blind to strategy and strategists who cannot take a step, and when the culture has finished its work the institutions handcuff the infirmity. A delegate is a man who picks a candidate for the largest office in the land, a President who must live with problems whose borders are in ethics, metaphysics, and now ontology; the delegate is prepared for this office of selection by emptying wastebaskets, toting garbage and saying yes at the right time for twenty years in the small political machine of some small or large town; his reward, one of them anyway, is that he arrives at an invitation to the convention. An expert on local catch-as-catch-can, a small-time, often mediocre practitioner of small-town political judo, he comes to the big city with nine-tenths of his mind made up, he will follow the orders of the boss who brought him. Yet of course it is not altogether so mean as that: his opinion is listened to—the boss will consider what he has to say as one interesting factor among five hundred, and what is most important to the delegate, he has the illusion of partial freedom. He can, unless he is severely honest with himself—and if he is, why sweat out the low levels of a political machine?—he can have the illusion that he has helped to choose the candidate, he can even worry most sincerely about his choice, flirt with defection from the boss, work out his own small political gains by the road of loyalty or the way of hard bargain. But even if he is there for no more than the ride, his vote a certainty in the mind of the political boss, able to be thrown here or switched there as the boss decides, still in some peculiar sense he is reality to the boss, the delegate is the great American public, the bar he owns or the law practice, the piece of the union he represents, or the real-estate office, is a part of the political landscape which the boss uses as his own image of how the votes will go, and if the people will like the candidate. And if the boss is depressed by what he sees, if the candidate does not feel right to him, if he has a dull intimation that the candidate is not his sort (as, let us say, Harry Truman was his sort, or Symington might be his sort, or Lyndon Johnson), then vote for him the boss will if he must; he cannot be caught on the wrong side, but he does not feel the pleasure of a personal choice. Which is the center of the panic. Because if the boss is depressed, the delegate is doubly depressed, and the emotional fact is that Kennedy is not in focus, not in the old political focus, he is not comfortable; in fact it is a mystery to the boss how Kennedy got to where he is, not a mystery in its structures; Kennedy is rolling in money, Kennedy got the votes in primaries, and, most of all, Kennedy has a jewel of a political machine. It is as good as a crack Notre Dame team, all discipline and savvy and go-go-go, sound, drilled, never dull, quick as a knife, full of the salt of hipper-dipper, a beautiful machine; the boss could adore it if only a sensible candidate were driving it, a Truman, even a Stevenson, please God a Northern Lyndon Johnson, but it is run by a man who looks young enough to be coach of the Freshman team, and that is not comfortable at all. The boss knows political machines, he knows issues, farm parity, Forand health bill, Landrum-Griffin, but this is not all so adequate after all to revolutionaries in Cuba who look like beatniks, competitions in missiles, Negroes looting whites in the Congo, intricacies of nuclear fallout, and NAACP men one does well to call Sir. It is all out of hand, everything important is off the center, foreign affairs is now the lick of the heat, and senators are candidates instead of governors, a disaster to the old family style of political measure where a political boss knows his governor and knows who his governor knows. So the boss is depressed, profoundly depressed. He comes to this convention resigned to nominating a man he does not understand, or let us say that, so far as he understands the candidate who is to be nominated, he is not happy about the secrets of his appeal, not so far as he divines these secrets; they seem to have too little to do with politics and all too much to do with the private madnesses of the nation which had thousands—or was it hundreds of thousands—of people demonstrating in the long night before Chessman was killed, and a movie star, the greatest, Marlon the Brando out in the night with them. Yes, this candidate for all his record, his good, sound, conventional liberal record has a patina of that other life, the second American life, the long electric night with the fires of neon leading down the highway to the murmur of jazz.

An Apparent Digression: A Vivid View of the
"City of Lost Angels"; The Democrats Defined;
A Pentagon of Traveling Salesmen;
Some Pointed Portraits of the Politicians

   I was seeing Pershing Square, Los Angeles, now for the first time . . . the nervous fruithustlers darting in and out of the shadows, fugitives from Times Square, Market Street SF, the French Quarter—masculine hustlers looking for lonely fruits to *score from, anything from the legendary $20 to a pad at night and breakfast in the morning and whatever you can clinch or clip; and the heat in their holy cop uniforms, holy because of the Almighty Stick and the Almightier Vagrancy Law; the scattered junkies, the small-time pushers, the queens, the sad panhandlers, the lonely, exiled nymphs haunting the entrance to the men's head, the fruits with the hungry eyes and the jingling coins; the tough teen-age chicks—"dittybops"— making it with the lost hustlers . . . all amid the incongruous piped music and the flowers—twin fountains gushing rainbow colored: the world of Lonely America squeezed into Pershing Square, of the Cities of Terrible Night, downtown now trapped in the City of lost Angels . . . and the trees hang over it all like some type of apathetic fate.*

—JOHN RECHY, *Big Table 3*

Seeing Los Angeles after ten years away, one realizes all over again that America is an unhappy contract between the East (that Faustian thrust of a most determined human will which reaches up and out above the eye into the skyscrapers of New York) and those flat lands of compromise and mediocre self-expression, those endless half-pretty repetitive small towns of the Middle and the West, whose spirit is forever horizontal and whose marrow comes to rendezvous in the pastel monotonies of Los Angeles architecture.

So far as America has a history, one can see it in the severe heights of New York City, in the glare from the Pittsburgh mills, by the color in the brick of Louisburg Square, along the knotted greedy façades of the small mansions on Chicago's North Side, in Natchez' antebellum homes, the wrought-iron balconies off Bourbon Street, a captain's house in Nantucket, by the curve of Commercial Street in Provincetown. One can make a list; it is probably finite. What culture we have made and what history has collected to it can be found in those few hard examples of an architecture which came to its artistic term, was born, lived and so collected some history about it. Not all the roots of American life are uprooted, but almost all, and the spirit of the supermarket, that homogenous extension of stainless surfaces and psychoanalyzed people, packaged commodities and ranch homes, interchangeable, geographically unrecognizable, that essence of the new postwar SuperAmerica is found nowhere so perfectly as in Los Angeles' ubiquitous acres. One gets the impression that people come to Los Angeles in order to divorce themselves from the past, here to live or try to live in the rootless pleasure world of an adult child. One knows that if the cities of the world were destroyed by a new war, the architecture of the rebuilding would create a landscape which looked, subject to specifications of climate, exactly and entirely like the San Fernando Valley.

It is not that Los Angeles is altogether hideous, it is even by degrees pleasant, but for an Easterner there is never any salt in the wind; it is like Mexican cooking without chile, or Chinese egg rolls missing their mustard; as one travels through the endless repetitions of that city which is the capital of suburbia with its milky pinks, its washed-out oranges, its tainted lime-yellows of pastel on one pretty little architectural monstrosity after another, the colors not intense enough, the styles never pure, and never sufficiently impure to collide on the eye, one conceives the people who live here—they have come out to express themselves, Los Angeles is the home of self-expression, but the artists are middle-class and middling-minded; no passions will calcify here for years in the gloom to be revealed a decade later as the tessellations of a hard and fertile work, no, it is all open, promiscuous, borrowed, half bought, a city without iron, eschewing wood, a kingdom of stucco, the playground for mass men—one has the feeling it was built by television sets giving orders to men. And in this land of the pretty-pretty, the virility is in the bar-

barisms, the vulgarities, it is in the huge billboards, the screamers of the neon lighting, the shouting farm-utensil colors of the gas stations and the monster drugstores, it is in the swing of the sports cars, hot rods, convertibles, Los Angeles is a city to drive in, the boulevards are wide, the traffic is nervous and fast, the radio stations play bouncing, blooping, rippling tunes, one digs the pop in a pop tune, no one of character would make love by it but the sound is good for swinging a car, electronic guitars and Hawaiian harps.

So this is the town the Democrats came to, and with their unerring instinct (after being with them a week, one thinks of this party as a crazy, half-rich family, loaded with poor cousins, traveling always in caravans with Cadillacs and Okie Fords, Lincolns and quarter-horse mules, putting up every night in tents to hear the chamber quartet of Great Cousin Eleanor invaded by the Texas-twanging steel-stringing geetarists of Bubber Lyndon, carrying its own mean highschool principal, Doc Symington, chided for its manners by good Uncle Adlai, told the route of march by Navigator Jack, cut off every six months from the rich will of Uncle Jim Farley, never listening to the mechanic of the caravan, Bald Sam Rayburn, who assures them they'll all break down unless Cousin Bubber gets the concession on the garage; it's the Snopes family married to Henry James, with the labor unions thrown in like a Yankee dollar, and yet it's true, in tranquility one recollects them with affection, their instinct is good, crazy family good) and this instinct now led the caravan to pick the Biltmore Hotel in downtown Los Angeles for their family get-together and reunion.

The Biltmore is one of the ugliest hotels in the world. Patterned after the flat roofs of an Italian Renaissance palace, it is eighty-eight times as large, and one-millionth as valuable to the continuation of man, and it would be intolerable if it were not for the presence of Pershing Square, that square block of park with cactus and palm trees, the three-hundred-and-sixty five-day-a-year convention of every junkie, pothead, pusher, queen (but you have read that good writing already). For years Pershing Square has been one of the three or four places in America famous to homosexuals, famous not for its posh, the chic is round-heeled here, but because it is one of the avatars of the good old masturbatory sex, dirty with the crusted sugars of smut, dirty rooming houses around the corner where the score is made, dirty book and photograph stores down the street, old-fashioned out-of-the-Thirties burlesque houses, cruising bars, jukeboxes, movie houses; Pershing Square is the town plaza for all those lonely, respectable, small-town homosexuals who lead a family life, make children, and have the Philbrick psychology (How I Joined the Communist Party and Led Three Lives). Yes, it is the open-air convention hall for the small-town inverts who live like spies, and it sits in the center of Los Angeles, facing the Biltmore, that hotel which is a mausoleum, that Pentagon of traveling salesmen the Party chose to house the headquarters of the Convention.

So here came that family, cursed before it began by the thundering absence of Great-Uncle Truman, the delegates dispersed over a run of thirty miles and twenty-seven hotels: the Olympian Motor Hotel, the Ambassador, the Beverley Wilshire, the Santa Ynez Inn (where rumor has it the delegates from Louisiana had some midnight swim), the Mayan, the Commodore, the Mayfair, the Sheraton-West, the Huntington-Sheraton, the Green, the Hayward, the Gates, the Figueroa, the Statler Hilton, the Hollywood Knickerbocker—does one have to be a collector to list such names?—beauties, all with that up-from-the-farm Los Angeles décor, plate-glass windows, patio and terrace, foam-rubber mattress, pastel paints, all of them pretty as an ad in full-page color, all but the Biltmore where everybody gathered every day—the newsmen, the TV, radio, magazine, and foreign newspapermen, the delegates, the politicos, the tourists, the campaign managers, the runners, the flunkies, the cousins and aunts, the wives, the grandfathers, the eight-year-old girls, and the twenty-eight-year-old girls in the Kennedy costumes, red and white and blue, the Symingteeners, the Johnson Ladies, the Stevenson Ladies, everybody —and for three days before the convention and four days into it, everybody collected at the Biltmore, in the lobby, in the grill, in the Biltmore Bowl, in the elevators, along the corridors, three hundred deep always outside the Kennedy suite, milling everywhere, every dark-carpeted grey-brown hall of the hotel, but it was in the Gallery of the Biltmore where one first felt the mood which pervaded all proceedings until the convention was almost over, that heavy, thick, witless depression which was to dominate every move as the delegates wandered and gawked and paraded and set for a spell, there in the Gallery of the Biltmore, that huge depressing alley with its inimitable hotel color, that faded depth of chiaroscuro which unhappily has no depth, that brown which is not a brown, that grey which has no pearl in it, that color which can be described only as hotel-color because the beiges, the tans, the walnuts, the mahoganies, the dull blood rugs, the moaning yellows, the sick greens, the greys and all those dumb browns merge into that lack of color which is an over-large hotel at convention time, with all the small-towners wearing their set, starched faces, that look they get at carnival, all fever and suspicion, and proud to be there, eddying slowly back and forth in that high block-long tunnel of a room with its arched ceiling and square recesses filling every rib of the arch with art work, escutcheons and blazons and other art, pictures I think, I cannot even remember, there was such a hill of cigar smoke the eye had to travel on its way to the ceiling, and at one end there was galvanized-pipe scaffolding and workmen repairing some part of the ceiling, one of them touching up one of the endless squares of painted plaster in the arch, and another worker, passing by, yelled up to the one who was working on the ceiling: "Hey, Michelangelo!"

Later, of course, it began to emerge and there were

portraits one could keep, Symington, dogged at a press conference, declaring with no conviction that he knew he had a good chance to win, the disappointment eating at his good looks so that he came off hard-faced, mean, and yet slack—a desperate dullness came off the best of his intentions. There was Johnson who had compromised too many contradictions and now the contradictions were in his face: when he smiled the corners of his mouth squeezd gloom; when he was pious, his eyes twinkled irony; when he spoke in a righteous tone, he looked corrupt; when he jested, the ham in his jowls looked to quiver. He was not convincing. He was a Southern politician, a Texas Democrat, a liberal Eisenhower; he would do no harm, he would do no good, he would react to the machine, good fellow, nice friend—the Russians would understand him better than his own.

Stevenson had the patina. He came into the room and the room was different, not stronger perhaps (which is why ultimately he did not win), but warmer. One knew why some adored him; he did not look like other people, not with press lights on his flesh; he looked like a lover, the simple truth, he had the sweet happiness of an adolescent who has just been given his first major kiss. And so he glowed, and one was reminded of Chaplin, not because they were the least alike in features, but because Charlie Chaplin was luminous when one met him and Stevenson had something of that light.

There was Eleanor Roosevelt, fine, precise, handworked like ivory. Her voice was almost attractive as she explained in the firm, sad tones of the first lady in this small town why she could not admit Mr. Kennedy, who was no doubt a gentleman, into her political house. One had the impression of a lady who was finally becoming a woman, which is to say that she was just a little bitchy about it all; nice bitchy, charming, it had a touch of art to it, but it made one wonder if she were not now satisfying the last passion of them all, which was to become physically attractive, for she was better-looking than she had ever been as she spurned the possibilities of a young suitor.

Jim Farley. Huge. Cold as a bishop. The hell he would consign you to was cold as ice.

Bobby Kennedy, that archetype Bobby Kennedy, looked like a West Point cadet, or, better, one of those unreconstructed Irishmen from Kirkland House one always used to have to face in the line in Harvard house football games. "Hello," you would say to the ones who looked like him as you lined up for the scrimmage after the kickoff, and his type would nod and look away, one rock glint of recognition your due for living across the hall from one another all through Freshman year, and then bang, as the ball was passed back, you'd get a bony king-hell knee in the crotch. He was the kind of man never to put on the gloves with if you wanted to do some social boxing, because after two minutes it would be a war, and ego-bastards last long in a war.

Carmine DeSapio and Kenneth Galbraith on the same part of the convention floor. DeSapio is bigger than one expects, keen and florid, great big smoked glasses, a suntan like Mantan—he is the kind of heavy-weight Italian who could get by with a name like Romeo—and Galbraith is tall-tall, as actors say, six foot six it could be, terribly thin, enormously atten-tive, exquisitely polite, birdlike, he is sensitive to the stirring of reeds in a wind over the next hill. "Our grey eminence," whispered the intelligent observer next to me.

Bob Wagner, the mayor of New York, a little man, plump, groomed, blank. He had the blank, pomaded, slightly worried look of the first barber in a good barbershop, the kind who would go to the track on his day off and wear a green transparent stone in a gold ring.

And then there was Kennedy, the edge of the mys-tery. But a sketch will no longer suffice.

*Perspective from the Biltmore Balcony: The
Colorful Arrival of the Hero with the Orange-
brown Suntan and Amazingly White Teeth;
Revelation of the Two Rivers Political Theory*

> *... It can be said with a fair amount of certainty
> that the essence of his political attractiveness is his
> extraordinary political intelligence. He has a
> mind quite unlike that of any other Democrat of
> this century. It is not literary, metaphysical and
> moral, as Adlai Stevenson's is. Kennedy is artic-
> ulate and often witty, but he does not seek verbal
> polish. No one can doubt the seriousness of his
> concern with the most serious political matters,
> but one feels that whereas Mr. Stevenson's politi-
> cal views derive from a view of life that holds pol-
> itics to a mere fraction of existence, Senator Ken-
> nedy's primary interest is in politics. The easy way
> in which he disposes of the question of Church
> and State—as if he felt that any reasonable man
> could quite easily resolve any possible conflict of
> loyalties—suggests that the organization of society
> is the one thing that really engages his interest.*
> —RICHARD ROVERE, *The New Yorker*, July 23, 1960

The afternoon he arrived at the convention from the
airport, there was of course a large crowd on the street
outside the Biltmore, and the best way to get a view
was to get up on an outdoor balcony of the Biltmore,
two flights above the street, and look down on the
event. One waited thirty minutes, and then a honking
of horns as wild as the getaway after an Italian wed-
ding sounded around the corner, and the Kennedy cor-
tege came into sight, circled Pershing Square, the men
in the open and leading convertibles sitting backwards
to look at their leader, and finally came to a halt in a
space cleared for them by the police in the crowd. The

television cameras were out, and a Kennedy band was playing some circus music. One saw him immediately. He had the deep orange-brown suntan of a ski instructor, and when he smiled at the crowd his teeth were amazingly white and clearly visible at a distance of fifty yards. For one moment he saluted Pershing Square, and Pershing Square saluted him back, the prince and the beggars of glamour staring at one another across a city street, one of those very special moments in the underground history of the world, and then with a quick move he was out of the car and by choice headed into the crowd instead of the lane cleared for him into the hotel by the police, so that he made his way inside surrounded by a mob, and one expected at any moment to see him lifted to its shoulders like a matador being carried back to the city after a triumph in the plaza. All the while the band kept playing the campaign tunes, sashaying circus music, and one had a moment of clarity, intense as a *déjà vu,* for the scene which had taken place had been glimpsed before in a dozen musical comedies; it was the scene where the hero, the matinee idol, the movie star comes to the palace to claim the princess, or what is the same, and more to our soil, the football hero, the campus king, arrives at the dean's home surrounded by a court of open-singing students to plead with the dean for his daughter's kiss and permission to put on the big musical that night. And suddenly I saw the convention, it came into focus for me, and I understood the mood of depression which had lain over the convention, because finally it was simple: the Democrats were going to nominate a man who, no matter how serious his political dedication might be, was indisputably and willy-nilly going to be seen as a great box-office actor, and the consequences of that were staggering and not at all easy to calculate.

Since the First World War Americans have been leading a double life, and our history has moved on two rivers, one visible, the other underground; there has been the history of politics which is concrete, factual, practical and unbelievably dull if not for the consequences of the actions of some of these men; and there is a subterranean river of untapped, ferocious, lonely and romantic desires, that concentration of ecstasy and violence which is the dream life of the nation.

The twentieth century may yet be seen as that era when civilized man and underprivileged man were melted together into mass man, the iron and steel of the nineteenth century giving way to electronic circuits which communicated their messages into men, the unmistakable tendency of the new century seeming to be the creation of men as interchangeable as commodities, their extremes of personality singed out of existence by the psychic fields of force the communicators would impose. This loss of personality was a catastrophe to the future of the imagination, but billions of people might first benefit from it by having enough to eat—one did not know—and there remained citadels of resistance in Europe where the culture was deep and roots were visible in the architecture of the past.

Nowhere, as in America, however, was this fall from individual man to mass man felt so acutely, for America was at once the first and most prolific creator of mass communications, and the most rootless of countries, since almost no American could lay claim to the line of a family which had not once at least severed its roots by migrating here. But, if rootless, it was then the most vulnerable of countries to its own homogenization. Yet America was also the country in which the dynamic myth of the Renaissance—that every man was potentially extraordinary—knew its most passionate persistence. Simply, America was the land where people still believed in heroes: George Washington; Billy the Kid; Lincoln, Jefferson; Mark Twain, Jack London, Hemingway; Joe Louis, Dempsey, Gentleman Jim; America believed in athletes, rum-runners, aviators; even lovers, by the time Valentino died. It was a country which had grown by the leap of one hero past another—is there a county in all of our ground which does not have its legendary figure? And when the West was filled, the expansion turned inward, became part of an agitated, overexcited, superheated dream life. The film studios threw up their searchlights as the frontier was finally sealed, and the romantic possibilities of the old conquest of land turned into a vertical myth, trapped within the skull, of a new kind of heroic life, each choosing his own archetype of a neo-renaissance man, be it Barrymore, Cagney, Flynn, Bogart, Brando or Sinatra, but it was almost as if there were no peace unless one could fight well, kill well (if always with honor), love well and love many, be cool, be daring, be dashing, be wild, be wily, be resourceful, be a brave gun. And this myth, that each of us was born to be free, to wander, to have adventure and to grow on the waves of the violent, the perfumed, and the unexpected, had a force which could not be tamed no matter how the nation's regulators—politicians, medicos, policemen, professors, priests, rabbis, ministers, *idéologues,* psychoanalysts, builders, executives and endless communicators—would brick-in the modern life with hygiene upon sanity, and middle-brow homily over platitude; the myth would not die. Indeed a quarter of the nation's business must have depended upon its existence. But it stayed alive for more than that— it was as if the message in the labyrinth of the genes would insist that violence was locked with creativity, and adventure was the secret of love.

Once, in the Second World War and in the year or two which followed, the underground river returned to earth, and the life of the nation was intense, of the present, electric; as a lady said, "That was the time when we gave parties which changed people's lives." The Forties was a decade when the speed with which one's own events occurred seemed as rapid as the history of the battlefields, and for the mass of people in America a forced march into a new jungle of emotion was the result. The surprises, the failures, and the dangers of that life must have terrified some nerve of awareness in the power and the mass, for, as if stricken by the orgiastic vistas the myth had carried up from underground, the retreat to a more conservative existence was disorderly, the fear of communism spread like an irrational hail of boils. To anyone who could see, the excessive hysteria of the Red wave was no preparation to face an enemy, but rather a terror of the national self: free-loving, lust-looting, atheistic, implacable—absurdity beyond absurdity to label communism so, for the moral products of Stalinism had been Victorian sex and a ponderous machine of material theology.

Forced underground again, deep beneath all *Reader's Digest* hospital dressings of Mental Health in Your Community, the myth continued to flow, fed by television and the film. The fissure in the national psyche widened to the danger point. The last large appearance of the myth was the vote which tricked the polls and gave Harry Truman his victory in '48. That was the last. Came the Korean War, the shadow of the H-bomb, and we were ready for the General. Uncle Harry gave way to Father, and security, regularity, order, and the life of no imagination were the command of the day. If one had any doubt of this, there was Joe McCarthy with his built-in treason detector, furnished by God, and the damage was done. In the totalitarian wind of those days, anyone who worked in Government formed the habit of being not too original, and many a mind atrophied from disuse and private shame. At the summit there was benevolence without leadership, regularity without vision, security without safety, rhetoric without life. The ship drifted on, that enormous warship of the United States, led by a Secretary of State whose cells were seceding to cancer, and as the world became more fantastic—Africa turning itself upside down, while some new kind of machine man was being made in China—two events occurred which stunned the confidence of America into a new night: the Russians put up their Sputnik, and Civil Rights —that reluctant gift to the American Negro, granted for its effect on foreign affairs—spewed into real life at

Little Rock. The national Ego was in shock: the Russians were now in some ways our technological superiors, and we had an internal problem of subject populations equal conceivably in its difficulty to the Soviet and its satellites. The fatherly calm of the General began to seem like the uxorious mellifluences of the undertaker.

Underneath it all was a larger problem. The life of politics and the life of myth had diverged too far, and the energies of the people one knew everywhere had slowed down. Twenty years ago a post-Depression generation had gone to war and formed a lively, grousing, by times inefficient, carousing, pleasure-seeking, not altogether inadequate army. It did part of what it was supposed to do, and many, out of combat, picked up a kind of private life on the fly, and had their good time despite the yaws of the military system. But today in America the generation which respected the code of the myth was Beat, a horde of half-begotten Christs with scraggly beards, heroes none, saints all, weak before the strong, empty conformisms of the authority. The sanction for finding one's growth was no longer one's flag, one's career, one's sex, one's adventure, not even one's booze. Among the best in this newest of the generations, the myth had found its voice in marijuana, and the joke of the underground was that when the Russians came over they could never dare to occupy us for long because America was too Hip. Gallows humor. The poorer truth might be that America was too Beat, the instinct of the nation so separated from its public mind that apathy, schizophrenia, and private beatitudes might be the pride of the welcoming committee any underground could offer.

Yes, the life of politics and the life of the myth had diverged too far. There was nothing to return them to one another, no common danger, no cause, no desire, and, most essentially, no hero. It was a hero America needed, a hero central to his time, a man whose personality might suggest contradictions and mysteries which could reach into the alienated circuits of the underground, because only a hero can capture the secret imagination of a people, and so be good for the vitality of his nation; a hero embodies the fantasy and so allows each private mind the liberty to consider its fantasy and find a way to grow. Each mind can become more conscious of its desire and waste less strength in hiding from itself. Roosevelt was such a hero, and Churchill, Lenin and De Gaulle; even Hitler, to take the most odious example of this thesis, was a hero, the hero-as-monster, embodying what had become the monstrous fantasy of a people, but the horror upon which the radical mind and liberal temperament foundered was that he gave outlet to the energies of the Germans and so presented the twentieth century with an index of how horrible had become the secret heart of its desire. Roosevelt is of course a happier example of the hero; from his paralytic leg to the royal elegance of his geniality he seemed to contain the country within himself; everyone from the meanest starving cripple to an ambitious young man could expand into the optimism of an improving future because the man offered an unspoken promise of a future which would be rich. The sexual and the sex-starved, the poor, the hardworking and the imaginative well-to-do could see themselves in the President, could believe him to be like themselves. So a large part of the country was able to discover its energies because not as much was wasted in feeling that the country was a poisonous nutrient which stifled the day.

Too simple? No doubt. One tries to construct a simple model. The thesis is after all not so mysterious; it would merely nudge the notion that a hero embodies his time and is not so very much better than his time, but he is larger than life and so is capable of giving direction to the time, able to encourage a nation to discover the deepest colors of its character. At bottom the concept of the hero is antagonistic to impersonal social progress, to the belief that social ills can be solved by social legislating, for it sees a country as all-but-trapped in its character until it has a hero who reveals the character of the country to itself. The implication is that without such a hero the nation turns sluggish. Truman for example was not such a hero, he was not sufficiently larger than life, he inspired familiarity without excitement, he was a character but his proportions came from soap opera: Uncle Harry, full of salty common-sense and small-minded certainty, a storekeeping uncle.

Whereas Eisenhower has been the anti-Hero, the regulator. Nations do not necessarily and inevitably seek for heroes. In periods of dull anxiety, one is more likely to look for security than a dramatic confrontation, and Eisenhower could stand as a hero only for that large number of Americans who were most proud of their lack of imagination. In American life, the unspoken war of the century has taken place between the city and the small town: the city which is dynamic, orgiastic, unsettling, explosive and accelerating to the psyche; the small town which is rooted, narrow, cautious and planted in the life-logic of the family. The need of the city is to accelerate growth; the pride of the small town is to retard it. But since America has been passing through a period of enormous expansion since the war, the double-four years of Dwight Eisenhower could not retard the expansion, it could only denude it of color, character, and the development of novelty. The small-town mind is rooted—it is rooted in the small town—and when it attempts to direct history the results are disastrously colorless because the instrument of world power which is used by the small-town mind is the committee. Comittees do not create, they merely proliferate, and the incredible dullness wreaked upon the American landscape in Eisenhower's eight years has been the triumph of the corporation. A tasteless, sexless, odorless sanctity in architecture, manners, modes, styles has been the result. Eisenhower embodied half the needs of the nation, the needs of the timid, the petrified, the sanctimonious, and the sluggish. What was even worse, he did not divide the nation as a hero might (with a dramatic dialogue as the result); he merely excluded one part of the nation from the other. The result was an alienation of the best minds and bravest impulses from the faltering history which was made. America's need in those years was to take an existential turn, to walk into the nightmare, to face into that terrible logic of history which demanded that the country and its people must become more extraordinary and more adventurous, or else perish, since the only alternative was to offer a false security in the power and the panacea of organized religion, family, and the FBI, a totalitarianization of the psyche by the stultifying techniques of the mass media which would seep into everyone's most private associations and so leave the country powerless against the Russians even if the denouement were to take fifty years, for in a competition between totalitarianisms the first maxim of the prizefight manager would doubtless apply: "Hungry fighters win fights."

The Hipster as Presidential Candidate: Thoughts on a Public Man's Eighteenth-Century Wife; Face-to-Face with the Hero; Significance of a Personal Note, or the Meaning of His Having Read an Author's Novel

Some part of these thoughts must have been in one's mind at the moment there was that first glimpse of Kennedy entering the Biltmore Hotel; and in the days which followed, the first mystery—the profound air of depression which hung over the convention—gave way to a second mystery which can be answered only by history. The depression of the delegates was understandable: no one had too much doubt that Kennedy would be nominated, but if elected he would be not only the youngest President ever to be chosen by voters, he would be the most conventionally attractive young man ever to sit in the White House, and his wife— some would claim it—might be the most beautiful first lady in our history. Of necessity the myth would emerge once more, because America's politics would now be also America's favorite movie, America's first soap opera, America's best-seller. One thinks of the talents of writers like Taylor Caldwell or Frank Yerby, or is it rather *The Fountainhead* which would contain such a fleshing of the romantic prescription? Or is it indeed one's own work which is called into question? "Well, there's your first hipster," says a writer one knows at the convention, "Sergius O'Shaugnessy born rich," and the temptation is to nod, for it could be true, a war hero, and the heroism is bona-fide, even exceptional, a man who has lived with death, who, crippled in the back, took on an operation which would kill him or restore him to power, who chose to marry a lady whose face might be too imaginative for the taste of a democracy which likes its first ladies to be executives of home-management, a man who courts political suicide by choosing to go all out for a nomination four, eight, or twelve years before his political elders think he is ready, a man who announces a week prior to the convention that the young are better fitted to direct history than the old. Yes, it captures the attention. This is no routine candidate calling every shot by safety's routine book ("Yes," Nixon said, naturally but terribly tired an hour after his nomination, the TV cameras and lights and microphones bringing out a sweat of fatigue on his face, the words coming very slowly from the tired brain, somber, modest, sober, slow, slow enough so that one could touch emphatically the cautions behind each word, "Yes, I want to say," said Nixon, "that whatever abilities I have, I got from my mother." A tired pause . . . dull moment of warning, ". . . and my father." The connection now made, the rest comes easy, ". . . and my school and my church." Such men are capable of anything).

One had the opportunity to study Kennedy a bit in the days that followed. His style in the press conferences was interesting. Not terribly popular with the reporters (too much a contemporary, and yet too difficult to understand, he received nothing like the rounds of applause given to Eleanor Roosevelt, Stevenson, Humphrey, or even Johnson), he carried himself nonetheless with a cool grace which seemed indifferent to applause, his manner somehow similar to the poise of a fine boxer, quick with his hands, neat in his timing, and two feet away from his corner when the bell ended the round. There was a good lithe wit to his responses, a dry Harvard wit, a keen sense of proportion in disposing of difficult questions—invariably he gave enough of an answer to be formally satisfactory without ever opening himself to a new question which might go further than the first. Asked by a reporter, "Are you for Adlai as vice-president?" the grin came forth and the voice turned very dry, "No, I cannot say we have considered *Adlai* as a vice-president." Yet there was an elusive detachment to everything he did. One did not have the feeling of a man present in the room with all his weight and all his mind. Johnson gave you all of himself, he was a political animal, he breathed like an animal, sweated like one, you knew his mind was entirely absorbed with the compendium of political fact and maneuver; Kennedy seemed at times like a young professor whose manner was adequate for the classroom, but whose mind was off in some intricacy of the Ph.D. thesis he was writing. Perhaps one can give a sense of the discrepancy by saying that he was like an actor who had been cast as the candidate, a good actor, but not a great one—you were aware all the time that the role was one thing and the man another—they did not coincide, the actor seemed a touch too aloof (as, let us say, Gregory Peck is usually too aloof) to become the part. Yet one had little sense of whether to value this elusiveness, or to beware of it. One could be witnessing the fortitude of a superior sensitivity or the detachment of a man who was not quite real to himself. And his voice gave no clue. When Johnson spoke, one could separate what was fraudulent from what was felt, he would have been satisfying as an actor the way Broderick Crawford or Paul Douglas are satisfying; one saw into his emotions, or at least had the illusion that one did. Kennedy's voice, however, was only a fair voice, too reedy, near to strident, it had the metallic snap of a cricket in it somewhere, it was more impersonal than the man, and so became the least-impressive quality in a face, a body, a selection of language, and a style of movement which made up a better-than-decent presentation, better than one had expected.

With all of that, it would not do to pass over the quality in Kennedy which is most difficult to describe. And in fact some touches should be added to this hint of a portrait, for later (after the convention), one had a short session alone with him, and the next day, another. As one had suspected in advance the interviews were not altogether satisfactory, they hardly could have been. A man running for President is altogether different from a man elected President: the hazards of the campaign make it impossible for a candidate to be as interesting as he might like to be (assuming he has such a desire). One kept advancing the argument that this campaign would be a contest of personalities, and Kennedy kept returning the discussion to politics. After a while one recognized this was an inevitable caution for him. So there would be not too much point to reconstructing the dialogue since Kennedy is hardly inarticulate about his political attitudes and there will be a library vault of text devoted to it in the newspapers. What struck me most about the interview was a passing remark whose importance was invisible on the scale of politics, but was altogether meaningful to my particular competence. As we sat down for the first time, Kennedy smiled nicely and said that he had read my books. One muttered one's pleasure. "Yes," he said, "I've read . . ." and then there was a short pause which did not last long enough to be embarrassing in which it was yet obvious no title came instantly to his mind, an omission one was not ready to mind altogether since a man in such a position must be obliged to carry a hundred thousand facts and names in his head, but the hesitation lasted no longer than three seconds or four, and then he said, "I've read *The Deer Park* and . . . the others," which startled me for it was the first time in a hundred similar situations, talking to someone whose knowledge of my work was casual, that the sentence did not come out, "I've read *The Naked and the Dead* . . . and the others." If one is to take the worst and assume that Kennedy was briefed for this interview (which is most doubtful), it still speaks well for the striking instincts of his advisers.

What was retained later is an impression of Kennedy's manners which were excellent, even artful, better than the formal good manners of Choate and Harvard, almost as if what was creative in the man had been given to the manners. In a room with one or two people, his voice improved, became low-pitched, even pleasant—it seemed obvious that in all these years he had never become a natural public speaker and so his voice was constricted in public, the symptom of all orators who are ambitious, throttled, and determined.

His personal quality had a subtle, not quite describable intensity, a suggestion of dry pent heat perhaps, his eyes large, the pupils grey, the whites prominent, almost shocking, his most forceful feature: he had the eyes of a mountaineer. His appearance changed with his mood, strikingly so, and this made him always more interesting than what he was saying. He would seem at one moment older than his age, forty-eight or fifty, a tall, slim, sunburned professor with a pleasant weathered face, not even particularly handsome; five minutes later, talking to a press conference on his lawn, three microphones before him, a television camera turning, his appearance would have gone through a metamorphosis, he would look again like a movie star, his coloring vivid, his manner rich, his gestures strong and quick, alive with that concentration of vitality a successful actor always seems to radiate. Kennedy had a dozen faces. Although they were not at all similar as people, the quality was reminiscent of someone like Brando whose expression rarely changes, but whose appearance seems to shift from one person into another as the minutes go by, and one bothers with this comparison because, like Brando, Kennedy's most characteristic quality is the remote and private air of a man who has traversed some lonely terrain of experience, of loss and gain, of nearness to death, which leaves him isolated from the mass of others.

> The next day while they waited in vain for rescuers, the wrecked half of the boat turned over in the water and they saw that it would soon sink. The group decided to swim to a small island three miles away. There were other islands bigger and nearer, but the Navy officers knew that they were occupied by the Japanese. On one island, only one mile to the south, they could see a Japanese camp. McMahon, the engineer whose legs were disabled by burns, was unable to swim. Despite his own painfully crippled back, Kennedy swam the three miles with a breast stroke, towing behind him by a life-belt strap that he held between his teeth the helpless McMahon . . . it took Kennedy and the suffering engineer five hours to reach the island.

The quotation is from a book which has for its dedicated unilateral title, *The Remarkable Kennedys,* but the prose is by one of the best of the war reporters, the former *Yank* editor, Joe McCarthy, and so presumably may be trusted in such details as this. Physical bravery does not of course guarantee a man's abilities in the White House—all too often men with physical courage are disappointing in their moral imagination—but the heroism here is remarkable for its tenacity. The above is merely one episode in a continuing saga which went on for five days in and out of the water, and left Kennedy at one point "miraculously saved from drowning (in a storm) by a group of Solomon Island natives who suddenly came up beside him in a large dugout canoe." Afterward, his back still injured (that precise back injury which was to put him on crutches eleven years later, and have him search for "spinal-fusion surgery" despite a warning that his chances of living through the operation were "extremely limited") afterward, he asked to go back on duty and became so bold in the attacks he made with his PT boat "that the crew didn't like to go out with him because he took so many chances."

It is the wisdom of a man who senses death within him and gambles that he can cure it by risking his life. It is the therapy of the instinct, and who is so wise as to call it irrational? Before he went into the Navy, Kennedy had been ailing. Washed out of Freshman year at Princeton by a prolonged trough of yellow jaundice, sick for a year at Harvard, weak already in the back from an injury at football, his trials suggest the self-hatred of a man whose resentment and ambition are too large for his body. Not everyone can discharge their furies on an analyst's couch, for some angers can be relaxed only by winning power, some rages are sufficiently monumental to demand that one try to become a hero or else fall back into that death which is already within the cells. But if one succeeds, the energy aroused can be exceptional. Talking to a man who had been with Kennedy in Hyannis Port the week before the convention, I heard that he was in a state of deep fatigue.

"Well, he didn't look tired at the convention," one commented.

"Oh, he had three days of rest. Three days of rest for him is like six months for us."

One thinks of that three-mile swim with the belt in his mouth and McMahon holding it behind him. There are pestilences which sit in the mouth and rot the teeth —in those five hours how much of the psyche must have been remade, for to give vent to the bite in one's jaws and yet use that rage to save a life: it is not so very many men who have the apocalyptic sense that heroism is the First Doctor.

If one had a profound criticism of Kennedy it was that his public mind was too conventional, but that seemed to matter less than the fact of such a man in

office because the law of political life had become so
dreary that only a conventional mind could win an
election. Indeed there could be no politics which gave
warmth to one's body until the country had recovered
its imagination, its pioneer lust for the unexpected
and incalculable. It was the changes that might come
afterward on which one could put one's hope. With
such a man in office the myth of the nation would
again be engaged, and the fact that he was Catholic
would shiver a first existential vibration of consciousness into the mind of the White Protestant. For the
first time in our history, the Protestant would have the
pain and creative luxury of feeling himself in some
tiny degree part of a minority, and that was an experience which might be incommensurable in its value to
the best of them.

A Vignette of Adlai Stevenson; The Speeches:
What Happened When the Teleprompter
Jammed: How U. S. Senator Eugene McCarthy
Played the Matador. An Observation
on the Name Fitzgerald

As yet we have said hardly a word about Stevenson.
And his actions must remain a puzzle unless one dares
a speculation about his motive, or was it his need?

So far as the people at the convention had affection
for anyone, it was Stevenson, so far as they were able
to generate any spontaneous enthusiasm, their cheers
were again for Stevenson. Yet it was obvious he never
had much chance because so soon as a chance would
present itself he seemed quick to dissipate the opportunity. The day before the nominations, he entered the
Sports Arena to take his seat as a delegate—the demonstration was spontaneous, noisy and prolonged; it was
quieted only by Governor Collins' invitation for
Stevenson to speak to the delegates. In obedience perhaps to the scruple that a candidate must not appear
before the convention until nominations are done,

Stevenson said no more than: "I am grateful for this tumultuous and moving welcome. After getting in and out of the Biltmore Hotel and this hall, I have decided I know whom you are going to nominate. It will be the last survivor." This dry reminder of the ruthlessness of politics broke the roar of excitement for his presence. The applause as he left the platform was like the dying fall-and-moan of a baseball crowd when a home run curves foul. The next day, a New York columnist talking about it said bitterly, "If he'd only gone through the motions, if he had just said that now he wanted to run, that he would work hard, and he hoped the delegates would vote for him. Instead he made that lame joke." One wonders. It seems almost as if he did not wish to win unless victory came despite himself, and then was overwhelming. There are men who are not heroes because they are too good for their time, and it is natural that defeats leave them bitter, tired, and doubtful of their right to make new history. If Stevenson had campaigned for a year before the convention, it is possible that he could have stopped Kennedy. At the least, the convention would have been enormously more exciting, and the nominations might have gone through half-a-dozen ballots before a winner was hammered into shape. But then Stevenson might also have shortened his life. One had the impression of a tired man who (for a politician) was sickened unduly by compromise. A year of maneuvering, broken promises, and detestable partners might have gutted him for the election campaign. If elected, it might have ruined him as a President. There is the possibility that he sensed his situation exactly this way, and knew that if he were to run for president, win and make a good one, he would first have to be restored, as one can indeed be restored, by an exceptional demonstration of love—love, in this case, meaning that the Party had a profound desire to keep him as their leader. The emotional truth of a last-minute victory for Stevenson over the Kennedy machine might have given him new energy; it would certainly have given him new faith in a country and a party whose good motives he was possibly beginning to doubt. Perhaps the fault he saw with his candidacy was that he attracted only the nicest people to himself and there were not enough of them. (One of the private amusements of the convention was to divine some of the qualities of the candidates by the style of the young women who put on hats and clothing and politicked in the colors of one presidential gent or another. Of course, half of them must have been hired models, but someone did the hiring and so it was fair to look for a common denominator. The Johnson girls tended to be plump, pie-faced, dumb sexy Southern; the Symingteeners seemed a touch mulish, stubborn, good-looking pluggers; the Kennedy ladies were the handsomest; healthy, attractive, tough, a little spoiled—they looked like the kind of girls who had gotten all the dances in high school and/or worked for a year as an airline hostess before marrying well. But the Stevenson girls looked to be doing it for no money; they were good sorts, slightly horsy-faced, one had the impression they played field hockey in college.) It was indeed the pure, the saintly, the clean-living, the pacifistic, the vegetarian who seemed most for Stevenson, and the less humorous in the Kennedy camp were heard to remark bitterly that Stevenson had nothing going for him but a bunch of Goddamn Beatniks. This might even have had its sour truth. The demonstrations outside the Sports Arena for Stevenson seemed to have more than a fair proportion of tall, emaciated young men with thin, wry beards and three-string guitars accompanied (again in undue proportion) by a contingent of ascetic, face-washed young Beat ladies in sweaters and dungarees. Not to mention all the Holden Caulfields one could see from here to the horizon. But of course it is unfair to limit it so, for the Democratic gentry were also committed half en masse for Stevenson, as well as a considerable number of movie stars, Shelley Winters for one: after the convention she remarked sweetly, "Tell me something nice about Kennedy so I can get excited about him."

What was properly astonishing was the way this horde of political half-breeds and amateurs came within distance of turning the convention from its preconceived purpose, and managed at the least to bring the only hour of thorough-going excitement the convention could offer.

But then nominating day was the best day of the week and enough happened to suggest that a convention out of control would be a spectacle as extraordinary in the American scale of spectator values as a close seventh game in the World Series or a tied fourth quarter in a professional-football championship. A political convention is after all not a meeting of a corporation's board of directors; it is a fiesta, a carnival, a pig-rooting, horse-snorting, band-playing, voice-screaming medieval get-together of greed, practical lust, compromised idealism, career-advancement, meeting, feud, vendetta, conciliation, of rabble-rousers, fist fights (as it used to be), embraces, drunks (again as it used to be) and collective rivers of animal sweat. It is a reminder that no matter how the country might pretend it has grown up and become tidy in its manners, bodiless in its legislative language, hygienic in its separation of high politics from private life, that the roots still come grubby from the soil, and that politics in America is still different from politics anywhere else because the politics has arisen out of the immediate needs, ambitions, and cupidities of the people, that our politics still smell of the bedroom and the kitchen, rather than having descended to us from the chill punctilio of aristocratic negotiation.

So. The Sports Arena was new, too pretty of course, tasteless in its design—it was somehow pleasing that the acoustics were so bad for one did not wish the architects well; there had been so little imagination in their design, and this arena would have none of the harsh grandeur of Madison Square Garden when it was aged by spectators' phlegm and feet over the next twenty years. Still it had some atmosphere; seen from the streets, with the spectators moving to the ticket gates, the bands playing, the green hot-shot special editions of the Los Angeles newspapers being hawked by the newsboys, there was a touch of the air of promise that precedes a bullfight, not something so good as the approach to the Plaza Mexico, but good, let us say, like the entrance into El Toreo of Mexico City, another architectural monstrosity, also with seats painted, as I remember, in rose-pink, and dark, milky sky-blue.

Inside, it was also different this nominating day. On Monday and Tuesday the air had been desultory, no one listened to the speakers, and everybody milled from one easy chatting conversation to another—it had been like a tepid Kaffeeklatsch for fifteen thousand people. But today there was a whip of anticipation in the air, the seats on the floor were filled, the press section was working, and in the gallery people were sitting in the aisles.

Sam Rayburn had just finished nominating Johnson as one came in, and the rebel yells went up, delegates started filing out of their seats and climbing over seats, and a pullulating dance of bodies and bands began to snake through the aisles, the posters jogging and whirling in time to the music. The dun color of the floor (faces, suits, seats and floor boards), so monotonous the first two days, now lit up with life as if an iridescent caterpillar had emerged from a fold of wet leaves. It was more vivid than one had expected, it was right, it felt finally like a convention, and from up close when one got down to the floor (where your presence was illegal and so consummated by sneaking in one time as demonstrators were going out, and again by slipping a five-dollar bill to a guard) the nearness to the demonstrators took on high color, that electric vividness one feels on the side lines of a football game when it is necessary to duck back as the ballcarrier goes by, his face tortured in the concentration of the moment, the thwomp of his tackle as acute as if one had been hit oneself.

That was the way the demonstrators looked on the floor. Nearly all had the rapt, private looks of a passion or a tension which would finally be worked off by one's limbs, three hundred football players, everything from seedy delegates with jowl-sweating shivers to livid models, paid for their work that day, but stomping out their beat on the floor with the hypnotic adulatory grimaces of ladies who had lived for Lyndon these last ten years.

Then from the funereal rostrum, whose color was not so rich as mahogany nor so dead as a cigar, came the last of the requests for the delegates to take their seats. The seconding speeches began, one minute each; they ran for three and four, the minor-league speakers running on the longest as if the electric antenna of television was the lure of the Sirens, leading them out. Bored cheers applauded their concluding Götterdämmerungen and the nominations were open again. A favorite son, a modest demonstration, five seconding speeches, tedium.

Next was Kennedy's occasion. Governor Freeman of Minnesota made the speech. On the second or third sentence his television prompter jammed, an accident. Few could be aware of it at the moment; the speech seemed merely flat and surprisingly void of bravura. He was obviously no giant of extempore. Then the demonstration. Well-run, bigger than Johnson's, jazzier, the caliber of the costumes and decorations better chosen: the placards were broad enough, "Let's Back Jack," the floats were garish, particularly a papier-mâché or plastic balloon of Kennedy's head, six feet in diameter, which had nonetheless the slightly shrunken, over-red, rubbery look of a toy for practical jokers in one of those sleazy off–Times Square magic-and-gimmick stores; the band was suitably corny; and yet one had the impression this demonstration had been designed by some hands-to-hip interior decorator who said, "Oh, joy, let's have fun, let's make this *true* beer hall."

Besides, the personnel had something of the Kennedy *élan*, those paper hats designed to look like straw boaters with Kennedy's face on the crown, and small photographs of him on the ribbon, those hats which had come to symbolize the crack speed of the Kennedy team, that Madison Avenue cachet which one finds in bars like P. J. Clarke's, the elegance always giving its subtle echo of the Twenties so that the raccoon coats seem more numerous than their real count, and the colored waistcoats are measured by the charm they would have drawn from Scott Fitzgerald's eye. But there, it occurred to one for the first time that Kennedy's middle name was just that, Fitzgerald; and the tone of his crack lieutenants, the unstated style, was true to Scott. The legend of Fitzgerald had an army at last, formed around the self-image in the mind of every superior Madison Avenue opportunist that he was hard, he was young, he was In, his conversation was lean as wit, and if the work was not always scrupulous, well the style could aspire. If there came a good day . . . he could meet the occasion.

The Kennedy snake dance ran its thirty lively minutes, cheered its seconding speeches, and sat back. They were so sure of winning, there had been so many victories before this one, and this one had been scouted and managed so well, that hysteria could hardly be the mood. Besides, everyone was waiting for the Stevenson barrage which should be at least diverting. But now came a long tedium. Favorite sons were nominated, fat mayors shook their hips, seconders told the word to constituents back in Ponderwaygot County, treacly demonstrations tried to hold the floor, and the afternoon went by; Symington's hour came and went, a good demonstration, good as Johnson's (for good cause —they had pooled their demonstrators). More favorite sons, Governor Docking of Kansas declared "a genius" by one of his lady speakers in a tense go-back-to-religion voice. The hours went by, two, three, four hours, it seemed forever before they would get to Stevenson. It was evening when Senator Eugene McCarthy of Minnesota got up to nominate him.

The gallery was ready, the floor was responsive, the demonstrators were milling like bulls in their pen wait-

ing for the *toril* to fly open—it would have been hard
not to wake the crowd up, not to make a good speech.
McCarthy made a great one. Great it was by the measure of convention oratory, and he held the crowd like
a matador, timing their *oles!*, building them up, easing
them back, correcting any sag in attention, gathering
their emotion, discharging it, creating new emotion on
the wave of the last, driving his passes tighter and
tighter as he readied for the kill. "Do not reject this
man who made us all proud to be called Democrats,
do not leave this prophet without honor in his own
party." One had not heard a speech like this since
1948 when Vito Marcantonio's voice, his harsh, shrill,
bitter, street urchin's voice screeched through the loud-
speakers at Yankee Stadium and lashed seventy thousand people into an uproar.

"There was only one man who said let's talk sense
to the American people," McCarthy went on, his
muleta furled for the *naturales*. "There was only one
man who said let's talk sense to the American people,"
he repeated. "He said the promise of America is the
promise of greatness. This was his call to greatness. . . .
Do not forget this man. . . . Ladies and Gentlemen, I
present to you not the favorite son of one state, but the
favorite son of the fifty states, the favorite son of every
country he has visited, the favorite son of every country which has not seen him but is secretly thrilled by
his name." Bedlam. The kill. "Ladies and Gentlemen,
I present to you Adlai Stevenson of Illinois." Ears and
tail. Hooves and bull. A roar went up like the roar
one heard the day Bobby Thomson hit his home run
at the Polo Grounds and the Giants won the pennant
from the Dodgers in the third playoff game of the 1951
season. The demonstration cascaded onto the floor, the
gallery came to its feet, the Sports Arena sounded like
the inside of a marching drum. A tidal pulse of hysteria, exaltation, defiance, exhilaration, anger and
roaring desire flooded over the floor. The cry which
had gone up on McCarthy's last sentence had not
paused for breath in five minutes, and troop after

troop of demonstrators jammed the floor (the Stevenson people to be scolded the next day for having collected floor passes and sent them out to bring in new demonstrators) and still the sound mounted. One felt the convention coming apart. There was a Kennedy girl in the seat in front of me, the Kennedy hat on her head, a dimpled healthy brunette; she had sat silently through McCarthy's speech, but now, like a woman paying her respects to the power of natural thrust, she took off her hat and began to clap herself. I saw a writer I knew in the next aisle; he had spent a year studying the Kennedy machine in order to write a book on how a nomination is won. If Stevenson stampeded the convention, his work was lost. Like a reporter at a mine cave-in I inquired the present view of the widow. "Who can think," was the answer, half frantic, half elated, "just watch it, that's all." I found a cool one, a New York reporter, who smiled in rueful respect. "It's the biggest demonstration I've seen since Wendell Wilkie's in 1940," he said, and added, "God, if Stevenson takes it, I can wire my wife and move the family on to Hawaii."

"I don't get it."

"Well, every story I wrote said it was locked up for Kennedy."

Still it went on, twenty minutes, thirty minutes, the chairman could hardly be heard, the demonstrators refused to leave. The lights were turned out, giving a sudden theatrical shift to the sense of a crowded church at midnight, and a new roar went up, louder, more passionate than anything heard before. It was the voice, it was the passion, if one insisted to call it that, of everything in America which was defeated, idealistic, innocent, alienated, outside and Beat, it was the potential voice of a new third of the nation whose psyche was ill from cultural malnutrition, it was powerful, it was extraordinary, it was larger than the decent, humorous, finicky, half-noble man who had called it forth, it was a cry from the Thirties when Time was simple, it was a resentment of the slick technique, the oiled gears, and the superior generals of Fitzgerald's Army; but it was also—and for this reason one could not admire it altogether, except with one's excitement —it was also the plea of the bewildered who hunger for simplicity again, it was the adolescent counterpart of the boss's depression before the unpredictable dynamic of Kennedy as President, it was the return to the sentimental dream of Roosevelt rather than the approaching nightmare of history's oncoming night, and it was inspired by a terror of the future as much as a revulsion of the present.

Fitz's Army held; after the demonstration was finally down, the convention languished for ninety minutes while Meyner and others were nominated, a fatal lapse of time because Stevenson had perhaps a chance to stop Kennedy if the voting had begun on the echo of the last cry for him, but in an hour and a half depression crept in again and emotions spent, the delegates who had wavered were rounded into line. When the vote was taken, Stevenson had made no gains. The brunette who had taken off her hat was wearing it again, and she clapped and squealed when Wyoming delivered the duke and Kennedy was in. The air was sheepish, like the mood of a suburban couple who forgive each other for cutting in and out of somebody else's automobile while the country club dance is on. Again, tonight, no miracle would occur. In the morning the papers would be moderate in their description of Stevenson's last charge.

*A Sketch of the Republicans Gathered
in Convention: The Choice Between the
Venturesome and the Safe; What May
Happen at Three O'clock in the Morning
on a Long Dark Night*

One did not go to the other convention. It was seen on television, and so too much cannot be said of that. It did however confirm one's earlier bias that the Republican Party was still a party of church ushers, undertakers, choirboys, prison warden, bank presidents, small-town police chiefs, state troopers, psychiatrists, beauty-parlor operators, corporation executives, Boy-Scout leaders, fraternity presidents, taxboard assessors, community leaders, surgeons, Pullman porters, head nurses and the fat sons of rich fathers. Its candidate would be given the manufactured image of an ordinary man, and his campaign, so far as it was a psychological campaign (and this would be far indeed), would present him as a simple, honest, dependable, hard-working, ready-to-learn, modest, humble, decent, sober young man whose greatest qualification for president was his profound abasement before the glories of the Republic, the stability of the mediocre, and his own unworthiness. The apocalyptic hour of Uriah Heep.

It would then be a campaign unlike the ones which had preceded it. Counting by the full spectrum of complete Right to absolute Left, the political differences would be minor, but what would be not at all minor was the power of each man to radiate his appeal into some fundamental depths of the American character. One would have an inkling at last if the desire of America was for drama or stability, for adventure or monotony. And this, this appeal to the psychic direction America would now choose for itself was the element most promising about this election, for it gave the possibility that the country might be able finally to rise above the deadening verbiage of its issues, its politics, its jargon, and live again by an image of itself. For in some part of themselves the people might know (since these candidates were not old enough to be revered) that they had chosen one young man for his mystery, for his promise that the country would grow or disintegrate by the unwilling charge he gave to the intensity of the myth, or had chosen another young man for his unstated oath that he would do all in his power to keep the myth buried and so convert the remains of Renaissance man as rapidly as possible into mass man.

One might expect them to choose the enigma in preference to the deadening certainty. Yet one must doubt America's bravery. This lurching, unhappy, pompous and most corrupt nation—could it have the courage finally to take on a new image for itself, was it brave enough to put into office not only one of its ablest men, its most efficient, its most conquistadorial (for Kennedy's capture of the Democratic Party deserves the word), but also one of its more mysterious men (the national psyche must shiver in its sleep at the image of Mickey Mantle-cum-Lindbergh in office, and a First Lady with an eighteenth-century face). Yes, America was at last engaging the fate of its myth, its consciousness about to be accelerated or cruelly depressed in its choice between two young men in their forties who, no matter how close, dull, or indifferent their stated politics might be, were radical poles apart, for one was sober, the apotheosis of opportunistic lead, all radium spent, the other handsome as a prince in the unstated aristocracy of the American dream. So, finally, would come a choice which history had never presented to a nation before—one could vote for glamour or for ugliness, a staggering and most stunning choice—would the nation be brave enough to enlist the romantic dream of itself, would it vote for the image in the mirror of its unconscious, were the people indeed brave enough to hope for an acceleration of Time, for that new life of drama which would come from choosing a son to lead them who was heir apparent to the psychic loins? One could pause: it might be more difficult to be a President than it ever had before. Nothing less than greatness would do.

Yet if the nation voted to improve its face, what an impetus might come to the arts, to the practices, to the lives and to the imagination of the American. If the nation so voted. But one knew the unadmitted specter in the minds of the Democratic delegates: that America would go to sleep on election eve with the polls promising Kennedy a victory on the day to come, yet in its sleep some millions of Democrats and Independents would suffer a nightmare before the mystery of uncharted possibilities their man would suggest, and in a terror of all the creativities (and some violences) that mass man might now have to dare again, the undetermined would go out in the morning to vote for the psychic security of Nixon the way a middle-aged man past adventure holds to the stale bread of his marriage. Yes, this election might be fearful enough to betray the polls and no one in America could plan the new direction until the last vote was counted by the last heeler in the last ambivalent ward, no one indeed could know until then what had happened the night before, what had happened at three o'clock in the morning on that long dark night of America's search for a security cheaper than her soul.

Postscript

This piece had more effect than any other single work of mine, and I think this is due as much to its meretriciousness as to its merits. I was forcing a reality, I was bending reality like a field of space to curve the time I wished to create. I was not writing with the hope that perchance I could find reality by being sufficiently honest to perceive it, but on the contrary was distorting reality in the hope that thereby I could affect it. I was engaging in an act of propaganda.

During the period after Kennedy was nominated, there was great indifference to him among the Democrats I knew; disaffection was general; outright aversion was felt by most of the liberal Left—the white collar SANE sort of professional who had been for Stevenson. The Kennedy machine worked well to overcome apathy and inertia; so did the debates with Nixon. Through the early Fall, before the election, people who had been going along with the Democratic Party for years began somewhat resignedly to accept their fate: they would go out after all and vote for John F. Kennedy. But there was no real enthusiasm, no drive. My piece came at the right time for him—three weeks before the election. It added the one ingredient Kennedy had not been able to find for the stew—it made him seem exciting, it made the election appear important. Around New York there was a turn in sentiment; one could feel it; Kennedy now had glamour.

As will be seen in the essay on Jackie Kennedy, I took to myself some of the critical credit for his victory. Whether I was right or wrong in fact may not be so important as its psychological reality in my own mind. I had invaded no-man's-land, I had created an archetype of Jack Kennedy in the public mind which might or might not be true, but which would induce people to vote for him, and so would tend to move him into the direction I had created. Naturally there would be forces thrusting him back out of No Man's Land, back to conventional politics, but so far as I had an effect, it was a Faustian one, much as if I had made a pact with Mephisto to give me an amulet, an art-work, which might arouse a djinn in history.

The night Kennedy was elected, I felt a sense of woe, as if I had made a terrible error, as if somehow I had betrayed the Left and myself. It was a spooky emotion. In the wake of the election, one note was clear—the strength the Left had been gaining in the last years of Eisenhower's administration would now be diluted, preempted, adulterated, converted and dissolved by the compromises and hypocrisies of a new Democratic administration. And so I began to follow Kennedy's career with obsession, as if I were responsible and guilty for all which was bad, dangerous, or potentially totalitarian within it. And the papers which follow are written under the shadow of this private fact, this conviction that I was now among the guilty, another genteel traitor in the land.

The Existential Heroine

I

A FEW OF YOU may remember that on February 14, last winter, our First Lady gave us a tour of the White House on television. For reasons to be explained in a while, I was in no charitable mood that night and gave Mrs. Kennedy a close scrutiny. Like anybody else, I have a bit of tolerance for my vices, at least those which do not get into the newspapers, but I take no pride in giving a hard look at a lady when she is on television. Ladies are created for an encounter face-to-face. No man can decide a lady is trivial until he has spent some minutes alone with her. Now while I have been in the same room with Jackie Kennedy twice, for a few minutes each time, it was never very much alone, and for that matter I do not think anyone's heart was particularly calm. The weather was too hectic. It was the Summer of 1960, after the Democratic Convention, before the presidential campaign had formally begun, at Hyannis Port, site of the Summer White House— those of you who know Hyannis ("High-anus," as the natives say) will know how funny is the title—all those motels and a Summer White House too: the Kennedy compound, an enclosure of three summer homes belonging to Joe Kennedy, Sr., RFK, and JFK, with a modest amount of lawn and beach to share among them. In those historic days the lawn was overrun with journalists, cameramen, magazine writers, politicians, delegations, friends, and neighboring gentry, government intellectuals, family, a prince, some Massachusetts state troopers, and red-necked hard-nosed tourists patrolling outside the fence for a glimpse of the boy. He was much in evidence, a bit of everywhere that morning, including the lawn, and particularly handsome at times as one has described elsewhere (*Es-*

quire, November, 1960), looking like a good version of
Charles Lindbergh at noon on a hot August day. Well,
Jackie Kennedy was inside in her living room sitting
around talking with a few of us, Arthur Schlesinger,
Jr. and his wife Marian, Prince Radziwill, Peter Maas
the writer, Jacques Lowe the photographer, and Pierre
Salinger. We were a curious assortment indeed, as
oddly assembled in our way as some of the do-gooders
and real baddies on the lawn outside. It would have
taken a hostess of broad and perhaps dubious gifts,
Perle Mesta, no doubt, or Ethel Merman, or Elsa
Maxwell, to have woven some mood into this occasion,
because pop! were going the flashbulbs out in the crazy
August sun on the sun-drenched terrace just beyond
the bay window at our back, a politician—a stocky machine type sweating in a dark suit with a white shirt
and white silk tie—was having his son, seventeeen perhaps, short, chunky, dressed the same way, take a picture of him and his wife, a Mediterranean dish around
sixty with a bright, happy, flowered dress. The boy
took a picture of father and mother, father took a picture of mother and son—another heeler came along to
take a picture of all three—it was a little like a rite sur-
rounding *droit du seigneur,* as if afterward the family
could press a locket in your hand and say, "Here, here
are contained three hairs from the youth of the Count,
discovered by me on my wife next morning." There
was something low and greedy about this picture-
taking, perhaps the popping of the flashbulbs in the
sunlight, as if everything monstrous and overreaching
in our insane public land were tamped together in the
foolproof act of taking a sun-drenched picture at
noon with no shadows and a flashbulb—do we sell insurance to protect our cadavers against the corrosion
of the grave?

And I had the impression that Jackie Kennedy was
almost suffering in the flesh from their invasion of her
house, her terrace, her share of the lands, that if the
popping of the flashbulbs went on until midnight on
the terrace outside she would have a tic forever in the

corner of her eye. Because that was the second impression of her, of a lady with delicate and exacerbated nerves. She was no broad hostess, not at all; broad hostesses are monumental animals turned mellow: hippopotami, rhinoceri, plump lion, sweet gorilla, warm bear. Jackie Kennedy was a cat, narrow and wild, and her fur was being rubbed every which way. This was the second impression. The first had been simpler. It had been merely of a college girl who was nice. Nice and clean and very merry. I had entered her house perspiring—talk of the politician, I was wearing a black suit myself, a washable, the only one in my closet not completely unpressed that morning, and I had been forced to pick a white shirt with button-down collar: all the white summer shirts were in the laundry. What a set-to I had had with Adele Mailer at breakfast. Food half-digested in anger, sweating like a goat, tense at the pit of my stomach for I would be interviewing Kennedy in a half hour, I was feeling not a little jangled when we were introduced, and we stumbled mutually over a few polite remarks, which was my fault I'm sure more than hers for I must have had a look in my eyes—I remember I felt like a drunk marine who knows in all clarity that if he doesn't have a fight soon it'll be good for his character but terrible for his constitution.

She offered me a cool drink—iced verbena tea with sprig of mint no doubt—but the expression in my face must have been rich because she added, still standing by the screen in the doorway, "We do have something harder of course," and something droll and hard came into her eyes as if she were a very naughty eight-year-old indeed. More than one photograph of Jackie Kennedy had put forward just this saucy regard—it was obviously the life of her charm. But I had not been prepared for another quality, of shyness conceivably. There was something quite remote in her. Not willed, not chilly, not directed at anyone in particular, but distant, detached as the psychologists say, moody and abstracted the novelists used to say. As we sat around the coffee table on summer couches, summer chairs, a pleasant living room in light colors, lemon, white and gold seeming to predominate, the sort of living room one might expect to find in Cleveland, may it be, at the home of a fairly important young executive whose wife had taste, sitting there, watching people go by, the group I mentioned earlier kept a kind of conversation going. Its center, if it had one, was obviously Jackie Kennedy. There was a natural tendency to look at her and see if she were amused. She did not sit there like a movie star with a ripe olive in each eye for the brain, but in fact gave conversation back, made some of it, laughed often. We had one short conversation about Provincetown, which was pleasant. She remarked that she had been staying no more than fifty miles away for all these summers but had never seen it. She must, I assured her. It was one of the few fishing villages in America which still had beauty. Besides it was the Wild West of the East. The local police were the Indians and the beatniks were the poor hardworking settlers. Her eyes turned merry. "Oh, I'd love to see it," she said. But how did one go? In three black limousines and fifty police for escort, or in a sports car at four A.M. with dark glasses? "I suppose now I'll never get to see it," she said wistfully.

She had a keen sense of laughter, but it revolved around the absurdities of the world. She was probably not altogether unlike a soldier who has been up at the front for two weeks. There was a hint of gone laughter. Soldiers who have had it bad enough can laugh at the fact some trooper got killed crossing an open area because he wanted to change his socks from khaki to green. The front lawn of this house must have been, I suppose, a kind of no-man's-land for a lady. The story I remember her telling was about Stash, Prince Radziwill, her brother-in-law, who had gone into the second-story bathroom that morning to take a shave and discovered, to his lack of complete pleasure, that a crush of tourists was watching him from across the road. Yes, the house had been besieged, and one knew she thought of the sightseers as a mob, a motley of gargoyles, like the horde who riot through the last pages in *The Day of the Locust*.

Since there was an air of self-indulgence about her, subtle but precise, one was certain she liked time to compose herself. While we sat there she must have gotten up a half-dozen times, to go away for two minutes, come back for three. She had the exasperated impatience of a college girl. One expected her to swear mildly. "Oh, Christ!" or "Sugar!" or "Fudge!" And each time she got up, there was a glimpse of her calves, surprisingly thin, not unfeverish. I was reminded of the legs on those adolescent Southern girls who used to go out together and walk up and down the streets of Fayetteville, North Carolina, in the Summer of 1944 at Fort Bragg. In the petulant Southern air of their boredom many of us had found something luminous that summer, a mixture of languor, heat, innocence and stupidity which was our cocktail vis-à-vis the knowledge we were going soon to Europe or the other war. One mentions this to underline the determinedly romantic aura in which one had chosen to behold Jackie Kennedy. There was a charm this other short Summer of 1960 in the thought a young man with a young attractive wife might soon become President. It offered possibilities and vistas; it brought a touch of life to the monotonies of politics, those monotonies so profoundly entrenched into the hinges and mortar of the Eisenhower administration. It was thus more interesting to look at Jackie Kennedy as a woman than as a probable First Lady. Perhaps it was out of some such motive, such a desire for the clean air and tang of unexpected montage, that I spoke about her in just the way I did later that afternoon.

"Do you think she's happy?" asked a lady, an old friend, on the beach at Wellfleet.

"I guess she would rather spend her life on the Riviera."

"What would she do there?"

"End up as the mystery woman, maybe, in a good murder case."

"Wow," said the lady, giving me my reward.

It had been my way of saying I liked Jackie Kennedy, that she was not at all stuffy, that she had perhaps a touch of that artful madness which suggests future drama.

My interview the first day had been a little short, and I was invited back for another one the following day. Rather nicely, Senator Kennedy invited me to bring anyone I wanted. About a week later I realized this was part of his acumen. You can tell a lot about a man by whom he invites in such a circumstance. Will it be a political expert or the wife? I invited my wife. The presence of this second lady is not unimportant, because this time she had the conversation with Jackie Kennedy. While I was busy somewhere or other, they were introduced. Down by the Kennedy family wharf. The Senator was about to take Jackie for a sail. The two women had a certain small general resemblance. They were something like the same height, they both had dark hair, and they had each been wearing it in a similar style for many years. Perhaps this was enough to create a quick political intimacy. "I wish," said Jackie Kennedy, "that I didn't have to go on this corny sail, because I would like very much to talk to you, Mrs. Mailer." A stroke. Mrs. M. did not like many people quickly, but Jackie now had a champion. It must have been a pleasant sight. Two attractive witches by the water's edge.

II

Jimmy Baldwin once entertained the readers of *Esquire* with a sweet and generously written piece called *The Black Boy Looks at the White Boy* in which he talked a great deal about himself and a little bit about me, a proportion I thought well-taken since he is on the best of terms with Baldwin and digs next to nothing about this white boy. As a method, I think it has its merits.

After I saw the Kennedys I added a few paragraphs to my piece about the convention, secretly relieved to have liked them, for my piece was most favorable to the Senator, and how would I have rewritten it if I had not liked him? With several mishaps it was printed three weeks before the election. Several days later, I received a letter from Jackie Kennedy. It was a nice letter, generous in its praise, accurate in its details. She remembered, for example, the color of the sweater my wife had been wearing, and mentioned she had one like it in the same purple. I answered with a letter which was out of measure. I was in a Napoleonic mood, I had decided to run for Mayor of New York; in a few weeks, I was to zoom and crash—my sense of reality was extravagant. So in response to a modestly voiced notion by Mrs. Kennedy that she wondered if the "impressionistic" way in which I had treated the convention could be applied to the history of the past, I replied in the cadence of a Goethe that while I was now engaged in certain difficulties of writing about the present, I hoped one day when work was done to do a biography of the Marquis de Sade and the "odd strange honor of the man."

I suppose this is as close to the edge as I have ever come. At the time, it seemed reasonable that Mrs. Kennedy, with her publicized interest in France and the eighteenth century, might be fascinated by de Sade. The style of his thought was, after all, a fair climax to the Age of Reason.

Now sociology has few virtues, but one of them is sanity. In writing such a letter to Mrs. Kennedy I was losing my sociology. The Catholic wife of a Catholic candidate for President was not likely to find de Sade as familiar as a tea cozy. I received no reply. I had smashed the limits of such letter-writing. In politics a break in sociology is as clean as a break in etiquette.

At the time I saw it somewhat differently. The odds

were against a reply, I decided, three-to-one against, or eight-to-one against. I did not glean they were eight-hundred-to-one against. It is the small inability to handicap odds which is family to the romantic, the desperate and the insane. "That man is going to kill me," someone thinks with fear, sensing a stranger. At this moment, they put the odds at even money, they may even be ready to die for their bet, when, if the fact could be measured, there is one chance in a thousand the danger is true. Exceptional leverage upon the unconscious life in other people is the strength of the artist and the torment of the madman.

Now if I have bothered to show my absence of proportion, it is because I want to put forward a notion which will seem criminal to some of you, but was believed in by me, is still believed in by me, and so affects what I write about the Kennedy's.

Jack Kennedy won the election by one hundred thousand votes. A lot of people could claim therefore to be the mind behind his victory. Jake Arvey could say the photo-finish would have gone the other way if not for the track near his Chicago machine. J. Edgar Hoover might say he saved the victory because he did not investigate the track. Lyndon Johnson could point to LBJ Ranch, and the vote in Texas. *Time* magazine could tell you that the abstract intrepidity of their support for Nixon gave the duke to Kennedy. Sinatra would not be surprised if the late ones who glommed onto Kennedy were not more numerous than the early-risers he scattered. And one does not even need to speak of the Corporations, the Mob, the money they delivered by messenger, the credit they would use later. So if I came to the cool conclusion I had won the election for Kennedy with my piece in *Esquire,* the thought might be high presumption, but it was not unique. I had done something curious but indispensable for the campaign—succeeded in making it dramatic. I had not shifted one hundred thousand votes directly, I had not. But a million people might have read my piece and some of them talked to other people. The cadres of

Stevenson Democrats whose morale was low might now revive with an argument that Kennedy was different in substance from Nixon. Dramatically different. The piece titled "Superman Comes to the Supermarket" affected volunteer work for Kennedy, enough to make a clean critical difference through the country. But such counting is a quibble. At bottom I had the feeling that if there were a power which made presidents, a power which might be termed Wall Street or Capitalism or The Establishment, a Mind or Collective Mind of some Spirit, some Master, or indeed *the* Master, no less, that then perhaps my article had turned that intelligence a fine hair in its circuits. This was what I thought. Right or wrong, I thought it, still do, and tell it now not to convince others (the act of stating such a claim is not happy), but to underline the proprietary tone I took when Kennedy invaded Cuba.

> "You've cut . . ." I wrote in *The Village Voice*, April 27, 1961, ". . . the shape of your plan for history, and it smells . . . rich and smug and scared of the power of the worst, dullest and most oppressive men of our land."

There was more. A good deal more. I want to quote more. Nothing could ever convince me the invasion of Cuba was not one of the meanest blunders in our history:

> You are a virtuoso in political management but you will never understand the revolutionary passion which comes to those who were one way or another too poor to learn how good they might have been; the greediness of the rich had already crippled their youth.
>
> Without this understanding you will never know what to do about Castro and Cuba. You will never understand that the man is the country, revolutionary, tyrannical . . . hysterical . . . brave as the best of animals, doomed perhaps to end in

tragedy, but one of the great figures of the twentieth century, at the present moment a far greater figure than yourself.

Later, through the grapevine which runs from Washington to New York, it could be heard that Jackie Kennedy was indignant at this piece, and one had the opportunity to speculate if her annoyance came from the postscript:

I was in a demonstration the other day . . . five literary magazines (so help me) which marched in a small circle of protest against our intervention in Cuba. One of the pickets was a very tall poetess with black hair which reached near to her waist. She was dressed like a medieval varlet, and she carried a sign addressed to your wife:

JACQUELINE, VOUS AVEZ
PERDU VOS ARTISTES

Tin soldier, you are depriving us of the Muse.

Months later, when the anger cooled, one could ask oneself what one did make of Washington now, for it was not an easy place to understand. It was intelligent, yes, but it was not original; there was wit in the detail and ponderousness in the program; vivacity, and dullness to equal it; tactical brilliance, political timidity; facts were still superior to the depths, criticism was less to be admired than the ability to be amusing—or so said the losers; equality and justice meandered; bureaucratic canals and locks; slums were replaced with buildings which looked like prisons; success was to be admired again, self-awareness dubious; television was attacked, but for its violence, not its mendacity, for its lack of educational programs, not its dearth of grace. There seemed no art, no real art in the new administration, and all the while the new administration proclaimed its eagerness to mother the arts. Or as Mr.

Collingwood said to Mrs. Kennedy, "This Administration has shown a particular affinity for artists, musicians, writers, poets. Is this because you and your husband just feel that way or do you think that there's a relationship between the Government and the arts?"

"That's so complicated," answered Mrs. Kennedy with good sense. "I don't know. I just think that everything in the White House should be the best."

Stravinsky had been invited of course and Robert Frost. Pablo Casals, Leonard Bernstein, Arthur Miller, Tennessee.

"But what about us?" growled the apes. Why did one know that Richard Wilbur would walk through the door before Allen Ginsberg; or Saul Bellow and J. D. Salinger long before William Burroughs or Norman Mailer. What special good would it do to found an Establishment if the few who gave intimations of high talent were instinctively excluded? I wanted a chance to preach to the President and to the First Lady. "Speak to the people a little more," I would have liked to say, "Talk on television about the things you do not understand. Use your popularity to be difficult and intellectually dangerous. There is more to greatness than liberal legislation." And to her I would have liked to go on about what the real meaning of an artist might be, of how the marrow of a nation was contained in his art, and one deadened artists at one's peril, because artists were not so much gifted as endowed; they had been given what was secret and best in their parents and in all the other people about them who had been generous or influenced them or made them, and so artists embodied the essence of what was best in the nation, embodied it in their talent rather than in their character, which could be small, but their talent—this fruit of all that was rich and nourishing in their lives— was related directly to the dreams and the ambitions of the most imaginative part of the nation. So the destiny of a nation was not separate at all from the fate of its artists. I would have liked to tell her that every time an artist failed to complete the full mansion, jungle, garden, armory, or city of his work the nation was subtly but permanently poorer, which is why we return so obsessively to the death of Tom Wolfe, the broken air of Scott Fitzgerald, and the gloomy smell of the vault which collects already about the horror of Hemingway's departure. I would have liked to say to her that a war for the right to express oneself had been going on in this country for fifty years, and that there were counterattacks massing because there were many who hated the artist now, that as the world dipped into the totalitarian trough of the twentieth century there was a mania of abhorrence for whatever was unpredictable. For all too many, security was the only bulwark against emptiness, eternity and death. The void was what America feared. Communism was one name they gave this void. The unknown was Communist. The girls who wore dungarees were Communist, and the boys who grew beards, the people who walked their dog off the leash. It was comic, but it was virulent, and there was a fanatic rage in much too much of the population. Detestation of the beatnik seethed like rabies on the mouths of small-town police officers.

Oh, there was much I wanted to tell her, even—exit sociology, enter insanity—that the obscene had a right to exist in the novel. For every fifteen-year-old who would be hurt by premature exposure, somewhere another, or two or three, would emerge from sexual experience which had been too full of moral funk onto the harder terrain of sex made alive by culture, that it was the purpose of culture finally to enrich all of the psyche, not just part of us, and damage to particular people in passing was a price we must pay. Thirty thousand Americans were killed each year by automobile crashes. No one talked of giving up the automobile: it was necessary to civilization. As necessary, I wanted to say, was art. Art in all its manifestations. Including the rude, the obscene, and the unsayable. Art was as essential to the nation as technology. I would tell her these things out of romantic abundance, because I liked her and thought she would understand what one was talking about, because as First Lady she was queen of the arts, she was our Muse if she chose to be. Perhaps it would not be altogether a disaster if America had a Muse.

Now it is not of much interest to most of you who read this that a small but distinct feud between the editors of *Esquire* and the writer was made up around the New Year. What is not as much off the matter was the suggestion, made at the time by one of these editors, that a story be done about Jackie Kennedy.

One liked the idea. What has been written already is curious prose if it is not obvious how much one liked the idea. Pierre Salinger was approached by the Magazine, and agreed to present the same idea to Mrs. Kennedy. I saw Salinger in his office for a few minutes. He told me: not yet a chance to talk to the Lady, but might that evening. I was leaving Washington. A few days later, one of the editors spoke to him. Mrs. Kennedy's answer: negative.

One didn't know. One didn't know how the idea had been presented, one didn't know just when it had been presented. It did not matter all that much. Whatever the details, the answer had come from the core. One's presence was not required. Which irritated the vanity. The vanity was no doubt outsize, but one thought of oneself as one of the few writers in the country. There was a right to interview Mrs. Kennedy. She was not only a woman looking for privacy, but an institution being put together before our eyes. If the people of America were to have a symbol, one had the right to read more about the creation. The country would stay alive by becoming more extraordinary, not more predictable.

III

Not with a kind eye then did I watch Mrs. Kennedy give the nation a tour. One would be fair. Fair to her and fair to the truth of one's reactions. There was now an advantage in not having had the interview.

I turned on the program a minute after the hour. The image on the screen was not of Mrs. Kennedy, but the White House. For some minutes she talked, reading from a prepared script while the camera was turned upon old prints, old plans, and present views of the building. Since Jackie Kennedy was not visible during this time, there was an opportunity to listen to her voice. It produced a small continuing shock. At first, before the picture emerged from the set, I thought I was turned to the wrong station, because the voice was a quiet parody of the sort of voice one hears on the radio late at night, dropped softly into the ear by girls who sell soft mattresses, depilatories, or creams to brighten the skin.

Now I had heard the First Lady occasionally on newsreels and in brief interviews on television, and thought she showed an odd public voice, but never paid attention, because the first time to hear her was in the living room at Hyannis Port and there she had been clear, merry and near excellent. So I discounted the public voice, concluded it was muffled by shyness perhaps or was too urgent in its desire to sound like other voices, to sound, let us say, like an attractive small-town salesgirl, or like Jackie Kennedy's version of one: the gentry in America have a dim ear for the nuances of accent in the rough, the poor, and the ready. I had decided it was probably some mockery of her husband's political ambitions, a sport upon whatever advisers had been trying for years to guide her to erase whatever was too patrician or cultivated in her speech. But the voice I was hearing now, the public voice, the voice after a year in the White House had grown undeniably worse, had nourished itself on its faults. Do some of you remember the girl with the magnificent sweater who used to give the weather reports on television in a swarmy sing-song tone? It was a self-conscious parody, very funny for a little while: "Temperature—forty-eight.   Humidity—twenty-eight. Prevailing winds." It had the style of the pinup magazine, it caught their prose: "Sandra Sharilee is 37-25-37, and likes to stay in at night." The girl who gave the weather report captured the voice of those pinup magazines, dreamy, narcissistic, visions of sex on the moon. And Jackie Kennedy's voice, her public voice, might as well have been influenced by the weather girl. What madness is loose in our public communication. And what self-ridicule that consciously or unconsciously, wittingly, willy-nilly, by the aid of speech teachers or all on her stubborn own, this was the manufactured voice Jackie Kennedy chose to arrive at. One had heard better ones at Christmastime in Macy's selling gadgets to the grim.

The introduction having ended, the camera moved onto Jackie Kennedy. We were shown the broad planes of the First Lady's most agreeable face. Out of the deep woods now. One could return to them by closing one's eyes and listening to the voice again, but the image was reasonable, reassuringly stiff. As the eye followed Mrs. Kennedy and her interlocutor, Charles Collingwood, through the halls, galleries and rooms of the White House, through the Blue Room, the Green Room, the East Room, the State Dining Room, the Red Room; as the listeners were offered a reference to Dolly Madison's favorite sofa, or President Monroe's Minerva clock, Nellie Custis' sofa, Mrs. Lincoln's later poverty, Daniel Webster's sofa, Julia Grant's desk, Andrew Jackson's broken mirror, the chest President Van Buren gave to his grandson; as the paintings were shown to us, paintings entitled *Niagara Falls, Grapes and Apples, Naval Battle of 1812, Indian Guides, A Mountain Glimpse, Mouth of the Delaware;* as one contemplated the life of this offering, the presentation began to take on the undernourished, overdone air of a charity show, a telethon for a new disease. It was not Mrs. Kennedy's fault—she strove honorably. What an agony it must have been to establish the sequence of all these names, all these objects. Probably she knew them well, perhaps she was interested in her subject— although the detached quality of her presence on this program made it not easy to believe—but whether or not she had taken a day-to-day interest in the booty now within the White House, still she had had a script partially written for her, by a television writer with black horn-rimmed glasses no doubt, she had been obliged to memorize portions of this script, she had trained for the part. Somehow it was sympathetic that she walked through it like a starlet who is utterly without talent. Mrs. Kennedy moved like a wooden horse. A marvelous horse, perhaps even a live horse, its feet hobbled, its head unready to turn for fear of a flick from the crop. She had that intense wooden lack of rest, that lack of comprehension for each word offered up which one finds only in a few of those curious movie stars who are huge box office. Jane Russell comes to mind, and Rita Hayworth when she was sadly cast, Jayne Mansfield in deep water, Brigitte Bardot before she learned to act. Marilyn Monroe. But one may be too kind. Jackie Kennedy was more like a starlet who will never learn to act because the extraordinary livid unreality of her life away from the camera has so beclouded her brain and seduced her attention that she is incapable of the simplest and most essential demand, which is to live and breathe easily with the meaning of the words one speaks.

This program was the sort of thing Eleanor Roosevelt could have done, and done well. She had grown up among objects like this—these stuffed armchairs, these candelabra—no doubt they lived for her with some charm of the past. But Jackie Kennedy was unconvincing. One did not feel she particularly loved the past of America—not all of us do for that matter, it may not even be a crime—but one never had the impression for a moment that the White House fitted her style. As one watched this tame, lackluster and halting show, one wanted to take the actress by the near shoulder. Because names, dates and objects were boring down into the very secrets of her being—or so one would lay the bet—and this encouraged a fraud which could only sicken her. By extension it would deaden us. What we needed and what she could offer us was much more complex than this public image of a pompadour, a tea-dance dress, and a Colonial window welded together in committee. Would the Kennedys be no more intelligent than the near past, had they not learned America was not to be saved by Madison Avenue, that no method could work which induced nausea faster than the pills we push to carry it away.

Afterward one could ask what it was one wanted of her, and the answer was that she show herself to us as she is. Because what we suffer from in America, in that rootless moral wilderness of our expanding life, is the unadmitted terror in each of us that bit by bit, year by year, we are going mad. Very few of us know really where we have come from and to where we are going, why we do it, and if it is ever worthwhile. For better or for worse we have lost our past, we live in that airless no-man's-land of the perpetual present, and so suffer doubly as we strike into the future because we have no roots by which to project ourselves forward, or judge our trip.

And this tour of the White House gave us precisely no sense of the past. To the contrary, it inflicted the past upon us, pummeled us with it, depressed us with facts. I counted the names, the proper names, and the dates in the transcript. More than two hundred items were dumped upon us during that hour. If one counts repetitions, the number is closer to four hundred. One was not being offered education, but anxiety.

We are in the Green Room—I quote from the transcript:

> MR. COLLINGWOOD: What other objects of special interest are there in the room now?
> MRS. KENNEDY: Well, there's this sofa which belonged to Daniel Webster and is really one of the finest pieces here in this room. And then there's this mirror. It was George Washington's and he had it in the Executive Mansion in Philadelphia, then he gave it to a friend and it was bought for

Mount Vernon in 1891. And it was there until Mount Vernon lent it to us this fall. And I must say I appreciate that more than I can say, because when Mount Vernon, which is probably the most revered house in this country, lends something to the White House, you know they have confidence it will be taken care of.

A neurotic may suffer agonies returning to his past; so may a nation which is not well. The neurotic recites endless lists of his activities and offers no reaction to any of it. So do we teach with empty content and by rigid manner where there is anxiety in the lore. American history disgorges this anxiety. Where, in the pleasant versions of it we are furnished, can we find an explanation for the disease which encourages us to scourge our countryside, stifle our cities, kill the physical sense of our past, and throw up excruciatingly totalitarian new office buildings everywhere to burden the vista of our end? This disease, is it hidden in the evasions, the injustices, and the prevarications of the past, or does it come to us from a terror of what is yet to come? Whatever, however, we do not create a better nation by teaching schoolchildren the catalogues of the White House. Nor do we use the First Lady decently if she is flattered in this, for catalogues are imprisonment to the delicate, muted sensitivity one feels passing across Jackie Kennedy from time to time like a small summer wind on a good garden.

Yes, before the tour was over, one had to feel compassion. Because silly, ill-advised, pointless, empty, dull, and obsequious to the most slavish tastes in American life, as was this show, still she was trying so hard, she wanted to please, she had given herself to this work, and it was hopeless there was no one about to tell her how very hopeless it was, how utterly without offering to the tormented adventurous spirit of American life. At times, in her eyes, there was a blank, full look which one could recognize. One had seen this look on a nineteen-year-old who was sweet and on the town and pushed too far. She slashed her wrists one night and tried to scar her cheeks and her breast. I had visited the girl in the hospital. She had blank eyes, a wide warm smile, a deadness in her voice. It did not matter about what she spoke—only her mouth followed the words, never her eyes. So I did not care to see that look in Jackie Kennedy's face, and I hoped by half—for more would be untrue—that the sense one got of her in newspaper photographs, of a ladygirl healthy and on the bounce, might come into her presence before our deadening sets. America needed a lady's humor to leaven the solemnities of our toneless power: finally we will send a man to Mars and the Martians will say, "God, he is dull."

Yes, it is to be hoped that Jackie Kennedy will come alive. Because I think finally she is one of us. By which I mean that she has not one face but many, not a true voice but accents, not a past so much as memories which cannot speak to one another. She attracts compassion. Somewhere in her mute vitality is a wash of our fatigue, of existential fatigue, of the great fatigue which comes from being adventurous in a world where most of the bets are covered cold and statisticians prosper. I liked her, I liked her still, but she was a phony —it was the cruelest thing one could say, she was a royal phony. There was something very difficult and very dangerous she was trying from deep within herself to do, dangerous not to her safety but to her soul. She was trying, I suppose, to be a proper First Lady and it was her mistake. Because there was no need to copy the Ladies who had come before her. Suppose America had not yet had a First Lady who was even remotely warm enough for our needs? Or sufficiently imaginative? But who could there be to advise her in all that company of organized men, weaned on the handbook of past precedent? If she would be any use to the nation she must first regain the freedom to look us in the eye. And offer the hard drink. For then three times three hurrah, and hats, our hats, in the air. If she were really interested in her White House, we would grant it to her, we would not begrudge her the tour, not if we could believe she was beginning to learn the difference between the arts and the safe old crafts. And indeed there was a way she could show us she was beginning to learn, it was the way of the hostess: one would offer her one's sword when Henry Miller was asked to the White House as often as Robert Frost and beat poetry's own Andy Hardy—good Gregory Corso—could do an Indian dance in the East Room with Archibald MacLeish. America would be as great as the royal rajah of her arts when the Academy ceased to be happy as a cherrystone clam, and the weakest of the beat returned to form. Because our tragedy is that we diverge as countrymen further and further away from one another, like a space ship broken apart in flight which now drifts mournfully in isolated orbits, satellites to each other, planets none, communication faint.

The Big Bite—March, 1963

THE NEWSPAPERS are rich in self-examination these last two mornings. Like beatniks or poets they are studying themselves, their digestion, their elimination, their neuroses, their arts. They are examining the secrets of their own formula for making history. They are trying to decide whether Adlai Stevenson is in serious disfavor with President Kennedy or is not. As in a laboratory experiment, they have a specimen to examine, tests to make.

The specimen is an article in *The Saturday Evening Post* by Stewart Alsop and Charles Bartlett. The article finds Stevenson guilty of expressing a *soft* policy toward Cuba during several *secret* conferences, those talks of the Executive Committee in which Kennedy discussed what to do about Soviet missiles in Cuba. Since Charles Bartlett is known to the newspaper business as a *leak* for the President, one basic theme proposes itself immediately: the President, or somebody very close to the President, gave Bartlett the idea that an attack upon Stevenson was not impermissible. It is an administrative way of seizing Stevenson by the throat and slamming him against a wall.

What? Soft on Cuba you son of a bitch?

Newspapers and politics are married. One cannot have a theme without its development. So a contrary and second hypothesis emerges from the first; it goes: Bartlett is not merely a leak for the President, but indeed has a set of spigots for a dozen different members of the administration. The President knew nothing in advance of Alsop and Bartlett's article, goes the second interpretation. On the contrary it is a plot by the Right Wing of the administration to eat up the Left Wing. Since this second conception is Liberal, it concludes that the President will not destroy Adlai Stevenson but rescue him.

Then there is a full theory in the center. It is created out of the other two theories. It supposes that Kennedy gave the secret of the conversations to Bartlett in order to rescue Adlai Stevenson later. By this supposition, John F. Kennedy must be much like Madame de Staël. It was remarked of this heroine that she liked to throw her friends into the pool in order to have the pleasure of fishing them out again.

I do not think the President throws his assistants into the pool for such a ladylike reason. Doubtless, he acts more like the pure moon man and good scientist he is. He knows that polls are not enough to test the pulse of the public. One needs a small explosion here, a bit of blast there. Hot ore to examine. Hot ants. One way to test the ferment of the extreme Right is to tie Adlai Stevenson to their anthill, put a splash of gasoline at his feet, and strike a match. Will he be burned? will he be bitten to death by ants? will he recover? If this last option shows vitality and Stevenson survives, one may assume the Right Wing is growing weak. On the other hand, if by the time you read this Stevenson is no longer our Ambassador to the U.N., then the

Right Wing has more strength now than it did before Cuba became the center of the world.

I make a prediction. I think Stevenson will still be Ambassador to the U.N. Once the President proved he was ready for an atomic war, the National Ticket was finally created. John F. Kennedy for President, Barry Goldwater for Vice-President. Adlai Stevenson and William F. Buckley, Jr. to stand on the platform beside them.

The only people who will vote against the National Ticket will be a few hundred unreconstructed Birchites, a few followers of George Lincoln Rockwell, fifty very old socialists loyal to Daniel De Leon, five or six junkies, eighty-two beatniks brave enough to keep wearing beards, a covey of vegetarians, a flying squad of pacifists, the three remaining bona-fide Communists of America, and the ten thousand members of the FBI who have infiltrated the Communist Party and will be afraid to vote for fear that one of the three bona-fide live Communists might see them and expose them to the wrath of the Party.

After the National Ticket is elected, we could have the Jack and Barry show. Edward Murrow might see his way clear to give us a tour of the Vice-President's electronic shack in Arizona.

Write me a letter. Tell me that what I do in this column is no more than nightclub smut and patter. Remind me that I am trying to deface the sanctity of America's institutions.

For fact, the only institutions which remain alive in American life are those which afford a press representative. The newspaper does not report history any longer. It must make it. The press representative helps them to make it. So the newspapers help to create institutions (that is to say: instrumentalities) which will supply them with news.

For the most part, newspapers tell nothing but lies. They prefer therefore to accept news from institutions which tell lies. Everyone knows that. The reason we still believe what we read in the papers is that we like to spend five cents, seven cents, or a dime, and relax for a while. We cannot relax if we admit to ourselves that a lie is entering the nervous system. Somewhere in the censor of the mind, one decides it is less debilitating to accept a ration of lies as a squad of facts.

It used to be, not very many years ago, that politicians could use the Washington Press Corps as a series of Certified Leaks. They could play the body politic like the strings of a harp. A piece of news was rarely what it presented itself to be—it was rather a lie which, put next to other lies, gave the intimation of a clue. At its best, a news story was the key to a cryptogram.

One offers a mythical example. *The New York Times* on a given day some ten or twelve years ago has a story with by-line on page three. It is trivial and it is dull. But it is on page three. So its importance is underlined. The story states that an "undisclosed reliable source" has said today that sentiment among the West Germans to end the Nuremberg Trials is increasing. One knows the "source" is the Secretary of State because the reporter is his Certified Leak. Now of course this story has no sociological bottom. The Secretary of State did not conduct a private poll of West Germans. Nor is he interested to serve the public with the latest information available to him. On the contrary he has no information: he is simply announcing to various experts in America, Europe, and West Germany that America is getting ready to end its de-Nazification program. Since the Secretary of State does not speak in his own name but through his Certified Leak, the experts are also advised to advise their particular institutions that the announcement of this new policy is several weeks to several months away. Objections by the separate institutions may be considered. Democratic process.

Those were the good old days of the Truman or Eisenhower Administration. With a code-breaking machine at hand, it was a high navigational pleasure to read a paper. Supplied with a handbook of Certified

Leaks, one could explore the news tributaries of the world. A genius could have put out a great newspaper without ever leaving his room. He just had to be a plumber with a plumber's snake.

But the Serpent entered Paradise. The Certified Leaks began to make news independently. Sometimes they were even known to betray their officials. The strings of the Goat's harp began to move in new ways. An official would try to play the harp, and a string would call, it would say, "Come here, index finger, touch me. If you don't, I'll start to vibrate without you." The Twist had entered History.

Who knows? Playing touch football, Kennedy gives the ball to Bartlett on an end around. "Don't give Adlai the ax," whispers the quarterback. "Oh, Jeez, dad," says Charley B. after his touchdown is called back, "I thought you said, *give* Adlai the ax." In such a game, which playmaker can know if his tongue is thickening or son is hip to Dad.

From an Open Letter to JFK

DURING that historic week in the fall of 1962 when America and Russia were on a collision course, and it was possible the death of all we had known could come at one minute or another, I would try to contemplate how iron must be your nerve, and I came to the conclusion that your nerve was either very great or that you were nerveless, which is another matter. If your secret aim has been to avoid war if possible, then your action was noble, your nerve worthy of the great generals of history. But if our existence is not essential to you, if in depth beneath depth of your mind there is not fear but a high calm joy at the thought of atomic war, then that week you were like a poker player with a royal flush, a revolver in his hand, unlimited money to raise each bet, and a string of carefully graded insults calculated to tip the table and let the shooting begin.

One does not know the answer. But the sensation is uneasy. There was an article in *Look,* December 18. Its title was "Washington in Crisis—154 hours that shook the world: the untold story of our plan to invade Cuba." Let me quote from it.

> Changes were made weekly as Castro's Cuba rattled with more rifles, tanks, and guns from Russia. By October 16, 1962, the invasion plan—a series of black loose-leaf notebooks in Pentagon safes—called for the massing of 100,000 men to take the island, a swarm of Air Force bombers and fighters and hundreds of Navy warships, from aircraft-laden carriers to assault landingcraft. This time, the pros would take no chances.
> *As part of the invasion plan, President Kennedy, his Cabinet, and top military and civilian leaders would repair to secret, atom-proof shelters in the mountains of Virginia and Maryland—for once the troops jumped off, no man could foretell with certainty the Kremlin's response.* [Italics mine.]

It is not your secret atom-proof shelters in the mountains of Virginia which cause terror—one can accept that by the logic of war, you would have to be protected. It's been true for almost half a century that the General with the highest rank is to be found in the deepest part of the ground. Besides, your physical bravery is not in question.

But there is panic at the thought that your own personal safety may affect the secret estimates of your mind. None of us can be certain that our own protection from death may not leave us secretly indifferent to the extinction of a million others. Which one of us can say we wept in childhood for the famine and death of ten million Chinese?

So I ask you this. Why not send us a hostage? Why not let us have Jacqueline Kennedy? The moment an invasion is let loose, and you as the Commander in Chief go to your deep bomb shelter, why not send us your wife and children to share our fate in this city? New York is the place where we have air-raid drills every year and no way at all to save a single body from a single Russian bomb. Yes, let your wife's helicopter land on the Hotel Carlyle, and we will know it is likely you are ready to suffer as we suffer, and that the weakness we feel before war is not merely our own pathetic inability to stare into the mountain passes of Heaven, or the stench of Hell, but is the impotence of men who would be brave, and yet must look at the children they have become powerless to protect. You see, we in New York are now like the ten million Chinese. Show us that you understand our condition, put a hostage from your flesh into our doomed city, or know that we can never trust you completely, for deep within yourself may be contained a bright mad voice which leaps to give the order that presses a button.

Yours respectfully,
NORMAN MAILER

The Big Bite—April, 1963

THE RITE OF SPRING is in the odor of the air. The nerve of winter which enters one's nose comes a long far way like a scythe from the peak of mountains. To the aged it can feel like a miasma up from the midnight corridors of a summer hotel, empty and out of season. Winter breath has the light of snow when the sun is on it, or the bone chill of a vault. But spring air comes up from the earth—at worst it can be the smell of new roots in bad slimy ground, at best the wine of late autumn frost is released from the old ice. Intoxication to the nostril, as if a filbert of fine sherbet had melted a sweet way into the tongue back of the throat down from the teeth. Spring is the season which marks the end of dread—so it is the season of profound dread for those who do not lose their fear.

Looking back on the winter and fall, one thinks of a long season of dread. There was that week toward the end of October when the world stood like a playing card on edge, and those of us who lived in New York wondered if the threat of war was like an exceptional dream which could end in a happy denouement (as indeed it did) or whether the events of each day would move, ante raised on ante, from boats on a collision course to invasions of Cuba, from threats of nuclear reprisal to the act itself, the Götterdämmerung of New York. Or would the end come instantly without prevision or warning, we would wonder as well, were we now heroes in a movie by Chaplin, was our house at the edge of the cliff, would we open the door and step into an abyss? There was dread that week. One looked at the buildings one passed and wondered if one was to see them again. For a week everyone in New York was like a patient with an incurable disease—would they be dead tomorrow or was it life for yet another year?

We sat that week in New York thinking of little. When movies are made of the last week on earth, the streets thrive with jazz, the juveniles are unrestrained, the adults pillage stores, there is rape, dancing, caterwauling laughter, sound of sirens and breaking glass, the roller coaster of a brave trumpet going out on its last ride. But we sat around. All too many watched television. Very few of us went out at night. The bars were half empty. The talk was quiet. One did not have the feeling great lovers were meeting that week, not for the first time nor for the last. An apathy came over our city. A muted and rather empty hour which lasted for a week. If it all blew up, if it all came to so little, if our efforts, our loves, our crimes added up to no more than a sudden extinction in a minute, in a moment, if we had not even time before the bomb (as civilians did once) to throw one quick look at some face, some trinket, some child for which one had love, well, one could not complain. That was our fate. That was what we deserved. We did not march in the street or shake our fists at the sky. We waited in our burrow like drunks in the bullpen pacing the floor of our existence, waiting for court in the morning while the floor was littered with the bile that came up in our spit and the dead butts of our dying lung's breath. Facing eternity we were convicts hanging on the dawn. There was no lust in the streets nor any defiance with which to roar at eternity. We were guilty.

We gave our freedom away a long time ago. We gave it away in all the revolutions we did not make, all the acts of courage we found a way to avoid, all the roots we destroyed in fury at that past which still would haunt our deeds. We divorced ourselves from the materials of the earth, the rock, the wood, the iron ore; we looked to new materials which were cooked in vats, long complex derivatives of urine which we called plastic. They had no odor of the living or of what once had lived, their touch was alien to nature. They spoke of the compromise of incompatibles. The plastic which had invaded our bathrooms, our kitchens, our clothing, our toys for children, our tools, our containers, our floor coverings, our cars, our sports, the world of our surfaces was the simple embodiment of social cowardice. We had tried to create a world in which all could live even if none could breathe. There had been a vast collective social effort in the twentieth century —each of us had tried to take back a critical bit more from existence than we had given to it.

There was a terror to contemplate in the logic of our apathy. Because if there was a God and we had come from Him, was it not the first possibility that each of us had a mission, one of us to create, another to be brave, a third to love, a fourth to work, a fifth to be bold, a sixth to be all of these. Was it not possible that we were sent out of eternity to become more than we had been?

What then if we had become less? There was a terror in the logic. Because if there was a God, there was also in first likelihood a Devil. If the God who sent us out demanded our courage, what would be most of interest to the other but our cowardice?

Which of us could say that nowhere in the secret debates of our dreams or the nightmare of open action, in those stricken instants when the legs are not as brave as the mind or the guts turn to water, which of us could say that never nor nowhere had we struck a pact with the Devil and whispered, Yes, let us deaden God, let Him die within me, it is too frightening to keep Him alive, I cannot bear the dread.

That is why we did not roar into the street and shout that it was unnatural for mankind to base its final hope on the concealed character of two men, that it was unnatural to pray that Kennedy and Khrushchev taken together were more good than evil. What an ignoble suppliant hope for civilization to rest its security on two men, no more, two men. What had happened to the dream of the world's wealth guarded by the world's talent, the world's resource?

We sat in apathy because most of us, in the private treacherous dialogues of our sleep, had turned our faith away from what was most vital in our mind, and had awakened in depression. We had drawn back in fright from ourselves, as if in our brilliance lay madness, and beyond the horizon dictated by others was death. We had been afraid of death. We had been afraid of death as no generation in the history of mankind has been afraid. None of us would need to scream as eternity recaptured our breath—we would be too deep in hospital drugs. We would die with deadened minds and twilight sleep. We had turned our back on the essential terror of life. We believed in the Devil, we hated nature.

So we watched the end approach with apathy. Because if he was God we had betrayed and the vision with which He had sent us forth, if our true terror now was not of life but of what might be waiting for us in death, then how much easier we might find it to be blasted into eternity deep in the ruin of ten million others, how much better indeed if the world went with us, and death was destroyed as completely as life. Yes, how many of the millions in New York had a secret prayer: that whomever we thought of as God be exploded with us, and Judgment cease.

Presidential Poems

ONE OF THE PRINCES *in the palace guard around the Kennedy's once saw fit to tell a wife of mine that I was "an intellectual adventurer." I was struck with the accuracy of the remark. Only an intellectual adventurer would write an open poem to the President. It came at a curious time in the inner life of JFK because he was contemplating the possibilities of an all-out fallout-shelter drive, which if successful (and the largest campaigns in America seem to be the easiest ones) would have left us Egyptian as a nation: a million underground one-room crypts stocked to the barrel top with canned goods, toys, and the beginnings (undertaken by children) of cave drawings. Something went wrong with the campaign; maybe the President had a bad dream. At any rate this poem was one of a hundred thousand items which might have been present to shift his mind.*

Open Poem to John Fitzgerald Kennedy

fallout
  is the hormone
    of the small town mind

a fallout shelter
    is sex

    think how warm
      at the thought

are all of U
and little Mrs. U S A
bonging the gong
                below

while bigcity flesh
all that blond hair
            and black hair
            straight and long
            short and highly curled
            floating in through
                        the trees
                a dew
                of homogenized bone
                and blood mist
            atom bombs
              are not so bad
              says small-time
                  in the town mind
              they disinfect
                  the big city
              and jazz us to the toes
                  out here in God's Country

        fingering is lovely
            on the edge of the grave.

Mr. President
  you realize of course
  that your shelter program
    for every home owner
    is sexing up the countryside
    and killing us in the
        bigcity bar.
  If this is good
    for the vitality
    of the nation
  (I mean that countryside
    could stand some sex)

then Mr. President
you are a genius
and corporation executives
living in the suburbs
with the five thousand
                    dollar
                    shelters
ought to salute you.
                    I do.

A few short poems. The first was written during a
week when the President was on a campaign to help
the dairy industries of America.

The President
    has asked us
    to drink a glass of milk
        each day.

I'm sure
    he doesn't ask
    us
    to do this
just because
    the milk is full
    of fallout now.

Men
who are not
    married
    and grow beards
    are insecure,
    said the CIA
before
    it went
    to Cuba.

Freedom of the Press

> Let every
> writer
> tell his
> > own
> > lies
> That's freedom
> of the
> press.

A plague is
   coming
   named
      Virus Y S X
      still unsolved
      promises to be
         proof
         against
         antibiotics
         psychoanalysis
         research projects
         vitamins
         awards
         crash programs
         crash diets
         symposiums
         foundations
         rest
         rehabilitation
         tranquilizers
         aspirin
         surgery
         brainwashing
         lobotomies

rises in status
box office boffo
perversions
and
even
a
good
piece
of

When that unhappy day
    comes to America
    let the Russians
    take over.
The best defense is
            infection.

A Debate with William F. Buckley—The Real Meaning of the Right Wing in America

WOULD YOU CARE to hear a story Robert Welch likes to tell?

"The minister has preached a superb sermon. It has moved his congregation to lead nobler and more righteous lives. Then the minister says, 'That, of course, was the Lord's side. For the next half hour, to be fair, I'll give equal time to the Devil.' "

Well, ladies and gentlemen, upon me has fallen the unhappy task of following Mr. Buckley. Mr. Buckley was so convincing in his speech that if I had not been forewarned that the Devil cannot know how far he has fallen from Paradise, I would most certainly have decided Mr. Buckley was an angel. A dishonest angel, perhaps, but then which noble speaker is not?

I did not come here, however, to give Mr. Buckley compliments. I appear, presumably, to discuss the real meaning of the Right Wing in America, a phenomenon which is not necessarily real in its meaning, for the Right Wing covers a spectrum of opinion as wide as the peculiarities one encounters on the Left. If we of the Left are a family of anarchists and Communists, socialists, pacifists, nihilists, beatniks, international spies, terrorists, hipsters and Bowery bums, secret agents, dope addicts, sex maniacs and scholarly professors, what indeed is one to make of the Right, which includes the president of a corporation or the Anglican headmaster of a preparatory school, intellectually attired in the fine ideas of Edmund Burke, down the road to the Eisenhower-is-a-Communist set of arguments, all the way down the road to an American Nazi like George Lincoln Rockwell, or to the sort of conservatives who attack property with bombs in California. On a vastly more modest and civilized scale, Mr. Buckley may commit a mild mayhem on the American sense of reality when he says McCarthy inaugurated no reign of terror. Perhaps, I say, it was someone else.

But it is easy to mock the Right Wing. I would rather put the best face one can on it. I think there are any number of interesting adolescents and young men and women going to school now who find themselves drawn to the Right. Secretly drawn. Some are drawn to conservatism today much as they might have been attracted to the Left 30 years ago. They are the ones who are curious for freedom, the freedom not only to make money but the freedom to discover their own nature, to discover good and to discover—dare I say it?—evil. At bottom they are ready to go to war with a ready-made world which they feel is stifling them.

I hope it is evident that I do not see the people in the Right Wing as a simple group of fanatics, but rather as a contradictory stew of reactionaries and individualists, of fascists and libertarians, libertarians like John Dos Passos for example. It could be said that most Right Wingers don't really know what they want. I would not include Mr. Buckley in this category, but I think it can be said the politics of the Right in America reflects an emotion more than an insight.

I think of a story told me by a Southerner about his aunt. She lived in a small town in South Carolina. She was a spinster. She came from one of the better families in town. Not surprisingly, the house where she lived had been in the family for a long time. She loved the trees on the walk which bordered each side of the street which ran by her house. They were very old trees.

The City Council passed a bill to cut down those trees. The street had to be widened. A bypass from the highway was being constructed around the old bypass of the business district. The reason for the new bypass was to create a new business district: a supermarket, a superpharmacy, a superservice station, a chromium-plated diner, a new cemetery with plastic tombstones, a new armory for the Army Reserve, an auto supply store, a farm implements shop, a store for Venetian blinds, a laundromat and an information booth for tourists who would miss the town on the new bypass but could read about it in the Chamber of Commerce's literature as they drove on to Florida.

Well, the old lady fought the bypass. To her, it was sacrilege that these trees be cut down. She felt that if there were any value to some older notions of grace and courtesy, courage under duress, and gallantry to ladies, of faith in God and the structure of His ways, that if there were any value at all to chivalry, tradition and manners, the children of the new generations could come to find it more naturally by walking down an avenue of old homes and trees than by reading the *National Review* in front of the picture window under the metal awning of the brand-new town library.

Secretly the old lady had some radical notions. She seemed to think that the old street and the trees on this old street were the property of everyone in the town, because everyone in the town could have the pleasure of walking down that street. At her gloomiest she even used to think that a new generation of Negroes growing up in the town, strong, hostile, too smart, and just loaded with Northern ideas, would hate the South forever and never forgive the past once the past was destroyed. If they grew up on the edge of brand-new bypasses in cement-brick homes with asbestos roofs and squatty hothouse bushes in the artificial fertilizer of the front yard, why then, how could they ever come to understand that not everyone in the old South was altogether evil and that there had been many whites who learned much from the Negro and loved him, that it was Negro slaves who had first planted these trees, and that it was Negro love of all that grew well which had set the trunks of these trees growing in so straight a route right into the air.

So the old lady fought the execution of these old trees. She went to see the Mayor, she talked to everyone on the City Council, she circulated a petition among her neighbors, she proceeded to be so active in the defense of these trees that many people in town began to think she was just naturally showing her age. Finally, her nephew took her aside. It was impossible to stop the bypass, he explained to her, because there was a man in town who had his heart set on it, and no one in town was powerful enough to stop this man. Not on a matter so special as these trees.

Who was this powerful and villainous man? Who would destroy the beauty of a fine old street? she wanted to know. Was it a Communist? No. Was it the leader for the National Association for the Advancement of Colored People? No. Was it perhaps a Freedom Rider? No. Was it a beatnik or a drug addict? No. Wasn't it one of those New York agitators? No, no, it wasn't even a Cuban. The sad fact of the matter was that the powerful and villainous man was married to the richest woman in the county, came himself from an excellently good family, owned half the real estate around, and was president of the biggest local corporation, which was a large company for making plastic luncheon plates. He was a man who had been received often in the old lady's house. He had even talked to her about joining his organization. He was the leader of the local council of the John Birch Society.

Mr. Buckley may say I am being unfair. The man who puts the new bypass through does not have to be the local leader of the John Birch Society. He can also be a liberal Republican, or a Democratic mayor, a white liberal Southerner, or—and here Mr. Buckley might tell my story with pleasure—he could be a Federal man. The bypass might be part of a national superhighway. The villain might even be a Federal man who is under scrutiny by the Senate Investigating Committee, the House Un-American Affairs Committee, the FBI, and the CIA. It seems not to matter—a man can be a fellow-traveler or a reactionary—either way those trees get chopped down, and the past is unreasonably destroyed.

The moral well may be that certain distinctions have begun to disappear. The average experience today is to meet few people who are authentic. Our minds belong to one cause, our hands manipulate a machine which works against our cause. We are not our own masters. We work against ourselves. We suffer from a disease. It is a disease which afflicts almost all of us by now, so prevalent, insidious and indefinable that I choose to call it a plague.

I think somewhere, at some debatable point in history, it is possible man caught some unspeakable illness of the psyche, that he betrayed some secret of his being and so betrayed the future of his species. I could not begin to trace the beginning of this plague, but whether it began early or late, I think it is accelerating now at the most incredible speed, and I would go so far as to think that many of the men and women who belong to the Right Wing are more sensitive to this disease than virtually any other people in this country. I thing it is precisely this sensitivity which gives power to the Right Wing's passions.

Now this plague appears to us as a sickening of our substance, an electrification of our nerves, a deterioration of desire, an apathy about the future, a detestation of the present, an amnesia of the past. Its forms are many, its flavor is unforgettable: It is the disease which destroys flavor. Its symptoms appear everywhere: in architecture, medicine, in the deteriorated quality of labor, the insubstantiality of money, the ravishment of nature, the impoverishment of food, the manipulation of emotion, the emptiness of faith, the displacement of sex, the deterioration of language, the reduction of philosophy, and the alienation of man from the product of his work and the results of his acts.

What a modest list! What a happy century. One could speak for hours on each of the categories of this plague. But we are here tonight to talk about other matters. So I will try to do no more than list the symptoms of this plague.

Even 25 years ago architecture, for example, still told one something about a building and what went on within it. Today, who can tell the difference between a modern school and a modern hospital, between a modern hospital and a modern prison, or a prison and a housing project? The airports look like luxury hotels, the luxury hotels are indistinguishable from a modern corporation's home office, and the home office looks like an air-conditioned underground city on the moon.

In medicine, not so long ago, just before the war, there still used to be diseases. Diphtheria, smallpox, German measles, scarlet fever. Today there are allergies, viruses, neuroses, incurable diseases. Surgery may have made some mechanical advances, but sickness is more mysterious than ever. No one knows quite what a virus is, nor an allergy, nor how to begin to comprehend an incurable disease. We have had an avalanche of antibiotics, and now we have a rampage of small epidemics with no name and no distinctive set of symptoms.

Nature is wounded in her fisheries, her forests. Airplanes spray insecticides. Species of insects are removed from the chain of life. Crops are poisoned just slightly. We grow enormous tomatoes which have no taste. Food is raised in artificial circumstances, with artificial nutrients, full of alien chemicals and foreign bodies.

Our emotions are turned like television dials by men in motivational research. Goods are not advertised to speak to our needs but to our secret itch. Our secondary schools have a curriculum as interesting as the wax paper on breakfast food. Our educational system teaches us not to think, but to know the answer. Faith is half-empty. Until the churches can offer an explanation for Buchenwald, or Siberia or Hiroshima, they are only giving solace to the unimaginative. They are neglecting the modern crisis. For all of us live today as divided men. Our hope for the future must be shared with the terror that we may go exploding into the heavens at the same instant 10,000,000 other souls are being exploded beside us. Not surprising, then, if many people no longer look to sex as an act whose final purpose is to continue the race.

Language is drowning in jargons of mud. Philosophy is in danger of becoming obsolescent. Metaphysics disappears, logical positivism arises. The mass of men begin to have respect not for those simple ideas which are mysteries, but on the contrary for those simple ideas which are certitudes. Soon a discussion of death will be considered a betrayal of philosophy.

Finally, there is a vast alienation of man from responsibility. One hundred years ago Marx was writing about the alienation of man from his tools and the product of his work. Today that alienation has gone deeper. Today we are alienated from our acts. A writer I know interviewed Dr. Teller, "the father of the hydrogen bomb." There was going to be a new test of that bomb soon. "Are you going to see it?" asked the reporter.

"Who is interested in that?" asked Teller. "That is just a big bang."

Face to face with a danger they cannot name, there are still many people on the Right Wing who sense that there seems to be some almost palpable conspiracy to tear life away from its roots. There is a biological rage at the heart of much Right Wing polemic. They feel as if somebody, or some group—in New York no doubt—are trying to poison the very earth, air and water of their existence. In their mind, this plague is associated with collectivism, and I am not so certain they are wrong. The essence of biology seems to be challenge and response, risk and survival, war and the lessons of war. It may be biologically true that life cannot have beauty without its companion—danger. Collectivism promises security. It spreads security the way a knife spreads margarine. Collectivism may well choke the pores of life.

But there is a contradiction here. Not all of the Right Wing, after all, is individual and strong. Far from it. The Right Wing knows better than I would know how many of them are collectivists in their own hearts, how many detest questions and want answers, loathe paradox, and live with a void inside themselves, a void of fear, a void of fear for the future and for what is unexpected, which fastens upon Communists as equal, one to one, with the Devil. The Right Wing often speaks of freedom when what it desires is iron law, when what it really desires is collectivism managed by itself. If the Right Wing is reacting to the plague, all too many of the powerful people on the Right—the presidents of more than a few corporations in California, for example—are helping to disseminate the plague. I do not know if this applies to Senator Goldwater who may be an honorable and upright man, but I think it can do no harm to take a little time to study the application of his ideas.

As a thoroughgoing conservative, the Senator believes in increasing personal liberty by enlarging economic liberty. He is well known for his views. He would reduce the cost of public welfare and diminish the present power of the unions, he would lower the income tax, dispense with subsidies to the farmer, decentralize the Federal Government and give states' rights back to the states, he would limit the Government's spending, and he would discourage any interference by Washington in the education of the young. It is a complete, comprehensive program. One may agree with it or disagree. But no doubt it is a working program. The reasonableness of this program is attractive. It might even reduce the depredations of the plague. There is just one trouble with it. It does not stop here. Senator Goldwater takes one further step. He would carry the cold war to the Soviet Union, he would withdraw diplomatic recognition, he would recognize, I quote, that:

> . . . If our objective is victory over communism, we must achieve superiority in all of the weapons —military, as well as political and economic— that may be useful in reaching that goal. Such a program costs money, but so long as the money is spent wisely and efficiently, I would spend it. I am not in favor of economizing on the nation's safety.

It is the sort of statement which inspires a novelist's imagination long enough to wonder what might happen to the Senator's program if he were elected President. For we may be certain he is sincere in his desire to achieve superiority in all the weapons, including such ideological weapons as arriving first on the moon. But what of the cost? There is one simple and unforgettable figure. More than 60 cents out of every dollar spent by the Government is spent on military security already. Near to two thirds of every dollar. And our national budget in 1963 will be in the neighborhood of $90,000,000,000. If we add what will be spent on foreign aid, the figure will come to more than 75 cents in every dollar.

Yet these expenditures have not given us a clear

superiority to the Soviet Union. On the contrary, Senator Goldwater points out that we must still *achieve* superiority. Presumably, he would increase the amount of money spent on defense. This, I suppose, would not hinder him from reducing the income tax, nor would it force him to borrow further funds. He could regain any moneys lost in this reduction by taking the money from welfare and education, that is he could if he didn't increase our defense efforts by more than 10 percent, for if he did that, we would be spending more already than the money we now spend on welfare. And of course that part of the population which would be most affected by the cessation of welfare, that is, so to speak, the impoverished part of the population, might not be happy. And it is not considered wise to have a portion of the populace unhappy when one is expanding one's ability to go to war, unless one wishes to put them in uniform. Perhaps Goldwater might not reduce the expenditures on welfare during this period. He might conceivably increase them a little in order to show that over the short period, during the crisis, during the arms buildup while we achieve superiority over the Russians, a conservative can take just as good care of the masses as a liberal. Especially since we may assume the Russians would be trying to achieve superiority over us at the same time we are trying to achieve superiority over them, so that an arms and munitions competition would be taking place and there would be enough money spent for everyone.

But let me move on to education where the problem is more simple. To achieve superiority over the Russians there, we simply need more technicians, engineers and scientists. We also have to build the laboratories in which to teach them. Perhaps, most reluctantly, just for the duration of the crisis, which is to say for the duration of his period in office, President Goldwater might have to increase the Federal budget for education. That would be contrary to his principles. But perhaps he could recover some of those expenditures by asking the farmer to dispense with subsidies. The farmer would not mind if additional Government funds were allocated to education and welfare, and he was not included. The farmer would not mind if the larger corporations of America, General Dynamics and General Motors, General Electric, United States Steel and A.T.&T., were engaged in rather large new defense contracts. No, the farmer would not mind relinquishing his subsidy. Not at all. Still, to keep him as happy as everyone else Goldwater might increase his subsidy. Just for the duration of the crisis. Just for the duration of enlightened conservatism in office. It would not matter about the higher income tax, the increased farm subsidies, the enlarged appropriation for welfare, the new magnified role of the Federal Government in education, President Goldwater could still give the states back their rights. He would not have to integrate the schools down South. He could drive the Russians out of the Congo, while the White Councils were closing the white colleges in order not to let a black man in. Yes, he could. For the length of a 20-minute speech in Phoenix, Arizona, he could. But you know and I know and he knows what he would do—he would do what President Eisenhower did. He would send troops in to integrate the schools of the South. He would do that if he wanted to keep the Russians out of the Congo.

Poor President Goldwater. At least he could cut down on the power of the unions. He could pass a Right-to-Work act. Indeed he could. He could carry the war to the Russians, he could achieve superiority, while the unions of America were giving up their power and agreeing not to strike. Yes. Yes. Of course he could. Poor President Goldwater. He might have to end by passing a law which would make it illegal ever to pass a Right-to-Work law. Under Goldwater, the American people would never have to be afraid of creeping socialism. They would just have state conservatism, creeping state conservatism. Yes, there are conservatives like the old lady who wished to save the trees and there are conservatives who talk of saving trees in order to get the power to cut down the trees.

So long as there is a cold war, there cannot be a conservative administration in America. There cannot for the simplest reason. Conservatism depends upon a huge reduction in the power and the budget of the central Government. Indeed, so long as there is a cold war, there are no politics of consequence in America. It matters less each year which party holds the power. Before the enormity of defense expenditures, there is no alternative to an ever-increasing welfare state. It can be an interesting welfare state like the present one, or a dull welfare state like President Eisenhower's. It can even be a totally repressive welfare state like President Goldwater's well might be. But the conservatives might recognize that greater economic liberty is not possible so long as one is building a greater war machine. To pretend that both can be real is hypocritical beyond belief. The conservatives are then merely mouthing impractical ideas which they presume may bring them power. They are sufficiently experienced to know that only liberalism can lead America into total war without popular violence, or an active underground.

There is an alternative. Perhaps it is ill-founded. Perhaps it is impractical. I do not know enough to say. I fear there is no one in this country who knows enough to say. Yet I think the time may be approaching for a great debate on this alternative. I say that at least this alternative is no more evil and no more visionary than Barry Goldwater's promise of a conservative America with superiority in all the weapons. So I say—in modesty and in doubt, I say—the alternative may be to end the cold war. The cold war has been an instrument of megalomaniacal delusion to this country. It is the poison of the Right Wing. It is the poison they feed themselves and it is the poison they feed the nation. Comunism may be evil incarnate, but it is a most complex evil which seems less intolerable today than it did under Stalin. I for one do not understand an absolute evil which is able to ameliorate its own evil. I say an evil which has captured the elements of the good is complex. To insist communism is a simple phenomenon can only brutalize the minds of the American people. Already, it has given this country over to the power of every huge corporation and organization in America. It has helped to create an America run by committees. It has stricken us with secret waste and hatred. It has held back the emergence of an America more alive and more fantastic than any America yet created.

So I say: End the cold war. Pull back our boundaries to what we can defend and to what wishes to be defended. There is one dread advantage to atomic war. It enables one powerful nation to be the equal of many nations. We do not have to hold every loose piece of real estate on earth to have security. Let communism come to those countries it will come to. Let us not use up our substance trying to hold onto nations which are poor, underdeveloped, and bound to us only by the depths of their hatred for us. We cannot equal the effort the Communists make in such places. We are not dedicated in that direction. We were not born to do that. We have had our frontier already. We cannot be excited to our core, our historic core, by the efforts of new underdeveloped nations to expand their frontiers. No, we are better engaged in another place, we are engaged in making the destiny of Western man, a destiny which seeks now to explore out beyond the moon and in back into the depths of the soul. With some small fraction of the money we spend now on defense we can truly defend ourselves and Western Europe, we can develop, we can become extraordinary, we can go a little further toward completing the heroic vision of Western man. Let the Communists flounder in the countries they acquire. The more countries they hold, the less supportable will become the contradictions of their ideology, the more bitter will grow the divisions in their internal interest, and the more enormous their desire to avoid a war which could only destroy the economies they will have developed at such vast labor and such vast waste. Let it be their waste, not ours. Our mission may be not to raise the level of minimum subsistence in the world so much as it may be to show the first features and promise of that incalculable renaissance men may someday enter. So let the true war begin. It is not a war between West and East, between capitalism and communism, or democracy and totalitarianism; it is rather the deep war which has gone on for six centuries in the nature of Western man, it is the war between the conservative and the rebel, between authority and instinct, between the two views of God which collide in the mind of the West, the ceremonious conservative view which believes that if God allows one man to be born wealthy and another poor, we must not tamper unduly with this conception of place, this form of society created by God, for it is possible the poor man is more fortunate than the rich, since he may be judged less severely on his return to eternity. That is the conservative view and it is not a mean nor easy view to deny.

The rebel or the revolutionary might argue, however, that the form of society is not God's creation, but a result of the war between God and the Devil, that this form is no more than the line of the battlefield upon which the Devil distributes wealth against God's best intention. So man must serve as God's agent, seeking to shift the wealth of our universe in such a way that the talent, creativity and strength of the future, dying now by dim dull deaths in every poor man alive, will come to take its first breath, will show us what a mighty renaissance is locked in the unconscious of the dumb. It is the argument which claims that no conservative can ever be certain those imbued with the value of tradition did not give more devotion to their garden, their stable, their kennel, the livery of their servant and the oratorical style of their clergy-man than God intended. Which conservative indeed can be certain that if his class once embodied some desire of the Divine Will, that it has not also now incurred God's displeasure after all these centuries of organized Christianity and enormous Christian greed? Which conservative can swear that it was not his class who gave the world a demonstration of greed so complete, an expropriation and spoliation of backward lands and simple people so avid, so vicious, so insane, a class which finally gave such suck to the Devil, that the most backward primitive in the darkest jungle would sell the grave and soul of his dearest ancestor for a machine with which to fight back?

That is the war which has meaning, that great and mortal debate between rebel and conservative where each would argue the other is an agent of the Devil. That is the war we can welcome, the war we can expect if the cold war will end. It is the war which will take life and power from the statistical congelations of the Center and give it over to Left and to Right, it is the war which will teach us our meaning, where we will discover ourselves and whether we are good and where we are not, so it is the war which will give the West what is great within it, the war which gives birth to art and furnishes strength to fight the plague. Art, free inquiry and the liberty to speak may be the only cure against the plague.

But first, I say, first there is another debate America must have. Do we become totalitarian or do we end the cold war? Do we accept the progressive collectivization of our lives which eternal cold war must bring, or do we gamble on the chance that we have armament enough already to be secure and to be free, and do we seek therefore to discover ourselves, and Nature willing, discover the conservative or rebellious temper of these tortured times? And when we are done, will we know truly who has spoken within us, the Lord, or the Fallen Prince?

The Leading Man: A Review of J.F.K.: The Man and the Myth

CO-AUTHOR of *Seeds of Treason,* a book on the Hiss-Chambers case, Victor Lasky has now written a giant political biography of John Fitzgerald Kennedy. It is a thoroughgoing performance which begins with the career of Joseph Kennedy Sr., then moves from Jack Kennedy's first political musings in college on through the separate stations of his career all the way into the first years of the Presidency. A considerable number of vignettes are offered as well of other members of the Kennedy family and such figures in the New Frontier as Theodore Sorensen, Arthur Schlesinger, Jr., and John Kenneth Galbraith. It is close to being a monumental study of Jack Kennedy's stops and starts, dips and swoops, turns to Right and Left as he advanced along his political life, and the work becomes an indispensable if not altogether trustworthy reference to anyone who would study the peculiar logic of political success, the practical details in the art of the possible.

Lasky has done an impressive amount of work. He has hunted down a thousand anecdotes in newspapers and magazines (half of them sufficiently apocryphal to be worthless, we can suspect), he has talked to everyone who knew Kennedy and would agree to talk to Lasky, he has come up with much of the goods and a hundred goodies. Did Jack Kennedy ever kiss a baby in the congressional campaign of 1946 and turning to a friend to say, "Kissing babies gives me asthma"? Well, you may be certain Lasky has found the item and put it in. *J. F. K.: The Man and the Myth* is a book which will give pleasure to every Kennedy-hater who reads it—they will feel as if they are dipping into a box of creamy chocolate. Indeed, at his best and worst, Lasky is reminiscent of Lait and Mortimer—he could have called his job *John F. Kennedy—Confidential.*

And there is value in such an undertaking: a man *is* responsible for his past. It is not fitting that Jack Kennedy should get away with all of it. The Republicans will employ these pages as a running handbook for the '64 campaign, and it will be of inestimable use to them, good use and dirty use, but ideally the book can be worth even more for liberal Democrats, since their chronic disease is hero worship, and Lasky's pages are effective antitoxin. For example:

> In 1950, John F. Kennedy made a personal contribution to Richard M. Nixon in his Senate campaign against the California Congresswoman [Helen Gahagan Douglas]. . . . Like any other contribution it was turned over to the Nixon Senate Campaign Committee in California.

On the preceding page is one of numerous references to the President's not unfavorable attitude toward McCarthy in the early Fifties: "He thought he 'knew Joe pretty well, and he [McCarthy] may have something.' "

But then the Kennedy of 1948 was making these sorts of headlines in the Boston *Herald:* "Kennedy says Roosevelt sold Poland to Reds." F.D.R. had done this "because he did not understand the Russian mind." So had gone a modest speech Congressman Kennedy had given to the *Polish-*American Citizens Club in Roxbury.

Lasky is unrelenting. A letter from the President to his father, written in 1937 when he was 20, goes in part (note the fence straddling):

> . . . while I felt that perhaps it would be far better for Spain if Franco should win—as he would strengthen and unite (sic) Spain—yet at the beginning the government was in the right morally speaking as its program was similar to the New Deal.

A little later, in his undergraduate thesis, "Appeasement at Munich," he was defending the Munich Pact: "The state of British opinion and the condition of Britain's armaments . . . made 'surrender' inevitable."

But these, after all, were the somewhat Right Wing views of a very young man. The embarrassment for liberals is that the attitude persisted almost up to his nomination. Calculated, in retrospect, seems J.F.K.'s courtship of President Eisenhower, his announcement in 1955 that he was only in "moderate opposition" to the White House, and Lasky's evidence that all through the late Fifties Jack Kennedy was doing his best to seduce the South. "Georgia loves him," reported the political editor of the Atlanta *Constitution*.

This catalogue of Right Wing sins and stances does, however, a violence to the balance. Kennedy's real political art—Lasky's documentation is more than adequate here—came from his ability to occupy the political Center yet move simultaneously to the Right and to the Left. He committed himself, for example, to the legislative programs of Walter Reuther and George Meany while engaging at the same time in an all-out attack on Dave Beck and Jimmy Hoffa. Thus he could nail down the support of the most powerful sectors of organized labor in the Democratic Party for his nomination while advancing himself in the public eye as a militant crusader against union rackets. At the junction of these two prongs is pure political sugar. The instrument of his attack on Hoffa had been the McClellan Labor Rackets Committee; Jack and Bobby Kennedy dominated the committee to the point where other senators would arrive for hearings to find witnesses called without their knowledge. Lasky's explanation is that the brothers were able to attain this exceptional power over a commitee only because they possessed "the blessing of the Majority Leader of the Senate, Lyndon B. Johnson." It was Johnson's notion presumably to bind Jack Kennedy over to the idea of a Johnson-Kennedy ticket for President. The shade of

Frankenstein falls dark on the shoulder of a politician.

Barry Goldwater once remarked bitterly that the Kennedys had nothing working for them but "money and gall," and when one thinks of the devoted work Bobby Kennedy gave to the McCarthy committee as a lawyer on McCarthy's staff, quitting finally only because he refused, according to Lasky, "to play second fiddle to Roy Cohn," there is either high comedy or the suspicion of horror in Bobby Kennedy's subsequent attack on Hubert Humphrey's tactics as McCarthyite during the West Virginia primaries seven years later.

The political point, of course, is that one can usually get away with it. For every man who would remember that Bobby Kennedy was once a McCarthyite, there would be a dozen others who would forget and call the first man a liar. A speech made in one city does not have the same magic when it is read about in another city. A promise made in private to a politician will not interfere with a contradictory promise made to another politician. When the time comes to fulfill the promise, one can reward the man who did the most for you, or is strongest, or indeed one can break both promises and make a deal with a third politician. One can promise the Negro his rights in the North while giving intimations to the South that one is secretly sympathetic to their fears. The art is to practice duplicity and double-dealing with a sense of moderation, taste, and personal style; the secret is to remain alert to the subtler shifting realities of mass communication: what sort of news in this season is likely to become national, which oratory will happily or unhappily remain local.

These are some of the lessons to be elucidated from the political career of John Fitzgerald Kennedy. If Lasky's work had been an objective study, if Kennedy had been considered merely the first among equals, if it had been understood that such men as Barry Goldwater, Hubert Humphrey, and Dick Nixon are all in their way equally adept as political operators—if Lasky's work had risen into an unbiased exploration of political mendacity in general and President Kennedy in particular, there might have been a hard remaining substance to the book. He could have left us with a classic in political biography. (A badly written classic, be it said—the prose is left without comment.) Instead, Lasky's pretense to be objective, which keeps the first half of his book interesting, begins even as pretense to disappear about the time Jack Kennedy begins to work for his nomination. Lasky's bias shows itself. He is, we discover, a Nixon man, an all-out Nixon man. The moral judgments slide over into propaganda. Nixon is invariably presented as honest, self-effacing, put upon, unjustly rejected; Kennedy grows into a villain of the first proportions. So a work which might have reminded us that we take the politician too seriously is replaced by Lasky's more specific objective—which is to stitch up a campaign flag for the return of Richard M. Nixon; so a work which could have reminded Jack Kennedy that there is still a public conscience becomes instead a campaign tract to be overpraised by Republicans and damned by Democrats. That is the crime of commission in *J. F. K.: The Man and the Myth*.

The void of omission is more grave. For, with all his documentation of Jack Kennedy's political life, the large disappointment in the book is that Lasky has no intimation of the curious depths in the President's nature. J.F.K. is a divided man, and only half his nature is political. Even through the lenses of his bias, Lasky understands that half very well—that half-man comes through the pages as one of the most consummate political animals in the history of America. But the half omitted is more crucial. For Jack Kennedy is a new kind of political leader, and a study of his past political sins will not help us to comprehend his future. The likelihood is that our President is a new kind of Commander in Chief. He is not a father, nor a god, nor a god-figure, nor an institution, nor a symbol. He is in fact—permit the literary conceit—a metaphor. Which is to say that Jack Kennedy is more like a hero of uncertain moral grandeur: is his ultimate nature tragic or epic? Is he a leading man or America's brother? A symbol is static. It exists eternally, immutably. It is the circle of the sun or the wave of the sea. But a metaphor is a relation. It changes as our experience changes. We say for example: the sun was burning with hate. A day later the meaning alters and we say to ourselves that it is only our own hatred we perceived in the sun; in a week the metaphor has come to mean something else again, something deeper perhaps—between the sun and ourselves is a celestial terrain of hatreds which alter our understanding of the sun at every moment.

These poetic mechanics are of course far indeed from Victor Lasky's prose, stance, and intention. But *J. F. K.: The Man and the Myth* is an irritating, frustrating, and finally disappointing book because it offered the promise of becoming a first-rate job, and was spoiled—this spoliation being a first-rate loss —by Lasky's incapacity to entertain a poetic concept of his subject. Jack Kennedy is somewhat more and considerably less after all than a hero or a villain— he is also an empty vessel, a man of many natures, not all of them necessarily rooted in granite. He is, it must be said, a Kierkegaardian hero. One can assume that in the private stricken moments of his life, those moments all of us know at rare and best-forgotten times, it is impossible for him to be certain of his moral bedrock. Kierkegaard was probably the first Western mind to have an intimation that either the nature of man was changing or had never been properly understood, that it was just as natural for man to be flooded with sensations of goodness when he was most evil as it was for him to taste his evil, and that a man in the act of being good could equally be depressed with an awareness of his profound evil. In this sense one did not have a nature which was formed already—on the contrary, one created one's

nature by the depth or power of one's acts. Kierkegaard had divined that there was probably no anguish
on heaven or earth so awful as the inability to create
one's nature by daring, exceptional, forbidden, or
socially impossible acts.

This impulse—to create and forever re-create his
nature—has been the President's dominant passion.
There is no other way to comprehend him. From the
Hairbreadth Harry of his P. T. boat exploits through
the political campaigns with their exceptional chances
(who could beat Cabot Lodge in Massachusetts in
1952?) through the lively bachelordom, through the
marriage to the impossibly beautiful and somewhat
madcap wife, the decision to run for President, a decision worthy of Julien Sorel, the adventure in Cuba,
the atomic poker game with Khrushchev last October
when the biggest bluff in the history of the world was
called—yes, each is a panel of scenes in the greatest
movie ever made.

The President is not a great mind, and it may be
that he will prove ultimately not to be a good man—
those who are forever re-creating their personalities
can end with a mediocre nature even more naturally
than a great one—but he had genius in one respect.
Jack Kennedy understood that the most important,
probably the only dynamic culture in America, the
only culture to enlist the imagination and change the
character of Americans, was the one we had been given
by the movies. Therefore a void existed at the center
of American life. No movie star had the mind, courage
or force to be national leader, and no national leader
had the epic adventurous resonance of a movie star.
So the President nominated himself. He would fill
the void. He would be the movie star come to life as
President. That took genius. For Jack Kennedy grew
up in the kind of milieu which was so monumental
with finance and penurious with emotion that everybody's breath smelled like they had been swallowing
pennies and you were considered mentally disturbed if
you did not bet on the New York Yanks. He had a char-

acter thus created of the most impossible ingredients
for his venture: overweening ambition and profound
political caution—he had been taught never to commit himself to a political idea since ideas often pass,
weaken, and die long before the men who believed
in them.

Yes, John F. Kennedy was without principles or
political passions except for one. He knew the only
way he could re-create the impoverished circuits which
lay between himself and the depths of his emotions
was to become President. *He* was his own idea, and
he had the luck to have a powerful father who agreed
entirely with his venture. So he combined the two
halves of his nature, the Faustian adventurer and the
political opportunist, and behind him left a record
of deceits, evasions, broken promises, Congressional
absenteeism, political pusillanimities, after-dinner
clichés, amoral political negotiations and a complete
absence on the record of a single piece of important
legislation. Or the utterance of a single exciting
political idea. He didn't have to. He was on the trail
of something else and the people who gathered to his
support were in quest of something else.

His impulse, that profound insight into the real
sources of political power in America, came from a
conscious or unconscious cognition that the nation
could no longer use a father; it was Kennedy's genius
to appreciate that we now required a leading man.
The contradictions of our national character had become so acute that no symbol of authority could satisfy our national anxiety any longer. We had become
a Kierkegaardian nation. In the deep mills of our
crossed desires, in the darkening ambiguities of our
historic role, we could know no longer whether we
were good or evil as an historic force, whether we
should prosper or decline, whether we were the seed
of freedom or the elaboration of a new tyranny. We
needed to discover ourselves by an exploration
through our ambiguity. And that precise ambiguity
is embodied in the man we chose for our President.

His magnetism is that he offers us a mirror of ourselves, he is an existential hero, his end is unknown,
it is even unpredictable, even as our end is unpredictable, and so in this time of crisis he is able to per-
form the indispensable psychic act of a leader, he
takes our national anxiety so long buried and re-
leases it to the surface—where it belongs.

Now we must live again as a frontier nation, out
on a psychic frontier without the faith of children
or the security of answers. So the country, for better
or for worse, is now again on the move, and the President is the living metaphor of our change. It is this
power in him to excite—whether he desires it or no—
our change, our discord, and our revolt, which Victor
Lasky has failed most resolutely to comprehend. He
does not see that Kennedy is the agent of our ferment
and that we now go forth into the future ignorant of
whether the final face of the Presidency and America shall prove to be Abraham Lincoln or Dorian
Gray.

A Political Miscellany for Existentialists

divided into two parts:

A.   The Critique

B.   The Action

with a sexual appendix
to follow and explanatory
note.

THESE WRITINGS for the miscellany vary in style: as advertised previously, they offer hints of irony, brutal simplicity of dialogue, adjuration, naïveté, invective, pomposity, slam-bang, even innocence. There is, however, a common denominator more common than the fact that these writings issue from the same author —it is their vector: they are all excursions into existential politics. Three cheers. Existentialism, you see, is built on the sort of perception which makes for legendary children. "But can't you see, Daddy, the emperor has no clothes." That is the beginning of existentialism. As a philosophy, existentialism was embattled before it was even created—one could go far arguing that the major attempt of all academic philosophy (which is to say all philosophy preceding existentialism) was precisely to keep existential concepts from ever entering the schools of philosophy. For existentialism is the perception of the child, the savage, the primitive, the lover, the warrior, the hunter, the saint, the criminal, the athlete, and the poet—at least insofar as his poem comes to exist (before it is analyzed somewhat later). If animals had philosophy they would be, of necessity, existentialists, for the first instinct of this philosophy is instinct. It would insist over and over that the truth is never known again so clearly as in the incandescence of the instant. At a critical moment, that which smells bad is bad, that indeed is how we know a complex experience is finally bad—we have the authority of our senses. What a danger to philosophy! It offers no enclaves, no moderation, no escape from judgment; it insists upon a courage larger than life, it permits no sentimental escape, it offers no respite in any authority higher than oneself, and what is worst, it elevates the self. There is no Godhead or authority without;

all Godhead is within. Thus, every time the potentiality of a man is lost, so too is the Godhead diminished. Therefore, note: it is not arrogant. It is the opposite of arrogance. We are arrogant when we see ourselves possessed of a secret others lack. A man armed with the authority of a true faith living somewhere external to himself, a *revealed* faith in existence before he was born, can be arrogant more easily—his responsibility is not so large if he is wrong. He may conform or not conform to authority—if he conforms, he is presumably safe; if he transgresses, he may yet be forgiven, he can always conform again. When, however, we are not anything but our own authority, when we are possessed of no given moral substance other than our own authority, we can never rest, for the existential nature of our own particular existence—I wish to say: the *feel* of our existence—is impermanence. Fix on this irony. Our body changes each day, so do our ideas. Our existential notion of authority must then of necessity sooner or later perceive that our own authority is a private truth forever in flux. It changes; if we are not alert enough, it changes within us, but it changes unhappily without us. Is the play on words here irritating?—we are talking of schizophrenia, the disease at the seat of disease. When schizophrenia attacks the body we use another name—cancer. That, after all, is the schizophrenia of the body cells. So, talk of existentialism inspires fear—it is too moral. Once we are each our own authority, we are therefore each our own failure, our own doom. There is no displacement. We know we are sick because we do not have the courage to be well—therefore we do not feel compassion for ourselves when we are ill.

It is this implicit emphasis upon self-development, upon extraordinary development in each of us, which forms the central principle of existential politics. For a corollary would claim that the plague of civilization derives from the monstrously unequal development of man, not by nations or economic areas, but by the dichotomies of our modern psyche which makes forced marches into science and relinquishes the senses. Take a metaphor of the plague—a man with poor eyesight who runs quickly. The equation within this metaphor is that the faster he runs, the less he sees. That is the machine of our plague.

So existential politics would look ultimately to restore a vision. And a first approach to its stance might come best by considering the necessity to regard all the social phenomena of man as machines and cages which will certainly destroy him until he comes to look at them with the eye of the emperor's child. So it is not square feet of living space we must ask for, but living quarters not devoid of art, *even if the plaster is cracked;* it is not the equality of man, but his self-development which is critical; not uniformed safeguards but physical arts; not wage scales but skill in work; not sexual permissiveness as the end in itself, but promiscuity as a dangerous possibility in the search for love— one grows pious. The art of politics is quickly becoming the art of the hero, for unless man proceeds rapidly to become his own work of art, there may be neither art nor politics nor even too many of the living. Of course we will swell before we cease.

A. The Critique

On Architectural Plague

THE ACT OF TRAVELING is never a casual act. It inspires an anxiety which no psychoanalyst can relieve in a hurry, for if travel is reminiscent of the trauma of birth, it is also suggestive of some possible migrations after death.

It suggests: death may not be peace but an expedition into the terror and melancholy we sought to avoid in our lives. To some part of the unconscious the act of travel is a grave hour; on a trip we prepare a buried corner of ourselves to be ready for what happens once we are dead.

By this logic, the end of a trip is a critical moment, a transition. Railroad stations in large cities should properly be monumental, heavy with dignity, reminiscent of the past. We learn little from travel, not nearly so much as we need to learn, if everywhere we are assaulted by the faceless surfaces of everything plastic which has been built in America since the war, that new architecture of giant weeds and giant boxes, of children's colors on billboards and jagged electric signs. Like the metastases of cancer cells, the plastic shacks, the motels, the drive-in theatres, the highway restaurants and the gas stations proliferate year by year until they are close to covering the highways of America with a new country which is laid over the old one the way a transparent sheet with new drawings is set upon the original plan. It is an architecture with no root to the past and no suggestion of the future, for one cannot conceive of a modern building growing old (does it turn dingy or will the colors stain?); there is no way to age, it can only cease to function. No doubt these buildings will live for twenty years and then crack in two. They will live like robots, or television sets which go out of order with one whistle of the wind.

On Totalitarianism and Modern Architecture

TOTALITARIANISM has haunted the twentieth century, haunted the efforts of intellectuals to define it, of politicians to withstand it, and of rebels to find a field of war where it could be given battle. Amoeboid, insidious, totalitarianism came close to conquering the world twenty years ago. In that first large upheaval the Nazis sang of blood and the deep roots of blood and then proceeded to destroy the essential intuition of the primitive, the umbilical idea that death and the appropriate totems of burial are as essential to life as life itself.

That first wave of totalitarianism was a tide which moved in two directions at once. It broke upon the incompatible military force of Russia and of America. But it was an ocean of plague. It contaminated whatever it touched. If Russia had been racing into totalitarianism before the war, it was pervasively totalitarian after the war, in the last half-mad years of Stalin's court. And America was altered from a nation of venture, exploitation, bigotry, initiative, strife, social justice and social injustice, into a vast central swamp of tasteless toneless authority whose dependable heroes were drawn from FBI men, doctors, television entertainers, corporation executives, and athletes who could cooperate with public-relations men.

One must recognize the features of the plague. If it appeared first in Nazi Germany as a political juggernaut, and in the Soviet Union as a psychosis in ideology, totalitarianism has slipped into America with no specific political face. There are liberals who are totalitarian, and conservatives, radicals, rightists, fanatics, hordes of the well-adjusted. Totalitarianism has come to America with no concentration camps and no need for them, no political parties and no desire for new parties, no, totalitarianism has slipped into the body cells and psyche of each of us. It has been transported, modified, codified, and inserted into each of us by way of the popular arts, the social crafts, the political crafts, and the corporate techniques. It sits in the image of the commercials on television which use phallic and vaginal symbols to sell products which are otherwise useless for sex, it is heard in the jargon of educators, in the synthetic continuums of prose with which public-relations men learn to enclose the sense and smell of an event, it resides in the taste of frozen food, the pharmaceutical odor of tranquilizers, the planned obsolescence of automobiles, the lack of workmanship in the mass, it lives in the boredom of a good mind, in the sexual excess of lovers who love each other into apathy, it is the livid passion which takes us to sleeping pills, the mechanical action in every household appliance which breaks too often, it vibrates in the sound of an air conditioner or the flicker of fluorescent lighting. And it proliferates in that new architecture which rests like an incubus upon the American landscape, that new architecture which cannot be called modern because it is not architecture but opposed to architecture. Modern architecture began with the desire to use the building materials of the twentieth century —steel, glass, reinforced concrete—and such techniques as cantilevered structure to increase the sculptural beauty of buildings while enlarging their function. It was the first art to be engulfed by the totalitarians, who distorted the search of modern architecture for simplicity and converted it to monotony. The essence of totalitarianism is that it beheads. It beheads individuality, variety, dissent, extreme possibility, romantic faith, it blinds vision, deadens instinct, it obliterates the past. Since it is also irrational, it puts up buildings with flat roofs and huge expanses of glass in northern climates and then suffocates the inhabitants with super-heating systems. Since totalitarianism is a cancer within the body of history, it obliterates distinctions. It makes factories look like college campuses. It makes the new buildings on college campuses look like factories. It depresses the average American with the unconscious recognition that he is installed in a gelatin of totalitarian environment which is bound to deaden his most individual efforts. This new architecture, this totalitarian architecture, destroys the past. There is no trace of the forms which lived in the centuries before us, none of their arrogance, their privilege, their aspirations, their canniness, their creations, their vulgarities. We are left with less and less sense of the lives of men and women who came before us. So we are less able to judge the sheer psychotic values of the present.

On Totalitarianism

TOTALITARIANISM: one aspect of the subject might be underlined again—it is that totalitarianism is better understood as a plague than an ideology. There was a time when simple totalitarianism seemed synonymous with dictatorship. People were forced to obey a governmental authority which was not only inhumane, but invariably antagonistic to the history of the nation's immediate past. A tension was still visible between the government as the oppressor and the people as the oppressed.

The kind of modern totalitarianism which we find in America, however, is as different from classical Fascism as is a plastic bomb from a hand grenade. The hand grenade makes an imprecise weapon. Thrown into a room full of people, one cannot know who will be hurt, who will be killed, who will escape. But the aggression is still direct: a man must throw the grenade, and so, in the French sense of the word, he must "assist" at the performance of the act. He would have some idea of whom he was throwing it at. Whereas, the *bombe plastique,* used in the streets of Paris by terrorists in the O.A.S. toward the end of the Algerian War, consisted of a kind of putty which could be left in a trashbasket or stuck onto a wall. When it went off, an hour or two after its placement, only laws of chance were operating. The bomber could not know whom he was killing for he was usually miles away. Some of his own people might even be passing the intersection when the explosion came. The actor was now wholly separated from his act.

The crucial characteristic of modern totalitarianism is that it is a moral disease which divorces us from guilt. It came into being as a desire to escape the judgments of the past and our responsibility for past injustice—in that sense it is a defense against eternity, an attempt to destroy that part of eternity which is death, which is punishment or reward. It arose from the excesses of theology, the exploitation of theology, and the oppressions of theology, but in destroying theology, the being of man and his vision may be reduced to a thousand-year apathy, or to extinction itself. The words are abstract, but the meaning by now is I hope not altogether hidden. In our flight from the consequence of our lives, in our flight from adventure, from danger, and from the natural ravages of disease, in our burial of the primitive, it is death the twentieth century is seeking to avoid.

On Modern Architecture and Cancer

WE HAVE BEEN SAYING: totalitarianism came to birth at the moment man turned incapable of facing back into the accumulated wrath and horror of his historic past. Now note: we sink into cancer after we have gorged on all the medicines which cheated all the diseases we have fled in our life, we sink into cancer when the organs, deadened by chemical rescues manufactured outside the body, became too biologically muddled to dominate their cells. Departing from the function of the separate organs, cancer cells from separate organs grow to look more like one another than the cells they have departed from. So, too, as society bogs into hypocrisies so elaborate they can no longer be traced, then do our buildings, those palpable artifacts of social cells, come to look like one another and cease to function with the mysterious proportion of the past.

On Existential Definition

DEFINITION has a value. If an experience is precise, one can know a little more of what is happening to oneself. It is in those marriages and love affairs which are neither good nor bad, nor quite interesting nor altogether awful that anxiety flows like a muddy river. It is in those housing projects which look like prisons that juvenile delinquency increases at a greater rate than it used to do in the slums.

On the Root of Modern Architecture

PEOPLE WHO ADMIRE new architecture find it of value because it obliterates the past. They wish to avoid the consequences of the past. Which is not to say that they see themselves as totalitarian. The totalitarian passion is an unconscious one. Which liberal fighting for bigger housing and additional cubic feet of air space in elementary schools does not see himself as a benefactor? Can he comprehend that the somewhat clammy pleasure he obtains from looking at the completion of the new school—that architectural horror!— is a reflection of a buried and ugly pleasure, a totalitarian glee that the Gothic knots and Romanesque oppressions which entered his psyche through the schoolhouses of his youth have now been excised? But those architectural wounds, those forms from his childhood not only shamed him and scored him, but marked upon him as well a wound from culture itself —its buried message of the cruelty and horror which were rooted in the majesties of the past. Now the flat surfaces, blank ornamentation and pastel colors of the new schoolhouses will maroon his children in an endless hallway of the present. A school is an arena to a child. Let it be mysterious, exciting, even gladiatorial, rather than a musical comedy's notion of a reception center for war brides. The totalitarian impulse not only washed away distinctions but looks for a style in buildings, in clothing, and in the ornamentations of tools, appliances, and daily objects which will diminish one's sense of function, and reduce one's sense of reality by reducing to jargon such emotions as awe, dread, beauty, pity, terror, calm, horror, and harmony. By dislocating us from the most powerful emotions, totalitarianism leaves us further isolated in the empty landscapes of psychosis, precisely that inner landscape of void and dread which we flee by turning to totalitarian styles of life.

Yes, people who admire new architecture are unconsciously totalitarian. They are looking to eject into their environment and landscape the same deadness and monotony life has put into them. A vast deadness and a huge monotony, a nausea without spasm, has been part of the profit of American life in the last fifteen years—we will pay in the next fifteen as this living death is disgorged into the buildings our totalitarian managers will manage to erect for us. The landscape of America is going to be stolen for half a century if a Resistance does not form. Indeed it may be stolen forever if we do not enter the depression of contemplating what we have already lost and what we have yet to lose.

On Totalitarianism and Social Action

(In partial answer to a question.)

A. There's something pompous about people who join peace movements, SANE, and so forth. They're the radical equivalent of working for the FBI. You see, nobody can criticize you. You're doing God's work, you're clean. How can anyone object to anybody who works for SANE, or is for banning the bomb?

Q. You're not questioning their motives, are you?

A. I *am* questioning their motives. I think there's something doubtful about these people. I don't trust them. I think they're totalitarian in spirit. Now of course I'm certainly not saying they're Communist, and they most obviously are not Fascists, but there are new kinds of totalitarians. A most numerous number since World War II.

I think, for example, most of the medical profession is totalitarian by now. At least those who push antibiotics are totalitarian. I think the FBI is totalitarian. I think pacifists are totalitarian. People on your own side are just as likely to be totalitarian as people on the other side.

Q. Yes, but totalitarian to me implies force—

A. A dull, moral, abstract force. There is just such a force in the campaign for "Ban the Bomb." It's too safe. You don't *lose* anything by belonging to a committee to ban the bomb. Who's going to hurt you? Is the FBI going to stick you in jail?

Q. There are certain employers who frown upon it—

A. Which employers? I think many good people are beginning to get a little complacent. The sort of good people who are militant and imaginative and active and brave, and want a world they're willing to fight for; if there were a revolution they would carry a gun; if there were an underground they would fight a guerrilla war. But there is no real action for them, and so they end up in what I think are essentially passive campaigns like "Ban the Bomb."

I'm against sit-down strikes. I'm against people sitting down in Trafalgar Square, and cops having to carry them off. I think if you're not ready to fight the police, you mustn't sit down and let them carry you off. You must recognize that you're not ready to fight to the very end for your principles. I was carried off in a chair not so long ago and I'm not proud of it. . . .

Q. Joe Heller told me that he admires you for—and may join you next time—just standing in City Hall Park and not taking shelter during the Civil Defense drill. Why is this any more manly than other activities?

A. I didn't stand there because I was a pacifist, but because I wanted to help demonstrate a complexity. It's a physical impossibility to save the people of New York in the event of atomic attack. Anyone who chooses to live in New York is doomed in such a case. That doesn't mean one should not live in New York, but I think it does mean one should know the possible price. Air-raid drills delude people into believing that they're safe in New York. That's what I object to, rounding up the psyches of New Yorkers and giving them mass close-order drill to the sound of an air-raid siren.

On the FBI

THE FBI HAS DONE more damage to America than the American Communist Party. It has done it for a variety of reasons, some well-intentioned, some delivered from pits of foul intention, but the FBI has chilled the potentiality of America to enrich the private lives of its people. It has put a sense of inhibition into the popular arts and the popular mind. It has been an evil force. What has made it even more deadening has been the personality of its director, which is to say, the *lack* of personality in its director. The FBI has been a political idea; its essence could be stated: America is in need of a secret police whose devotion, dedication, untiring effort, professional competence and political purity entitle it to scrutinize every aspect of American life it deems worthy to scrutinize. The idea is fearful enough, but when no personality embodies it, no other personality may contest it. The cause of secret-policeness advances like a plague.

On the FBI as a Religion

Q. You once referred in passing to the FBI as a religious movement; would you elaborate on that?

A. A lot of people need the FBI for their sanity. To become a saint one must dare insanity, but if one wishes instead to flee from insanity, one method is to join an organized religion. The FBI is an organized religion.

The FBI blots out everything which could bring dread into the average mediocrity's life. Like a lover who rushes to immolate himself for love, since that is easier than to fight a war for love, the mediocrity offers the FBI his complete conformity. He gives up his personal possibilities. He believes he is living for the sake of others. The trouble is that the others are as mediocre as he is. So such people not only use themselves up, their own lives, but if there *is* a God, they use *Him* up.

Naturally these lovers of the FBI can't think of the possibility they've wasted themselves. Instead they believe in that force which agrees with them, that force which is all-out for mediocrity. The only absolute organization in America, the FBI. At bottom, I mean, profoundly at bottom, the FBI has nothing to do with Communism, nothing to do with catching criminals, nothing to do with the Mafia, the syndicate, nothing to do with gangbusting, nothing to do with illegal interstate commerce, it has nothing to do with anything but serving as a church for the mediocre.

FREUD HAD an umbilical respect for the meanings of anxiety and dread. His epigones have reduced these concepts to little more than alarm bells and rattles of malfunction in a psychic machine. Anxiety and dread are treated by them as facts, as the clashing of gears in a neurotic act. The primitive understanding of dread —that one was caught in a dialogue with gods, devils, and spirits, and so was naturally consumed with awe, shame, and terror, has been all but forgotten. We are taught that we feel anxiety because we are driven by unconscious impulses which are socially unacceptable; dread we are told is a repetition of infantile experiences of helplessness. It is induced in us by situations which remind our unconscious of weaning and other early deprivations. What is never discussed: the possibility that we feel anxiety because we are in danger of losing some part or quality of our soul unless we act, and act dangerously; or the likelihood that we feel dread when intimations of our death inspire us with disproportionate terror, a horror not merely because we are going to die, but to the contrary because we are going to die badly and suffer some unendurable stricture of eternity. These explanations are altogether outside the close focus of the psychological sciences in the twentieth century. Our century, at least our American Century, is a convalescent home for the shell-shocked veterans of a two-thousand-year war—that huge struggle within Christianity to liberate or to destroy the vision of man.

Faced with our failure (for it would seem the war has gone against us) the investigators of the intellect have taken to intellectual tranquilizers. It is logical positivism, logicians, and language analysts who dominate Anglo-American philosophy rather than existentialists; it is Freudians instead of Reichians or Jungians who rule psychoanalysis; and it is journalism rather than art which forges the apathetic conscience of our time. But then politics, like journalism, is intended to hide from us the existential abyss of dread, the terror which lies beneath our sedation. Today, a successful politician is not a man who wrestles with the art of the possible in order to enrich life, alleviate hardship, or correct injustice—he is, on the contrary, a doctor of mass communications who may measure his success by the practice of a political ritual and vocabulary which diverts us temporarily from dread, from anxiety, from the mirror of the dream.

On Politics and Dread—B

OUR CENTURY, at least our American Century, is a convalescent home for the shell-shocked veterans of a two-thousand-year-war—that huge struggle within Christianity to liberate or to destroy the vision of man.

Faced with our failure (for it would seem the war has gone against us) the investigators of the intellect have taken to intellectual tranquilizers. It is logical positivism, logicians, and language analysts who dominate Anglo-American philosophy rather than existentialists; it is Freudians instead of Reichians or Jungians who rule psychoanalysis; and it is journalism rather than art which forges the apathetic conscience of our time. But then politics, like journalism, is intended to hide from us the existential abyss of dread, the terror which lies beneath our sedation. Today, a successful politician is not a man who wrestles with the art of the possible in order to enrich life, alleviate hardship, or correct injustice—he is, on the contrary, a doctor of mass communications who may measure his success by the practice of a political ritual and vocabulary which diverts us temporarily from dread, from anxiety, from the mirror of the dream.

On the Minds of Presidents

THE PRESIDENT SUFFERS from one intellectual malady—intellectual malnutrition. That particular anemia visits leaders surrounded by advisors who do not tell the truth. Advisors are dishonest because they are professional. By the developed habits of his craft, a professional automatically suppresses as much information as he divulges; nor is this to speak of the various kinds of information a professional is incapable of receiving because the language necessary for the inquiry does not belong to his vocational jargon. So a President suffers intellectual horrors. His information is predigested—his mind is allowed as much stimulation as the second stomach of a cow. He is given not nuances but facts; indeed he is given facts not in whole, but facts masticated, their backs broken.

The natural work of the modern Presidency destroys a man's ability for abstract thought. He becomes able to think not of the mystery in the atom bomb but of its engineering.

On the Cold War

IT COULD BE ARGUED that the impetus to America's cold war with Communism has come from a collective psychosis, from a monster which has borne almost no relation to the objective cold war going on in these years, a particular real cold war which has been concrete, limited, ugly, detailed, and shrewd in its encounters. The Russians have shown a tough tenacious sly somewhat dishonorable and never-tiring regard for local victory in each of their episodes with us. We have dealt with this in terms which are schizophrenic. We also have been tough tenacious sly somewhat dishonorable and have hardly ever slackened in our regard for local victory; but for domestic political consumption we present the Russians to the American public as implacable, insane and monolithic. We could have been talking equally of the plague or some exotic variety of sex. Obviously we were afraid of something more than the Communists. Dread has been loose in the twentieth century.

On Economic Waste

THERE HAVE BEEN political leaders who kept themselves functioning on medical drugs—Adolf Hitler is one who comes to mind—and our economy has been allowed to deteriorate in its very expansions by the fiduciary drug of the war economy. If the cold war were magically to cease next year, we would face an economic crisis whose proportions are beyond measure, even as a drug addict suffers paroxysms, apathy, and collapse when his drug is withdrawn. Some large part of such an economic crisis would derive from the huge proliferations of waste in the economy, which is to say: the concealed nature of the waste within industry, the poor workmanship, the deterioration of materials, the inflated value, the literal cancers (such as institutional advertising) which are to be found in industry's mode of production.

On the Mass Media

Q. Isn't it possible that the mass media which you call totalitarian are a reflection rather than a cause of this condition in society?

A. A reflection of what people want? No, I don't think so. That's like saying that the United States

Army was a reflection of what the soldiers wanted.

Q. But they were drafted—

A. And you're not drafted—your eye is not *drafted* when you turn on that TV set? To assume that people are getting what they want through the mass media also assumes that the men and women who direct the mass media know something about the people. But they don't know anything about the people. That's why I gave you the example of the Army. The Private exists in a world which is hermetically alienated from the larger aims of the Generals who are planning the higher strategy of the war. I mean part of the tragedy of modern war (or what used to be modern war) is that you could have a noble war which was utterly ignoble at its basic level because the people who directed the war couldn't reach the common man who was carrying the gun. As for example, Franklin Delano Roosevelt and the average infantryman.

And the reason they can't is because there *is* such a thing as class, finally. And the upper classes don't understand the lower classes, they're incapable of it. Every little detail of their upbringing turns them away from the possibility of such understanding.

The mass media is made up of a group of people who are looking for money and for power. The reason is not because they have any moral sense, any inner sense of a goal, of an ideal that's worth fighting for, dying for, if one is brave enough. No, the reason they want power is because power is the only thing which will relieve the profound illness which has seized them. Which has seized all of us. The illness of the twentieth century. There isn't psychic room for all of us. Malthus's law has moved from the excessive procreation of bodies to the excessive mediocritization of psyches. The deaths don't occur on the battlefield any longer, or through malnutrition; they occur within the brain, within the psyche itself. You see, one can have Fascism come in any form at all, through the church, through sex, through social welfare, corporatism, state capitalism, through organized medicine, the FBI, the Pentagon. Fascism is not a way of life but a murderous mode of deadening reality by smothering it with lies.

Every time one sees a bad television show, one is watching the nation get ready for the day when a Hitler will come. I think a reasonably good play on television that is truthful for the first two acts and becomes completely false in the third act is evil, because it arouses certain expectations in people, makes them start considering their lives, and just at the point when they're most open they're turned away with a lie. Of course the ideology of the show is not Fascistic; on the contrary its manifest ideology is invariably liberal, but the show still prepares Fascism because it is meretricious art and so sickens people a little further. Whenever people get collectively sick, the remedy becomes progressively more violent and hideous.

On Minorities

THE MODERN AMERICAN politician often begins his career with a modest passion to defend the rights of minorities. By the time he is successful, his passion has been converted to platitude.

Minority groups are the artistic nerves of a republic; like any phenomenon which has to do with art, they are profoundly divided. They are both themselves and the mirror of their culture as it reacts upon them. They are themselves and the negative truth of themselves. No white man, for example, can hate the Negro race with the same passionate hatred and detailed detestation that each Negro feels for himself and for his people; no anti-Semite can begin to comprehend the malicious analysis of his soul which every Jew indulges every day.

For decades the Jews have been militant for their rights; since the Second World War the Negroes have emerged as an embattled and disciplined minority. It is thus characteristic of both races that they have a more intense awareness of their own value and their own lack of value than the awareness of the white Anglo-Saxon Protestant for himself. Unlike the Protestant of the center, minorities have a nature which is polarized. So it is natural that their buried themes, precisely those preoccupations which are never mentioned by minority action groups like the Anti-Defamation League or the NAACP, are charged with paradox, with a search for psychic extremes. To a Protestant, secure in the middle of American life, God and the Devil, magic, death and eternity, are matters outside himself. He may contemplate them but he does not habitually absorb them into the living tissue of his brain. Whereas the exceptional member of any minority group feels as if he possesses God and the Devil within himself, that the taste of his own death is already in his cells, that his purchase on eternity rises and falls with the calm or cowardice of his actions. It is a life exposed to the raw living nerve of anxiety, and rare is the average Jew or Negro who can bear it for long—so the larger tendency among minorities is to manufacture a mediocre personality which is a dull replica of the manners of the white man in power. Nothing can be more conformist, more profoundly depressing that the Jew-in-the-suburb, or the Negro as member of the Black Bourgeoisie. It is the price they pay for the fact that not all self-hatred is invalid—the critical faculty turned upon oneself can serve to create a personality which is exceptional, which mirrors the particular arts and graces of the white gentry, but this is possible only if one can live with one's existential nerve exposed. Man's personality rises to a level of higher and more delicate habits only if he is willing to engage a sequence of painful victories and cruel defeats in his expedition through the locks and ambushes of social life. One does not copy the manner of someone superior; rather one works an art upon it which makes it suitable for oneself. Direct imitation of a superior manner merely produces a synthetic manner. The collective expression of this in a minority group is nothing other than assimilation.

To the degree each American Jew and American Negro is assimilated he is colorless, a part of a collective nausea which is encysted into the future.

B. The Action

On the Root of Existential Politics

CLASSICAL POLITICS begins with the notion that a great many facts and a few phenomena are hard, measurable, and statistical, and thus may be manipulated to produce corrective results. Existential politics, however, derives not from statistics as a prime phenomenon, but from existentialism. So it begins with the separate notion that we live out our lives wandering among mysteries, and can guide ourselves only by what our inner voice tells us is true to the relations between mysteries. The separate mysteries we may never seize, but to appropriate a meaning from their relationship is possible.

On the Concept of the Hero in Politics

POLITICS is the art of the possible, and what is always possible is to reduce the amount of real suffering in a bad time, and to enrich the quality of life in a good time. This is precisely what is not being done in America. We are in a good time in America, a prosperous time, a time of relative wealth and relative lack of poverty which was created not by Roosevelt, Truman, Eisenhower, or Kennedy, but by the economic mathematics of finding an ever-expanding market whose ultimate consumer is the enemy soldier. We have been living in the curious but prosperous hollow of planned military obsolescence. In fact we have built so many different airplanes since the Second World

War that soon there ought to be enough to give away an obsolete one to each high-school class in the land.

But we've done nothing to approach the center of the problem: life in America becomes more economically prosperous and more psychically impoverished each year.

Politics is arithmetic, but politics is also rhetoric, passion, and an occasional idea to fire the imagination of millions. It is the unspoken thesis of these pages that no President can save America from a descent into totalitarianism without shifting the mind of the American politician to existential styles of political thought.

If the question is now asked what can possibly be meant by "an existential grasp of the nature of reality," or "existential styles of political thought," the answer would rest in the notion that the disease of the state is intensified when large historic ideas come to power without men to personify them or dramatize their qualities.

Existential politics is rooted in the concept of the hero, it would argue that the hero is the one kind of man who *never* develops by accident, that a hero is a consecutive set of brave and witty self-creations. All heroes are leaders—even if, like Don Quixote, they have but one man to follow them—but not all leaders are heroes. An unheroic leader is a man who embodies his time but is not superior to it—he is historically faceless. Roosevelt was a hero, Calvin Coolidge or Herbert Hoover were leaders, nominal leaders. So was Eisenhower. Joe McCarthy, on the contrary, was a hero, a most distressing kind of hero, but because he was a hero he encountered opponents as well as attracted followers, and he was finally defeated. With his fall went the threat that his ideas would dominate America. How fortunate for the Left that a hero arose on the Right at that moment. For if not, the leaders of the Right might have strangled the liberties of America somewhat further by remaining a faceless force.

Politics is like a body of organs. When the body is

sick, it is usually because one or another organ has become too weak or too powerful in its function. If the disproportion is acute, a war goes on in the body, an inflammatory sickness, a fever, a crisis. The war decided, the organ subsides, different in size, stronger or weaker, it returns to its part of the body's function. Acute disease is cure. But it is the war itself which initiates such a restoration of balance. For war has features, symptoms, results.* Acute diseases are like political forces personified by heroes. And slack diseases, featureless symptomless diseases like virus and colds and the ubiquitous cancer are the appropriate metaphor of all those political forces like the FBI, or like the liberalism of the Democratic Party, which are historically faceless. That is why political rights like personal rights are best won by face-to-face confrontation. But since modern historical movements are now so huge, only a hero may lead them and still possess a face.

On the FBI

AN EXISTENTIAL PRESIDENT would look for a man with a salient personality to put as head of the FBI. Under such a man, the fortunes of the FBI would prosper or falter, but its activities would be dramatized, its victories would come from open struggle, and its success would cease to resemble the certainty of the house percentage in a gambling casino. The FBI would be forced to exist rather than proliferate. If its leader was not heroic as a man, the FBI would proceed to exist less, it would lose existence because it would be in open competition for existence with other organs of the

---

*Note that the war in Vietnam is without features (read: a battle-line) and seems to be without measurable results. Of symptoms it has many—they are all cancerous: wasteful growth in useless places.

government. But with a heroic leader it would prosper, it would *deserve* to prosper. The FBI has at present a leader, but not a hero. So it is faceless in history. And because it is faceless it is insidious, plague-like, an evil force. Power without a face is the disease of the state. But if the FBI had a hero for a leader and its fortunes prospered on open political market, then even if its ideas seemed odious, one would have to accept its prosperity as an historic event, a force with precise features.

On Leaders and New Revolutionaries

Q. How do you sap the energy of bad leaders who are caught up in their own bad time?

A. In a modern state, the forces of propaganda control leaders as well as citizens, because the forces of propaganda are more complex than the leader. In a bad time, the war to be fought is in the mass media.

If anyone is a leftist, or a radical, if a man becomes an anarchist, a hipster, some kind of proto-Communist, a rebel, a wild reactionary, I don't care what—if he's somebody who's got a sense that the world is wrong and he's more or less right, then the thing to do, if he wants political action, is not to look for organizations which he can join, nor to look for long walks he can go on with other picketeers, but rather it is to devote his life to working subtly, silently, steelfully, against the state.

And there's one best way he can do that. He can *join* the mass media. He can bore from within. He shouldn't look to form a sect or a cell—he should do it alone. The moment he starts to form sects and cells, he's beginning to create dissension and counterespionage agents.

The history of revolutionary movements is that they form cells, then defeat themselves. The worst and most paranoid kind of secret police—those split personalities who are half secret policemen and half revolutionaries (I'm talking of psychological types rather than of literal police agents)—enter these organizations and begin to manufacture them over again from within.

It's better to work alone, trusting no one, just working, working, working not to sabotage so much as to shift and to turn and to confuse the mass media and hold the mirror to its guilt, keep the light in its eye, never, never, never oneself beginning to believe that the legitimate work one is doing in the mass media has some prior value to it; always knowing that the work no matter how well intended is likely to be subtly hideous work. The mass media does diabolically subtle things to the morale and life of the people who do their work; few of us are strong enough to live alone in enemy territory. But it's work which must be done.

So long as the mass media are controlled completely by one's enemies, the tender life of all of us is in danger. And the way to fight back is not to look to start a group or a cell or to write a program, but instead it is to look for a job in the heart of the enemy.

On Violence and Political Violence

Q. In The Naked and the Dead, *there was a theme about the futility of violence on a grand scale; and yet, in "The White Negro," there's almost a justification of violence, at least on a personal level. How do you reconcile this apparent inconsistency?*

A. The ideas I had about violence changed 180 degrees over those years. Beneath the ideology in *The Naked and The Dead* was an obsession with violence. The characters for whom I had the most secret admiration, like Croft, were violent people.

Ideologically, intellectually, I did disapprove of

violence, though I didn't at the time of "The White Negro."

But what I still disapprove of is *inhuman* violence—violence which is on a large scale and abstract. I disapprove of bombing a city. I disapprove of the kind of man who will derive aesthetic satisfaction from the fact that an Ethiopian village looks like a red rose at the moment the bombs are exploding. I won't disapprove of the act of perception which witnesses that; I think that act of perception is noble.

What I'm getting at: a native village is bombed, and the bombs happen to be beautiful when they land; in fact it would be odd if all that sudden destruction did not liberate some beauty. The form a bomb takes in its explosion may be in part a picture of the potentialities it destroyed. So let us accept the idea that the bomb is beautiful.

If so, any liberal who decries the act of bombing is totalitarian if he doesn't admit that the bombs were indeed beautiful.

Because the moment we tell something that's untrue, it does not matter how pure our motives may be—the moment we start mothering mankind and decide that one truth is good for them to hear and another is not so good, because while *we* can understand, those poor ignorant unfortunates cannot—then we're depriving the minds of others of knowledge which may be essential.

Think of a young pilot who comes along later, some young pilot who goes out on a mission and isn't prepared for the fact that a bombing might be beautiful. If the pilot is totally unprepared he might never get over the fact that he was particularly thrilled by the beauty of that bomb.

But if our culture had been large enough to say that Ciano's son-in-law not only found that bomb beautiful, but that indeed this act of perception was *not* what was wrong; the evil was to think that this beauty was worth the lot of living helpless people who were wiped out broadside. Obviously, whenever there's destruction, there's going to be beauty implicit in it.

On Violence and Social Action

Q. At the risk of making you seem totalitarian, what would you substitute for sit-down strikes and other passive forms of protest?

A. Sketch the outline of a large argument. What I don't like about the "Ban the Bomb" program, for example, is that it is precisely the sort of political program which can enlist hundreds of thousands, and then millions of people. Half or two-thirds or even three-quarters of the world could belong to such an organization, and yet you could still have an atomic war. I'm not saying the "Ban the Bomb" program would *cause* an atomic war, but there's absolutely no proof it would prevent it. If you have people who are evil enough to lust for an atomic war, they are even more likely to force that war if there looks to be a real danger that they will never have a war.

Our best hope for no atomic war is that the complexities of political life at the summit remain complex. One has to assume the political leaders of the world are *halfway* decent, are not *necessarily* going to blow up the world, that indeed if everything else is equal they would just as soon *not* blow up the world. So I say create complexities, let art deepen sophistication, let complexities be demonstrated to our leaders, let us try to make *them* more complex. That is a manly activity. It offers more hope for saving the world then a gaggle of pacifists and vegetarians. The "Ban the Bomb" program is not manly. It is militant but it is not manly. So it is in danger of becoming totalitarian.

Action for Minorities

THE PROBLEM in a democracy is not to assimilate minorities but to avoid stifling them as they attain their equality. If the Jews and Negroes attain a brilliant equality with the white Anglo-Saxon Protestant and the Irish Catholic, then America will be different. Whatever it will become, it will be different from anything we can conceive. Whereas if the Negro and Jew are assimilated into the muted unimaginative level of present-day American life, then America will be very much like it is now, only worse.

An inflammation or rent in the body can heal in such a way that the limb or organ offers new powers of coordination which did not exist before; equally the inflammation can subside to a chronic leaden dullness of function.

So with minorities, one must look for more than the insurance of their rights—one must search to liberate the art which is trapped in the thousand acts of perception which embody their self-hatred, for self-hatred ignored must corrode the roots of one's past and leave one marooned in an alien culture. The liberal premise —that Negroes and Jews are like everybody else once they are given the same rights—can only obscure the complexity, the intensity, and the psychotic brilliance of a minority's inner life.

The argument of existential politics might be that one never understands a people or a time by contemplating a common denominator, for the average man in a minority group is no longer a member of that minority—he is instead a social paste which has been compounded out of the grinding stone of the society which contains him. He is not his own authentic expression. By this logic, the average Negro or Jew is not so much a black man or a Semite as a mediocre ersatz Protestant. That does not mean he is altogether an inferior man of the center—in his suppressed nerve, in his buried heart, exist the themes which the exceptional man of the minority can embody. So a politician, professionally sensitive to minority groups, cannot begin to be of real stature to that minority until he becomes aware of what is most extraordinary in a people as well as what is most pressing and ubiquitous in their need.

The problem is similar to the difficulty in dealing with juvenile delinquents—one can pacify them by any one of a number of unimaginative programs and be left with a human material which is apathetic if indeed not anchored to moronic expectations; or one can search for arts which transmute violence into heroic activity.

A Cure for Juvenile Delinquency

A LONG TIME AGO, back in 1960, I advanced the idea on a television show that the best way to combat juvenile delinquency was to give artistic outlet to the violence, creativity, and sense of pageantry which drives the juvenile delinquent toward disaster. Why not have medieval jousting tournaments in Central Park? I suggested. Some of the gangs of Harlem might spend a winter grooming their horses, designing their livery, learning how to ride, how to use the lance, how to oil the armor.

It was one of a set of suggestions. Why couldn't there be horse races through the downtown streets of Little Italy in New York, similar to the great horse race in Siena, or a municipal circus which would train young acrobats, trapeze artists, lion tamers, and high-wire acts? Once a year there might be stock-car races down Broadway from 205th Street to the Battery and back. Mountaineers could even be trained in New York. They would learn to make the ascent of difficult skyscrapers. We could build a pool one hundred feet deep and train juveniles in skindiving, or erect a great ski jump in Central Park.

Existential politics is simple. It has a basic argument: if there is a strong ineradicable strain in human nature, one must not try to suppress it, or anomaly, cancer, and plague will follow. Instead one must find an art into which it can grow. So a word to the ear of the President: a Peace Corps is not enough. Start an Adventurer's Corps as well. Let the louts who inhabit the crossroads and pharmacy doorways of every small town in America know that there is an amateur army they can join, a free men's club, an outfit where they may discover if they are potentially brave or fearfully lazy. Even the soul of a lout has anguish—it is the dull urgent apathy that there is something in his heart which is too large to be a bum and yet he does not know if he is of sufficient stature to claim he is a man. So give him the Adventurer's Corps where he can go to the Everglades and fight alligators with a knife or sit on the side of the swamp and watch, where he can learn to fly a glider or spit tobacco in the hangar, where he can ski the snow fields of mountains or go to sleep in the warming hut.

It is the mark of gentlemen that they are economically and spiritually free to go off on a season of expedition or adventure whenever their soul is stale or their spirit dead. Why should we leave that exceptional privilege to the rich in a democracy? The poor have as much right to novelty, to danger, to exploration and surprise. Let Congress commission two hundred yachts for the Adventurer Corps—they will cost no more than two hundred jet bombers and will not become obsolete for fifty years. Let the louts at the crossroads sail the seven seas and climb the mast in the middle of a storm.

On a Substitute for Housing Projects

GOVERNMENT to take a fraction of the money it costs to dispossess and relocate slum tenants, demolish buildings, erect twenty stories of massed barracks, and instead give a thousand or two thousand dollars to each slum tenant to spend on materials for improving his apartment and to pay for the wages of whatever skilled labor he needs for small specific jobs like a new toilet, a window, a fireplace, wiring, wallpaper, or a new wall. The tenant would be loaned or rented the tools he needed, he would be expected to work along with his labor. If he took the first hundred dollars he received and drank it up, he would get no more money.

By the time such a project was done, every slum apartment in the city would be different. Some would be worse, some would be improved, a few would be beautiful. But each man would know at least whether he wished to improve his home, or truly didn't care. And that might be better than moving into a scientifically allotted living space halfway between a hospital and a prison.

Housing projects radiate depression in two directions. The people who live in them are deadened by receiving a gift which has no beauty. The people who go past in their automobiles are gloomy for an instant, because the future, or that part of the future we sense in our architecture, is telling us much about the powers who erected these buildings. They expect us to become more like each other as the years go by.

The conservatives cry out that the welfare state will reduce us to a low and dull common denominator. Indeed it will, unless the welfare which reaches the poor reaches them in such a way that they can use their own hands to change their own life.

On Rebuilding the Cities

WHAT IS CALLED for is shelter which is pleasurable, substantial, intricate, intimate, delicate, detailed, foibled, rich in gargoyle, guignol, false closet, secret stair, witch's hearth, attic, grandeur, kitsch, a world of buildings as diverse as the need within the eye.

What we get is: commodities swollen in price by false, needless and useless labor. Modern architecture works with a currency which (measured in terms of the skilled and/or useful labor going into a building) is worth half the real value of nineteenth-century money. The mechanical advances in construction hardly begins to make up for the wastes of advertising, public relations, building-union covenants, city grafts, land costs, and the anemia of a dollar diminished by armaments and their taxes. In this context the formulas of modern architecture have triumphed, and her bastards—those new office skyscrapers—proliferate everywhere: one suspects the best reason is that modern architecture offers a pretext to a large real-estate operator to stick up a skyscraper at a fraction of the money it should cost, so helps him to conceal the criminal fact that we are being given a stricken building, a denuded, aseptic, unfinished work, stripped of ornament, origins, prejudices, not even a peaked roof or spire to engage the heavens.

Look at the depth of the problem in the root of the future:

> . . . Fifty years from now . . . there will be four hundred million Americans, four-fifths of them in urban areas. In the remainder of this century . . . we will have to build homes, highways, and facilities equal to all those built since this country was first settled. In the next forty years we must rebuild the entire urban United States.
> —*Lyndon Johnson*

If we are to spare the countryside, if we are to protect the style of the small town and of the exclusive suburb, keep the organic center of the metropolis and the old neighborhoods, maintain those few remaining streets where the tradition of the nineteenth century and the muse of the eighteenth century still linger on the mood in the summer cool of an evening, if we are to avoid a megalopolis five hundred miles long, a city without shape or exit, a nightmare of ranch houses, highways, suburbs and industrial sludge, if we are to save the dramatic edge of a city—that precise moment when we leave the outskirts and race into the country, the open country—if we are to have a keen sense of concentration and a breath of release, then there is only one solution: the cities must climb, they must not spread, they must build up, not by increments, but by leaps, up and up, up to the heavens.

We must be able to live in houses one hundred stories high, two hundred stories high, far above the height of buildings as we know them now. New cities with great towers must rise in the plain, cities higher than mountains, cities with room for 400,000,000 to live, or that part of 400,000,000 who wish to live high in a landscape of peaks and spires, cliffs and precipices. For the others, for those who wish to live on the ground and with the ground, there will be new room to live—the traditional small town will be able to survive, as will the old neighborhoods in the cities. But first a way must be found to build upward, to triple and triple again the height of all buildings as we know them now.

Picture, if you please, an open space where twenty acrobats stand, each locking hands with two different partners. Conceive then of ten acrobats standing on the shoulders of these twenty, and five upon the ten acrobats, and three more in turn above them, then two, then one. We have a pyramid of figures: six thousand to eight thousand pounds is supported upon a base of twenty pairs of shoes.

It enables one to think of structures more complex, of pyramids of steel which rise to become towers. Imagine a tower half a mile high and stressed to bear a vast load. Think of six or eight such towers and of bridges built between them, even as huge vines tie the branches of one high tree to another; think of groups of apartments built above these bridges (like the shops on the Ponte Vecchio in Florence) and apartments suspended beneath each bridge, and smaller bridges running from one complex of apartments to another, and of apartments suspended from cables, apartments kept in harmonious stress to one another by cables between them.

One can now begin to conceive of a city, or a separate part of a city, which is as high as it is wide, a city which bends ever so subtly in a high wind with the most delicate flexing of its near-to-numberless parts even as the smallest strut in a great bridge reflects the passing of an automobile with some fine-tuned quiver. In the subtlety of its swayings the vertical city might seem to be ready to live itself. It might be agreeable to live there.

The real question, however, has not yet been posed. It is whether a large fraction of the population would find it reasonable to live one hundred or two hundred stories in the air. There is the dread of heights. Would that tiny pit of suicide, planted like the small seed of murder in civilized man, flower prematurely into breakdown, terror and dread? Would it demand too much of a tenant to stare down each morning on a flight of 2,000 feet? Or would it prove a deliverance for some? Would the juvenile delinquent festering in the violence of his monotonous corridors diminish in his desire for brutality if he lived high in the air and found the intensity of his inexpressible and murderous vision matched by the chill intensity of the space through a fall?

That question returns us to the perspective of twentieth-century man. Caught between our desires to cling to the earth and to explore the stars, it is not impossible that a new life lived half a mile in the air, with streets in the clouds and chasms beyond each railing could prove nonetheless more intimate and more personal to us than the present congestions of the housing-project city. For that future man would be returned some individuality from his habitation. His apartment in the sky would be not so very different in its internal details from the apartments of his neighbors, no more than one apartment is varied from another in Washington Square Village. But his situation would now be different from any other. His windows would look out on a view of massive constructions and airy bridges, of huge vaults and fine intricacies. The complexity of our culture could be captured again by the imagination of the architect: our buildings could begin to look a little less like armored tanks and more like clipper ships. Would we also then feel the dignity of sailors on a four-master at sea? Living so high, thrust into space, might we be returned to that mixture of awe and elation, of dignity and self-respect and a hint of dread, that sense of zest which a man must have known working his way out along a yardarm in a stiff breeze at sea? Would the fatal monotony of mass culture dissolve a hint before the quiet swaying of a great and vertical city?

Existential Legislation

Coda

This terminal position paper, "Existential Legislation," is, of course, not serious. It is comic. It was written with comic intent. As the years go by, it becomes less comic. Soon its proposals will be commonplace. At least all but the first and the second.

Existential politics is in favor of legisation whose inner tendency would be to weaken the bonds of legislation. As examples:

1. A law passed which would abolish capital punishment, except for those states which insisted on keeping it. Such states would then be allowed to kill criminals provided that the killing is not impersonal but personal and a public spectacle: to wit, that the executioner be more or less the same size and weight as the criminal (the law could here specify the limits) and that they fight to death using no weapons, or weapons not capable of killing at a distance. Thus, knives or broken bottles would be acceptable. Guns would not.

This law might return us to the finer questions of moral judgment. The killer would carry the other man's death in his psyche. The audience, in turn, would experience a sense of tragedy, since the executioners, highly trained for this, would almost always win. In the flabby American spirit there is a buried sadist who finds the bullfight contemptible—what he really desires are gladiators. Since nothing is worse for a country than repressed sadism, this method of execution would offer ventilation for the more cancerous emotions of the American public.

2. Cancer is going to become the first political problem of America in twenty years. The man who finds a cure might run successfully for President. But it is doubtful if a cure will be found until all serious cancer researchers, and most especially the heads of departments are put under sentence of mortal combat (with a professional executioner) if they have failed to make progress in their part of the program after two years. This would keep committeemen out of the project—it would also help in the search for a cure, since one may suspect that only a brave man living in the illumination of approaching death could brood

sufficiently over the nature of disease to come up with a cure which was not worse than the illness.

3. Pass a bill making legal the sale of drugs. People who take drugs may burn up the best part of their minds and gut their sex, but the same is true for those who drink too much, and alcohol is in a favored legal position. While it would not necessarily be attractive to see a larger proportion of people destroy themselves with drugs, it must be recognized that the right to destroy oneself is also one of the inalienable rights, because others cannot know the reason for the self-destruction. It is possible many people take heroin because they sense unconsciously that if they did not, they would be likely to commit murder, get cancer, or turn homosexual. Choices.

4. Make every effort to pass the Communists our diseases. Encourage the long-term loan to them of countless committees of the best minds we have in Washington and on Madison Ave. If our hucksters have been able to leech the best blood of the American spirit, they should be able to debilitate the Communists equally; if not, admiration for Madison Ave. is misplaced.

5. Pass a bill abolishing all forms of censorship. Censorship is an insult to democracy because it makes men unequal—it assumes some have more sexual wisdom than others. Besides, pornography is debilitating —the majority of people might stay away from it. Given the force of the hangover, most people do not get drunk every night, and the same could apply here. It is possible this is indulgence of shallow liberal optimism, and America would become a cesspool of all-night pornograhic drive-in movies, the majority of the population becoming night people who meet for cocktails at one in the morning. But this could also serve as the salvation of the Republic, for America

would then become so wicked a land that no Communist nation would ever dare to occupy us, nor even to exterminate us by atom bomb, their scientists having by then discovered that people who are atomized disseminate their spirit into the conqueror.

A Sexual Appendix to the Miscellany on Existential Politics

THE STATED RELATION of sexuality to existential politics is burlesque, as all attachments of sex to a separate subject must be. Think only of sex and philosophy, sex and economics, sex and professional football, sex and master bridge tournament points, yes, we got it, we got the point. Still, existential politics will insist on reconnoitering sex. Sex is upon us. Not as a referendum to put up on the election ballot list—"Legalize Sex"—but as a set of problems to sharpen our political reflex. For instance, the birth-control pill is considered politically progressive—in an existential light, as the last notes which follow will attempt to show, it may be progressive but it is certainly deadening. Whatever deadens existence is bad politics—so goes the logic of existential politics. Therefore anything which deadens sex is ultimately on the side of bad politics, or—since we have simple minds here—is eventually equal to the spread of totalitarianism, for that political growth depends on a deadening of existence as its seed ground. Therefore, we add a section on sex to these position papers. And now, enough of apology. What strange fellow would apologize for adding a few pages on the sweet subject to a political tome?

On Masturbation and Procreation

Q. Do you think you're something of a puritan when it comes to masturbation?

A. I think masturbation is bad.

Q. In relation to heterosexual fulfillment?

A. In relation to everything—orgasm, heterosexuality, to style, to stance, to be able to fight. I think masturbation cripples people. It doesn't cripple them altogether, but it turns them askew, it sets up a bad and often enduring tension. I mean has anyone ever studied the correlation between cigarette smoking and masturbation? Anybody who spends his adolescence masturbating, generally enters his young manhood with no sense of being a man. The answer—I don't know what the answer is—sex for adolescents may be the answer, it may not. I really don't know.

Q. But can't one kid start young with heterosexual relations and yet develop all the wrong kinds of attitudes—while another kid will go through his adolescence masturbating and yet see the humor of it, see the absurdity of it, know it's temporary?

A. I wouldn't dream of laying down a law with no variation. But let me say it another way. At the time I was growing up, there was much more sexual repression than there is today. One knew sex was good and everything was in the way of it. And so one did think of it as one of the wars to fight, if not *the* war to fight—the war for greater sexual liberty.

Masturbation was one expression of that deprivation. No adolescent would ever masturbate, presumably, if he could have sex with a girl. A lot of adolescents masturbate because they don't want to take part in homosexuality.

Q. There are certain societies where masturbation—

A. All I'm talking about is the one society I *know.* I'll be damned if I'm going to be led around with a ring in my nose by anthropologists. I mean the few I've known personally have always struck me as slightly absurd. I'm sure they don't know A-hole from appetite about "certain societies."

But we were talking about masturbation as the result of sexual repression. I don't see any reason to defend it. If you have more sexual liberty, why the hell still defend masturbation?

One has to keep coming back to one notion: How do you make life? How do you *not* make life? You have to assume, just as a working stance, that life is probably good—if it isn't good, then our existence is such absurdity that *any* action immediately becomes absurd—but if you assume that life is good, then you have to assume that those things which keep life from happening—which tend to make life more complex without becoming more useful, more stimulating—are bad.

Anything that tends to make a man a machine without giving him the power to increase the real life in himself is bad.

Q. Is it possible that you have a totalitarian attitude against masturbation?

A. I wouldn't say all people who masturbate are evil, probably I would even say that some of the best people in the world masturbate.

Q. Well, we're getting right back now to this notion of absolutes. You know—to somebody, masturbation can be a thing of beauty—

A. To what end? To what end? Who is going to benefit from it?

Q. It's a better end than the beauty of a bombing.

A. Masturbation is bombing. It's bombing oneself.

Q. I see nothing wrong if the only person hurt from masturbation is the one who practices it. But it can

also benefit—look, Stekel wrote a book on autoerotic-
ism, and one of the points he made was that at least it
saved some people who might otherwise go out and
commit rape. He was talking about extremes, but—

A. It's better to commit rape than masturbate.
Maybe, maybe. The whole thing becomes very difficult.

Q. *But rape involves somebody else. The minute*
you—

A. Just talking about it on the basis of violence:
one is violence toward oneself; one is violence toward
others. And you don't recognize—let's follow your
argument and be speculative for a moment—if everyone becomes violent toward themselves, then past a
certain point the entire race commits suicide. But if
everyone becomes violent toward everyone else, you
would probably have one wounded hero-monster left.

Q. *And he'd have to masturbate.*

A. That's true . . . But—you use that to point out
how tragic was my solution, which is that he wins and
still has to masturbate. I reply that at least it was
more valuable than masturbating in the first place.
Besides he might have no desire to masturbate. He
might lie down and send his thoughts back to the root
of his being.

Q. *I think there's a basic flaw in your argument.*
Why are you assuming that masturbation is violence
unto oneself? Why is it not pleasure unto oneself? And
I'm not defending masturbation—well, I'm defending
masturbation, yes, as a substitute if and when—

A. All right, look. When you make love, whatever
is good in you or bad in you, goes out into someone
else. I mean this literally. I'm not interested in the bio-
chemistry of it, the electromagnetism of it, nor in how

the psychic waves are passed back and forth, and what psychic waves are. All I know is that when one makes love, one changes a woman slightly and a woman changes you slightly.

Q. Certain circumstances can change one for the worse.

A. But at least you have gone through a process which is part of life.

One can be better for the experience, or worse. But one has experience to absorb, to think about, one has literally to digest the new spirit which has entered the flesh. The body has been galvanized for an experience of flesh, a declaration of the flesh.

If one has the courage to think about every aspect of the act—I don't mean think mechanically about it, but if one is able to brood over the act, to dwell on it—then one is *changed* by the act. Even if one has been *jangled* by the act. Because in the act of restoring one's harmony, one has to encounter all the reasons one was jangled.

So finally one has had an experience which is nourishing. Nourishing because one's able to *feel* one's way into more difficult or more precious insights as a result of it. One's able to live a tougher, more heroic life if one can digest and absorb the experience.

But, if one masturbates, all that happens is, everything that's beautiful and good in one, goes up the hand, goes into the air, is *lost*. Now what the hell is there to *absorb*? One hasn't tested himself. You see, in a way, the heterosexual act lays questions to rest, and makes one able to build upon a few answers. Whereas if one masturbates, the ability to contemplate one's experience is disturbed. Instead, fantasies of power take over and disturb all sleep.

If you have, for example, the image of a beautiful sexy babe in masturbation, you still don't know whether you can make love to her in the flesh. All you know is that you can violate her in your *brain*. Well, a lot of good that is.

But if one has fought the good fight or the evil fight and ended with the beautiful sexy dame, then if the experience is good, your life is changed by it; if the experience is not good, one's life is also changed by it, in a less happy way. But at least one knows something of what happened. One has something real to build on.

The ultimate direction of masturbation always has to be insanity.

Q. But you're not man enough to take the other position which is sex for the young. Except for petting, what else is there between those two alternatives?

A. I'd say, between masturbation and sex for the young, I prefer sex for the young. Of course. But I think there may be still a third alternative: At the time I grew up, sex had enormous fascination for everyone, but it had no dignity, it had no place. It was not a value. It had nothing to do with procreation, it had to do with the bathroom—it was burning, it was feverish, it was dirty, cute, giggly.

The thought of waiting for sex never occurred—when I was young my parents did not speak about sex, and no one else I knew ever discussed the possibility of holding onto one's sex as the single most important thing one has. To keep one's sex until one got what one deserved for it—that was never suggested to me when I was young.

The possibilities were to go out and have sex with a girl, have homosexual sex, or masturbate. Those were the choices. The fourth alternative—chastity, if you will—was ridiculous and absurd. It's probably more absurd today. If you talked to kids of chastity today, they would not stop laughing, I'm certain.

But the fact of the matter is, if you get marvelous sex when you're young, all right; but if you're not ready to make a baby with that marvelous sex, then you may also be putting something down the drain forever, which is the ability that you had to make a baby; the most marvelous thing that was in you may have been shot into a diaphragm, or wasted on a pill. One might be losing one's future.

The point is that, so long as one has a determinedly atheistic and rational approach to life, then the only thing that makes sense is the most comprehensive promiscuous sex you can find.

Q. Well, since I do have an essentially atheistic and more or less rational approach to life, I think I can speak with at least my individual authority. As a matter of fact, the more rational I become, the more selective—

A. You know, "selective" is a word that sounds like a refugee from a group-therapy session.

Q. I've never been in any kind of therapy—

A. No, I know, but there's a *plague* coming out of all these centers—they go around *infecting* all of us. The words sit in one's vocabulary like bedbugs under glass.

Q. But I can't think of a better word. "Selective" is a word that means what I want to communicate to you.

A. Selective. It's arrogant—how do you know who's doing the selecting? I mean you're a modest man with a good sense of yourself, but suddenly it comes to sex and you're selective. Like you won't pick *this* girl; you'll pick *that* one. . . .

Q. Exactly. It's arrogant, but—

A. Yeah, yeah, yeah—but the fact that one girl wants you and the other girl *doesn't*—I mean, that has nothing to do with it?

Q. Well, they have a right to be selective, too.

A. Then it's mutually selective. Which means you fall in together or go in together. Now, those are better words than "selective." They have more to do with the body and much less to do with the machine. Electronic machines *select.*

Q. Well, what I'm saying is you make a choice. A human choice. It has nothing to do with a machine . . . I'll tell you what's bugging me—it's your mystical approach. You'll use an expression like "You may be sending the best baby that's in you out into your hand"—but even when you're having intercourse, how many unused spermatozoa will there be in one ejaculation of semen?

A. Look, America is dominated by a bunch of half-maniacal scientists, men who don't know anything about the act of creation. If science comes along and says there are one million spermatozoa in a discharge, you reason on that basis. That may not be a real basis.

We just don't know what the *real* is. We just don't know. Of the million spermatozoa, there may be only two or three with any real chance of reaching the ovum; the others are there like a supporting army, or if we're talking of planned parenthood, as a body of the electorate. These sperm go out with no sense at all of being real spermatozoa. They may appear to be real spermatozoa under the microscope, but after all, a man from Mars who's looking at us through a telescope might think that Communist bureaucrats and FBI men look exactly the same.

Q. Well, they are.

A. Krassner's jab piles up more points. The point is that the scientists don't know what's going on. That meeting of the ovum and the sperm is too mysterious for the laboratory. Even the electron microscope can't measure the striations of passion in a spermatozoon. Or the force of its will.

But we can trust our emotion. Our emotions are a better guide to what goes on in these matters than scientists.

Q. But in the act of pleasure—go back to your instincts, as you say—in the act of sex, you're not thinking in terms of procreation, you're thinking in terms of pleasure.

A. You are when you're young. As you get older, you begin to grow more and more obsessed with procreation. You begin to feel used up. Another part of oneself is fast diminishing. There isn't that much of oneself left. I'm not talking now in any crude sense of how much semen is left in the barrel. I'm saying that one's very *being* is being used up.

Every man has a different point where he gets close to his being. Sooner or later everything that stands between him and his being—what the psychoanalysts call defenses—is used up, because men have to work through their lives; just being a man they have to stand up in all the situations where a woman can lie down. Just on the simplest level . . . where a woman can cry, a man has to stand. And for that reason, men are often used more completely than women. They have more rights and more powers, and also they are used more.

Sooner or later, every man comes close to his being and realizes that even though he's using the act, the act is using him too. He becomes, as you say, more selective. The reason he becomes more selective is that you can get killed, you literally *can* fuck your head off, you can lose your brains, you can wreck your body, you can use yourself up badly, eternally—I know a little bit of what I'm talking about.

On the Womanization of America

BEFORE WORLD WAR I, America was not a place engaged in world history, but an island *sheltered* from world history, a place where people could go and be free of the deteriorating effects of the crises of history. But when America became a world power and began to have ambitions to become the only world power, American men began to want something else: not to be successful in the old way of building large families, a business, moving into new country, into the frontier, creating something that was going to expand; but rather, living in a relatively stratified society now, they wanted to rise through these strata and acquire more and more power in a world no longer open and viable but on the contrary like an enormously subtle and complex machine. Well, when they desired this, they began to look for something different in women. I think the womanization of America comes not only because women are becoming more selfish, more greedy, less romantic, less warm, more lusty, and more filled with hate—but because the men have collaborated with them. There's been a change in the minds of most men about the function of marriage— it isn't that they're necessarily becoming weaker vis-à-vis their wives, it's that they've married women who will be less good for them in the home and more good for them in the world. The kind of woman who doesn't wash a dish is usually a beauty who'll spend 10 to 12 hours in bed and will take two hours to make up; she has to have a nurse for the children, but she'll be a wow at a party and will aid the man in his career because when they both go to the party, everybody envies him, covets his woman, so forth. What he wants is a marvelous courtesan with social arts. A courtesan who can go out into the world with him.

On Homosexuality

I THINK THERE MAY BE more homosexuals today than there were 50 years ago. If so, the basic reason might have to do with a general loss of faith in the country, faith in the meaning of one's work, faith in the notion of oneself as a man. When a man can't find any dignity in his work, he loses virility. Masculinity is not something given to you, something you're born with, but something you gain. And you gain it by winning small battles with honor. Because there is very little honor left in American life, there is a certain built-in tendency to destroy masculinity in American men. The mass media, for instance—television first, movies second, magazines third, and newspapers running no poor fourth—tend to destroy virility slowly and steadily. They give people an unreal view of life. They give people a notion that American life is easier than it really is, less complex, more rewarding. The result is that Americans, as they emerge from adolescence into young manhood, are very much like green soldiers being sent into difficult terrain ignorant of the conditions. A lot of virility gets massacred.

On the Pill

Q. *What do you think of this remark by Dr. Ernest Dichter, founder and president of the Institute for Motivational Research? "We recently did a study in one of the European countries on birth-control. . . . There's a definite relationship between the social class and the use of birth-control techniques. I am talking primarily about the lower-income group.*

". . . Our statistical knowledge with the birth-control association has shown that the instruction reaches primarily the middle class and upper-middle class. The

real problem is reaching the lower-income-group people, for they are the ones who have many children."

A. Well, that's the trouble with motivational research. There's no attempt to consider the possibility that a woman might be right—biologically right, instinctively right—in *not* wanting to use a contraceptive. If you take ignorant women, they're not going to be able to express themselves at all. Their reasons for not wanting to use birth-control pills would be rather vague. Suppose unconsciously they feel a deep biological aversion to having sex without the possibility of conceiving. Maybe a woman obtains her deepest knowledge of herself and of the world by the way in which she conceives. You see, the fact that she *can* conceive alters the existential character of her sex. It makes it deeper. She's taking more of a risk. It's more dangerous, more responsible, it's graver. Because it's graver, it's deeper. Since it's deeper, it's better. The reason she may not want to use a contraceptive is because she senses somewhere within her—in dim fashion, no doubt—that there's something alien to the continuation of her, her species, and her family, if she uses a contraceptive. Yet she may also feel a great shame about all this, because, after all, here's this very impressive gentleman with the eyeglasses, taking down every word she says, and there's the attitude of her husband and all the people around her, and her children, about using contraceptives, and so she begins to feel that, well, maybe she's wrong, and confusion is the result. And this pitiful confusion is immediately processed into statistics, which are psychotic in their lack of attachment to the biological reality.

On Negro Sexuality

Q. In his book, Nobody Knows My Name, *James Baldwin—referring to your essay, "The White Negro"—*

complained about "the myth of the sexuality of Ne-
groes which Norman Mailer, like so many others, re-
fuses to give up." Are you still denying it's a myth?

A. Negroes are closer to sex than we are. By that
I don't mean that every Negro's a great stud, that
every Negro woman is great sex, that those black
people just got rhythm.

I'm willing to bet that if you pushed Jimmy hard
enough, he'd finally admit that he thought that the
Negroes had more to do with sexuality than the white
—but whether he really believes that or not, Baldwin's
buried point is that I shouldn't talk that way because
it's bad for the Negro people, it's going to slow them
up, going to hurt them; talk about Negro sexuality
hurts their progress because it makes the white man
nervous and unhappy and miserable.

But the white man is nervous and unhappy and miserable anyway. It's not I who think the Negro has such
profound sexuality, it's the average white man all
through the country. Why deny their insight? Why do
you think they react so violently in the South to having their little girls and boys go to school with Negro
kids if it isn't that they're afraid of sexuality in the
Negro?

That's the real problem. What's the use of avoiding
it?

Q. Are you saying that, whether it's a myth or not,
in effect—

A. First of all, I don't believe it's a myth at all, for
any number of reasons. I think *any* submerged class is
going to be more accustomed to sexuality than a leisure class. A leisure class may be more *preoccupied*
with sexuality; but a submerged class will be more
drenched in it.

You see, the upper classes are obsessed with sex, but
they contain very little of it themselves. They use up

much too much sex in their manipulations of power. In effect, they exchange sex for power. So they restrict themselves in their sexuality—whereas the submerged classes have to take their desires for power and plow them back into sex.

So, to begin with, there's just that much more sexual vitality at the bottom than there is at the top. Second of all, Africa, a tropical land. Now I don't care to hear how many variations there are in Africa, how complex is its geography, how there's not only jungle but pasture land, mountains, snow, and so forth—everybody knows that. Finally, Africa is, at bottom, the Congo. Now tropical people are usually more sexual. It's easier to cohabit, it's easier to stay alive. If there's more time, more leisure, more warmth, more —we'll use one of those machine words—more support-from-the-environment than there is in a northern country, then sex will tend to be more luxuriant.

Besides the Negro has been all but forbidden any sort of intellectual occupation here for a couple of centuries. So he has had to learn other ways of comprehending modern life.

Sexuality is the armature of Negro life. Without sexuality they would've perished. The Jews stayed alive by having a culture to which they could refer, in which, more or less, they could believe. The Negroes stayed alive by having sexuality.

Sex and Censors

Q. In G. Legman's classic study of censorship, Love and Death, he says: "Murder is a crime. Describing murder is not. Sex is not a crime. Describing sex is. Why?"

A. Reading about murder may often satisfy the desire, whereas reading about sex usually *increases* desire. Now it's obvious that censors are not interested in increasing the amount of sexual desire in a country. There seems to be some relation between high sexuality and low productive level. Countries with the most sexuality have the lowest productive level. In countries like India, where poor people—not intellectuals—are absorbed in sex, productivity has stayed at a very low level for centuries. The same was true in China, and in a lesser sense, perhaps, in Russia before the revolution. At any rate, there does seem to be some relation between sexual repression and the increase of productivity. Censors often feel that they are guarding the *health* of the nation by repressing sexuality.

I would argue with the censor on his own ground that there's no use trying to resist a wave of real interest and even perhaps of biological intensity by trying to suppress it. If there's going to be any censorship—and I'm not certain there should be—it ought to recognize that an intimate and serious evocation of sex is part of the very *marrow* of a nation's culture, and when the marrow is drained through brutal or stupid censorship, then the country begins to sicken. I won't say it *causes,* but it certainly *accelerates,* the sickness of the country.

On Lady Chatterley *and* Tropic of Cancer

I READ *Lady Chatterley's Lover* in college. The unabridged edition. In the Treasure Room at Widener. It changed my life. It was the first thing I'd ever read that gave me the idea sex could have beauty. I learned from Lawrence that the way to write about sex was not to strike poses, but be true to the logic of each moment. There's a subtle logic to love. I think one of the reasons people are absorbed in love is because it's one of the only ways in which they can find a logic to their lives. Looking back on it now, I think *Lady Chatterley's Lover* is not a very good book. It's probably one of the greatest of the bad books—it's much too simple—it tries to capture the essence of sex and yet has nothing to say about the violence which is part of sex. One doesn't arrive at love by getting into bed with a woman and getting better and better at it, and exploring more and more deeply. A man and woman can't *just* explore more and more deeply into one another. Any number of things keep happening—the world keeps impinging on sex. The lovers keep testing one another; lovers not only create but they also destroy one another; lovers change one another; lovers resist the change that each gives to the other. Lawrence, by avoiding these problems, wrote a book that was more mythical than novelistic and terribly sentimental. Yet, it's a book to defend to the death. If it had entered the general literature at the time it was written, our sexual literature today would be better. It was exactly because *Lady Chatterley's Lover* was kept in a state of suppression for many years that it took on a power it didn't really possess.

What is marvelous about *Tropic of Cancer* is that it is the exact opposite of *Lady Chatterley*. *Tropic of Cancer* gets the beauty of sex another way, the way people who care a great deal about prizefighting can go to a club fight and enjoy the blood, the cigar smoke, the spit on the floor, the body odor; it's part of something whose end is unforeseen. In *Lady Chatterley's Lover* as I remember, there was not even a description of Mellors' cottage—you don't know what the bed's like—but when you read about sex in Miller, you know how the sheets scratch. For anyone who's interested in getting sexual pleasure from a book, *Tropic of Cancer* is more exciting than *Lady Chatterley's Lover*. When one reads Lawrence there's a certain wistfulness, one feels. Most people don't find sex that pure, that deep, that organic. They find it sort of partial and hot and ugly and fascinating and filled with all sorts of day-to-day details.

THIRD PART

The Johnson Administration

IN AMERICA few people will trust you unless you are irreverent; there was a message returned to us by our frontier that the outlaw is worth more than the sheriff.

One was therefore irreverent to the President. But the extent of one's irreverence was discovered to be also the measure of one's unsuspected affection: that one discovered the day he was killed; discovered that again during the weeks of depression which followed. For he was no ordinary sheriff—he was an outlaw's sheriff, he was one sheriff who could have been an outlaw himself. Such Presidents can be quickly counted: Jefferson, Andrew Jackson, Lincoln, Franklin Delano Roosevelt, John F. Kennedy. One doubts if there are any others. While this is the only kind of sheriff for whom an outlaw can feel love, one should still of course not be excessively polite, for every sheriff must labor finally on the side of all those mediocrities who made a profit from mediocrity by extinguishing (let a new Marx rise up among us) the promise of others.

Still, John F. Kennedy was a remarkable man. A modern democracy is a tyranny whose borders are undefined; one discovers how far one can go only by traveling in a straight line until one is stopped; Kennedy was not in a hurry to stop us. I would not be surprised if he believed that the health of America (which is to say our vitality) depends in part on the inventiveness and passion of its outlaws.

Then, of course, he was killed by an outlaw. Which is tragic, but not startling. For heroism often gives life to a creation which is bound and determined to kill the hero. Ultimately a hero is a man who would argue with the gods, and so awakens devils to contest his vision. The more a man can achieve, the more he may be certain that the devil will inhabit a part of his creation.

These theological illuminations are of vast use to the reader, doubtless; but they lead the author astray from the point. He was trying to say that we have here a President and a presidential time which was neither conclusive nor legislatively active, but which was nonetheless a period not without a suspicion of greatness, greatness of promise at the very least, for it was a time when writers could speak across the land in intimate dialogue with their leader.

He was a good and serious man, one now suspects. Only such a man would neglect to cover himself with the pompous insulations of the state. Still, one would not retract what one has written: his faults were his faults, his lacks were his lacks, his political maneuverings were no better than the others, his dull taste was certainly his dull taste. But what one did not recognize sufficiently was the extent of his humor. That humor created an atmosphere in which one could attempt this book; now, as a document which circles mournfully about its subject, one can hear in the echoes of his absence the proportions of that humor, and thus feel the loss. Fifty years may go by before such a witty and promising atmosphere comes to life in America again. So the corridors are gloomy. "He was a great man," said a girl at a party the other night. "No, he wasn't a great man," I said. "He was a man who could have become great or could have failed, and now we'll never know. That's what's so awful." That is what is so awful. Tragedy is amputation; so many of the nerves of one's memory run back to the limb which is no longer there.

In the Red Light: A History of the Republican Convention in 1964

. . . He had drawn the burning city, a great bonfire of architectural styles, ranging from Egyptian to Cape Cod colonial. Through the center, winding from left to right, was a long hill street and down

it, spilling into the middle foreground, came the mob carrying baseball bats and torches. For the faces of its members, he was using the innumerable sketches he had made of the people who come to California to die; the cultists of all sorts, economic as well as religious, the wave, airplane, funeral and preview watchers—all those poor devils who can only be stirred by the promise of miracles and then only to violence. A super "Dr. Know-All Pierce-All" had made the necessary promise of miracles and they were marching behind his banner in a great united front of screwballs and screwboxes to purify the land. No longer bored, they sang and danced joyously in the red light of the flames.

 —NATHANAEL WEST, *The Day of the Locust*

NOW THE CITY was beautiful, it was still the most beautiful city in the United States, but like all American cities it was a casualty of the undeclared war. There had been an undisclosed full-scale struggle going on in America for twenty years—it was whether the country would go mad or not. And the battle line of that war (which showed that yes slowly the country was losing the war, we were indeed going mad) was of course the progress of the new roads, buildings, and supermarkets which popped out all over the cities of the nation. San Francisco was losing her beauty. Monstrous corporations in combine with monstrous realtors had erected monstrous boxes of Kleenex ten, twenty, thirty stories high through the downtown section, and the new view from Telegraph Hill had shards of glass the size of a mountain wall stuck into the soft Italian landscape of St. Francis' City. The San Francisco Hilton, for an example, while close to twenty stories high was near to a square block in size and looked from the street to have the proportions and form of a cube of sugar. It was a dirty sugar-white in color and its windows were set in an odd elongated checkerboard, a harlequin pattern in which each window was offset from the one above and beneath like the vents in a portable radio.

The Hilton was only six weeks old, but already it was one of the architectural wonders of the world, for its insides were composed in large part of an automobile ramp on which it was possible to drive all the way up to the eleventh floor, open a door and lo! you were in your hotel corridor, twenty feet from your own room door. It was a startling way to exhaust the internal space of a hotel, but it had one huge American advantage: any guest at the Hilton could drive all the way to his room without ever having to steer a lady through the lobby. Of course, after all those automobile ramps, there was not much volume left, so the rooms were small, the rooms were very small for seventeen dollars a day, and the windows were placed to the extreme left or right of the wall and ran from ceiling to floor, in order to allow the building to appear to the outside eye like a radio being carried by a model who worked in the high nude. The carpets and wallpapers, the drapes and the table tops were plastic, the bathroom had the odor of burning insecticide. It developed that the plastic cement used to finish the tiling gave off this odor during the months it took to dry. Molecules were being tortured everywhere.

Well, that was American capitalism gainfully employed. It had won the war. It had won it in so many places you could picture your accommodations before you arrived. Such is the nature of the promiscuous. Flying out, way out on the jet, on the way West, not yet at the Hilton but knowing it would be there, I got into a conversation with the man who sat at the window, an Australian journalist named Moffitt, a short fellow with a bushwhacker's moustache; and he scolded me for reading Buchanan's book, *Who Killed Kennedy?* He wanted to know why a man of my intelligence bothered with trash. Well, the country had never been the same since Kennedy was assassinated, courtesy was ready to reply; some process of derailment, begun with Hemingway's death and the death of Marilyn Monroe, had been racing on now through the months, through the heavens, faster than the contrails of our jet across the late afternoon mind of America; so one looked for clues where they could be found. It would be easier to know that Oswald had done it all by himself, or as an accomplice to ten other men, or was innocent, or twice damned; anything was superior to that sense of the ship of state battering its way down swells of sea, while in the hold cargo was loose and ready to slide.

This conversation did not of course take place—an Astrojet is not the vehicle for metaphorical transactions, it is after all still another of the extermination chambers of the century—slowly the breath gives up some microcosmic portion of itself, green plastic and silver-gray plastic, the nostrils breathe no odor of materials which existed once as elements of nature, no wood, no stone, no ore, time molders like a sponge in the sink. But Moffitt was Australian and fascinated with America, and had his quick comments to make, some provincial, some pure shrewd; finally he poked his finger on something I had never put together for myself, not quite: "Why is it," he asked, "that all the new stuff you build here, including the interior furnishings of this airplane, looks like a child's nursery?"

And that is what it was. The inside of our airplane was like a child's plastic nursery, a dayroom in the children's ward, and if I had been Quentin Compson, I might have answered, "Because we want to go back, because the nerves grew in all the wrong ways. Because we developed habits which are suffocating us to death. I tell you, man, we do it because we're sick, we're a sick nation, we're sick to the edge of vomit and so we build our lives with materials which smell like vomit, polyethylene and bakelite and fiberglas and styrene. Yes, our schools look like nurseries, and our factories and our temples, our kitchens and our johns, our airports and our libraries and our offices, we are one great big bloody nursery attached to a doctor's waiting room, and we are sick, we're very sick, maybe we always were sick, maybe the Puritans carried the virus and were so odious the British were right to drive them out, maybe we're a nation of culls and weeds and half-crazy from the start."

Nobody of course was Quentin Compson, nobody spoke that way any more, but the question was posed by a ghost and so had to linger: was there indeed a death in the seed which brought us here? was the country extraordinary or accursed, a junkyard where even the minnows gave caviar in the filthy pond in the fierce electric American night?

I

> *I must see the things; I must see the men.*
> —BURKE, *Reflections on the Revolution in France*

At the Mark Hopkins on Saturday morning two days before the convention would begin, the atmosphere had the same agreeable clean rather healthy excitement (that particular American excitement) one picks up on the morning of a big football game. The kids were out, the children who were for Goldwater and those who were for Scranton, and they milled about in the small open courtyard of the hotel, and in the small hopelessly congested lobby where lines one hundred long were waiting for each of the three overworked elevators beating up to the twelfth and fourteenth floors, Scranton and Goldwater Headquarters respectively. It was a clear day outside, one of those cool sunny days in July when San Francisco is as nice as New York on a beautiful day in October, and the city fell away from Nob Hill in a perfect throw. There were apples in the air. It was a perfect football day. There was even wistfulness to be eighteen and have a date for lunch before the game. So the teams lined up first this way in one's mind, the children, adolescents, and young men and women for Goldwater to one side, the Scrantons to the other, and you could tell a lot about the colleges and the teams by looking at the faces. The Goldwater girls and boys were for the most part innocent, and they tended to have large slightly protruded jaws, not unlike Big Barry himself, and blue eyes—an astonishing number had blue eyes (was the world finally coming to the war of the blue-eyed versus the brown-eyed?)—and they were simple, they were small-town, they were hicky, the boys tended to have a little acne, an introspective pimple or two by the corner of the mouth or the side of the chin, a lot of the boys looked solemn and serious, dedicated but slightly blank—they could fix a transistor radio, but a word like "Renaissance" would lay a soft wound of silence, stupefaction in their brain. They were idealists, nearly every last one of them, but they did not speak of the happier varieties of idealism; one thought of Lutherans from North Dakota, 4-H from Minnesota, and Eagle Scouts from Maine. Many of them wore eyeglasses. They were thrifty young men, hardworking young men, polite, slightly paralyzed before the variety of life, but ready to die for a cause. It was obvious they thought Goldwater was one of the finest men ever to be born into American life. And they were stingy, they wore store-bought ready-mades, skinny kids in twenty-dollar suits and that pinch of the jaw, that recidivism of the gums which speaks of false teeth before you are fifty.

The Goldwater girls ran to two varieties. There were the models who had been hired for the purpose, and they were attractive but not very imaginative, they looked like hookers on horses, and then there were the true followers, the daughters of delegates, the California children who belonged to one Goldwater club or another. They were younger than the models of course, they were most of them fifteen, sixteen, not even seventeen, wearing cowboy hats and white vests and shirts with fringes, white riding boots; nearly all of them were blonde and they had simple rather sweet faces, the sort of faces which television commercials used to use for such product fodder as biscuit batter before the commercials turned witty; these Goldwater girls had the faces of young ladies who listened to their parents, particularly to their fathers, they were full of character, but it was the character of tidiness, industry, subservience—unlike the Goldwater boys who looked on the whole not unintelligent though slightly maniacal in the singularity of their vision (the way young physicists look slightly maniacal), the girls seemed to be just about all quite dumb. There was one blonde little girl who was lovely, pretty enough to be a starlet, but she left a pang because her eyes when open were irremediably dim. Taken altogether, boys and girls, they were like the graduating class of a high school in Nebraska. The valedictorian would write his speech on the following theme: Why is the United States the Greatest Nation on Earth?

Whereas the kids who were for Scranton were prep-school or country-day. Some of the boys were plump and merry, some were mildly executive, but they shared in common that slightly complacent air of success which is the only curse of the fraternity president or leader of the student council. They were keen, they tended to be smooth, they had a penchant for bow ties and they were the kind to drive Triumphs or Pontiac convertibles, while the Goldwater boys would be borrowing their father's Dodge Dart (except for the one in a hundred who was automotive in his genius and so had built a dragster to top out at one-six-five). Then there were the Scranton boys who were still the descendants of Holden Caulfield. Faces like theirs had been seen for Stevenson in '60 in L.A. against J.F.K., and faces like theirs might appear (one would hope) in '68 for still another, but for now they were for the nearest candidate with wit, class, and the born fore-knowledge of defeat. Slim, slightly mournful, certainly acerb, and dubious of the fraternity presidents with whom they had made cause, the Holden Caulfields were out for Scranton, and looked a size overmatched by the girls who were for Scranton, good-looking most of them, slightly spoiled, saucy, full of peeves, junior debs doing their best to be cool and so wearing their hair long with a part down the center in such a way that the face, sexy, stripped of makeup (except for some sort of white libidinous wax on the lips) was half-concealed by a Gothic arch of falling tresses. Such were Scranton's parts, such were Goldwater's, as the children shaped up for the game.

> *In this state of . . . warfare between the noble ancient landed interest and the new monied interest, the . . . monied interest is in its nature more ready for any adventure; and its possessors more disposed to new enterprises of any kind. Being of a recent acquisition, it falls in more naturally with any novelties. It is therefore the kind of wealth which will be resorted to by all who wish for change.*
> —BURKE, *Reflections on the Revolution in France*

> *Among the young industrial and financial monopolies of the West and Southwest that want a "bigger slice of the capitalist profit pie," Mr. Vasilyev listed H. L. Hunt, the Texas multimillionaire, the Lockheed Aircraft Corporation, the Douglas Aircraft Company, the Boeing Company and the Northrup Corporation and the Giannini "financial empire" headed by the Bank of America.*
>
> *These are the forces, Mr. Vasilyev said, that overcame the last-minute effort by "Wall Street, the Boston financial group and the Pennsylvania industrial complex" to promote the candidacy of Governor William W. Scranton of Pennsylvania at the Republican convention last month.*
>
> *"But the 'new money' of the West proved to be stronger than the old money of the Northeast," the Soviet commentator said.*
> —*New York Times*, August 13, 1964

For a time it had been interesting history. You will remember that Scranton decided to run for nomination after a talk in Gettysburg on June 6 with President Eisenhower. He left with the solid assumption he would receive Eisenhower's support, solid enough for Governor Scranton's public-relations machine to announce this fact to the nation. That night or early next morning President Eisenhower received a phone call from George Humphrey. Eisenhower had been planning to visit Humphrey in Cleveland during the week of the Governor's Conference. But it developed Barry Goldwater had already been invited to be at Humphrey's home as well. A social difficulty thus presented itself. Humphrey resolved it in this fashion: Eisenhower would understand if, under the circumstances, Goldwater having been invited first . . .

Ike knew what that meant. If his old friend, crony, subordinate and private brain trust George Humphrey was willing to let the old gander-in-chief come out second on a collision of invitations, then Ike had picked a loser, Ike was in danger of being a loser himself. Well, Ike hadn't come out of Abilene, Kansas, all those years ago *ever* to end on the losing side. So he waddled back to the middle. He phoned Bill Scranton you will remember but an hour before Scranton was ready to announce his candidacy at the Governor's Conference on June 7, and told Scranton he could not be party to a "cabal." It was obvious to everybody in America that the old man had not labored through the night and through the day to make the truth of his first conversation with the young man stand out loud and clear in the high sun of ten A.M.

Still, one could not feel too sorry for the young man. It is never easy to grieve for a candidate of the Establishment, particularly the Republican Establishment of the East, which runs a spectrum from the Duke of Windsor to Jerome Zerbe, from Thomas E. Dewey to Lowell Thomas, from Drue Heinz to Tex and Jinx, from Maine to Nassau, New York to South of France, from Allen Dulles to Henry Luce, Igor Cassini to Joe

Alsop, from Sullivan & Cromwell to Cartier's, and from Arthur Krock to Tuxedo Park.

Well, the last two years, all the way from Arthur Krock to Tuxedo Park, you could hear that Bill Scranton was going to be the Republican candidate in '64. Attempts might be made to argue: Goldwater looks strong, somebody could say at a dinner table; hasn't got a chance, the Establishment would give back—it's going to be Scranton. What was most impressive is that the Establishment did not bother to photograph their man, immerse him in publicity, or seek to etch his image. It was taken for granted that when the time came, doors would open, doors would shut, figures would be inserted, heads would be removed, a whiff of incense, a whisk of wickedness—Scranton would be the candidate.

Of course, Goldwater, or the Goldwater organization, or *some* organization, kept picking up delegates for Goldwater, and from a year away there was a bit of sentiment that it might be easier to make a deal with Goldwater, it might be easier to *moderate* him than to excise him. Once upon a time, J.P. Morgan would doubtless have sent some bright young man out on the Southern Pacific with a bag full of hundred-dollar bills. Now, however, possessing a mass media, the buy-off could take place in public. Last November, three weeks before J.F.K. was assassinated, *Life* magazine put Goldwater on their cover wearing a pearl-gray Stetson and clean, pressed, faded blue work shirt and Levi's while his companion, a Palomino named Sunny, stood with one of the Senator's hands on his bridle, the other laid over the vein of his nose. It was Hopalong Cassidy all baby fat removed, it gave promise of the campaign to come: the image of Kennedy was now to be combated by Sheriff B. Morris Goldwater, the Silver Gun of the West. It was one of those pictures worth ten thousand speeches—it gave promise of delivering a million votes. It was also a way of stating that the Establishment was not yet unalterably opposed to Goldwater, and could yet help him, as it had with this cover. But inside the magazine across the heads of seven million readers, another message was delivered to the Senator.

> *Financial interests in Ohio, Illinois, Texas, Los Angeles and San Francisco—all centers of wealth independent of eastern ties—have been lining up money and intense local pressure for Goldwater. But . . . people fail to realize there's a difference in kinds of money. . . . Old money has political power but new money has only purchasing power. . . . When you get to a convention, you don't buy delegates. But you do put the pressure on people who control the delegates—the people who owe the old money for their stake.*

Which was a way to remind Goldwater there were concessions to make. It was in foreign affairs that Goldwater had the most to explain about his policies.

> *Barry Goldwater [went Life's conclusion] represents a valuable impulse in the American politics of '64. He does not yet clearly represent all that a serious contender for the Presidency should. "Guts without depth" and "a man of one-sentence solutions" are the epithets of his critics. The time has come for him to rebut them if he can.*

Two months later Goldwater announced his formal candidacy for the Republican nomination, and issued a pamphlet called "Senator Goldwater Speaks Out on the Issues." Written in that milk-of-magnesia style which is characteristic of such tracts, one could no longer be certain what he thought—he had moved from being a man of "one-sentence solutions" to a man who showed a preference for many imprecise sentences. Barry was treading water. As he did, his people, his organization, kept picking up delegates. It was not until he voted against the Civil Rights Bill that the open battle between old money and new was at last engaged. Too late on the side of the East. To anyone who knew a bit about the workings of the Establishment, a mystery was present. For unless the Establishment had become most suddenly inept, there was a buried motive in the delay, a fear, as if the Eastern money were afraid of some force in the American mind racing to power in defiance of them, some mystique from out the pure accelerating delirium of a crusade which would make cinder of the opposition. So they had waited, all candidates but Rockefeller had waited, none willing to draw the fires of the Right until Scranton was flushed by the ebb and flow, the mystery or murmur, in an old man's throat.

Somewhat later that morning, one saw Scranton in a press conference at the San Francisco Hilton. The Corinthian Room on the ballroom floor (Press Headquarters) was a white room, perhaps forty-five feet by forty feet with a low ceiling and a huge puff of a modern chandelier made up of pieces of plastic which looked like orange candy. The carpet was an electric plastic green, the bridge seats (some two hundred of them) were covered in a plastic the color of wet aspirin, and the walls were white, a hospital-sink white. The practical effect was to leave you feeling like a cold cut set in the white tray of a refrigerator.

The speaker, however, was like a fly annealed on the electric-light bulb of the refrigerator. The banks of lights were turned on him, movie lights, TV lights, four thousand watts in the eye must be the average price a politician pays for his press conference. It gives them all a high instant patina, their skin responding to the call of the wild; there is danger, because the press conference creates the moment when the actor must walk into the gears of the machine. While it is a hundred-to-one or a thousand-to-one he will make no mistake, his career can be extinguished by a blunder. Unless one is making news on a given day—which is to say an important announcement is to be made—the press conference is thus a virtuoso price to be paid for remaining in the game, since there are all too many days when it is to the interest of the speaker, or of his party, or his wing of the party, to make no particular news, but rather to repress news. Still, the speaker must not be too dull, or he will hurt his own position, his remarks will be printed too far back in the paper. So he must be interesting without being revealing. Whereas it is to the interest of the press to make him revealing. A delicate game of balance therefore goes on. Nixon used to play well until the day of his breakdown. Eisenhower was once good at it. Goldwater was considered bad at this game, sufficiently bad that at the convention he held but one press conference before his nomination, and in the six preceding weeks had given but two.

An opportunity to observe the game in operation came with Melvin Laird who tried to convince the Press Corps that the Republican platform was liberal, strong on civil rights, critical of extremists, and yet true to Goldwater. Laird, a smooth vigorous man with a bald domelike head, held the breech for half an hour, ducking questions with grace the way Negroes used once to duck baseballs in a carnival. When he got into trouble (it was after all a most untenable position), he called on one of the most necessary rules of the game, which is that you don't insult the good character of the speaker. So Laird would finally say, "We worked hard on this platform, it's a good platform, I'm proud of it." That made the questioners retreat and regroup for a new attack.

Now Scranton's press conferences were of course different—because no one could be certain if Scranton was part of the game or a wild hare diverting the chase from every true scent. The result was a choppiness to the questioning, a sense of irritation, a hint of vast contempt from the Press Corps; a reporter despises a politician who is not professional, for the game then becomes surrealistic, and it is the function of games to keep dreams, dread and surrealism out in the night where they belong. They would dog at Scranton, they would try to close: *Governor, Governor, could you give the name of any delegate who has moved over from Goldwater to you?* No, we are not prepared to say at this time, would come the answer. *Are there any?* (Titter from the audience.) Certainly. *But you do not care to say?* Not at this time. *Governor* (a new man now), *is there any truth to the rumor you are going to concede before the convention begins?* None whatsoever. *Governor, is it not true that you may be willing to run for Vice-President?* For the eighty-eighth time, it is certainly not true. *Unqualifiedly?* Yes (said Scranton sadly), unqualifiedly.

He stood there like a saint, most curious kind of saint. If he had been an actor he would have played the Dauphin to Ingrid Bergman's Joan of Arc. He was obviously, on superficial study, a weak and stubborn man. One felt he had been spoiled when he was young by a lack of testing. It was not that he lacked bravery, it was that he had lacked all opportunity to be brave for much too long, and now he was not so much engaged in a serious political struggle as in a puberty rite. It was incredible that this pleasant urbane man, so self-satisfied, so civilized, so reasonable, so innocent of butchers' tubs and spleens and guts (that knowledge which radiates with full ceremony off Khrushchev's halo), should be now in fact the man the Eastern Establishment had picked as their candidate for President. He had a fatal flaw to his style, he was just very slightly delicate the way, let us say, a young Madison Avenue executive will seem petulant next to the surly vigor of a president of a steel corporation. Scranton had none of the heft of a political jockstrapper like Goldwater; no, rather he had the big wide thin-lipped mouth of a clown—hopeless! If the roles had been reversed, if it had been Scranton with six hundred delegates and Goldwater who led a rush in the last four weeks to steal the land, why Goldwater might still have won. Scranton was decent but some part of his soul seemed to live in the void. Doubtless he had been more formidable when he began, but he had been losing for four weeks, one loss after another, delegates, delegations, caucuses, he had been losing with Eisenhower, he had lost with Dirksen, he had lost Illinois, he was losing Ohio, his wheeler-dealers stood by idle wheels; you cannot deal when you are losing delegates, there is nothing to offer the delegate but the salvation of his soul, and the delegate has put salvation in hock a long time ago. So Scranton had begun with the most resistant of missions—there are few works in life so difficult as to pry delegates loose from a man who has a nomination virtually won. To be a delegate and stick with the loser is a kind of life, but no delegate can face the possibility of going from a winner to a loser; the losses are not measurable. People are in politics to win. In these circumstances, consider the political weight lifting required of Scranton. He announces his candidacy four weeks before the convention, Goldwater within fifty votes of the nomination. Is Scranton to pull delegates loose from such a scene by an unhappy faculty for getting pictures taken with his legs in the air doing polkas, R.C.A.F. exercises, and backhands in tennis? One knows Scranton's the product of a good many evenings when Eastern gentry circled around cigars and brandy and decided on poor Bill because he was finally not offensive to any. But it would have taken Paul Bunyan to claw into Goldwater's strength from four weeks out. His two hundred plus of Southern delegates were firm as marble, firm as their hated of Civil Rights. And there was much other strength for Barry from the Midwest and the West, a hard core of delegates filled with hot scalding hatred for the Eastern Establishment. They were (unlike the children who were for Goldwater) the hard core of delegates, composed in large part of the kind of tourists who had been poisoning the air of hotel lobbies for twenty years. You could see them now with their Goldwater buttons, ensconced in every lobby, a WASP Mafia where the grapes of wrath were stored. Not for nothing did the White

Anglo-Saxon Protestant have a five-year subscription to *Reader's Digest* and *National Geographic,* high colonics and arthritis, silver-rimmed spectacles, punched-out bellies, and that air of controlled schizophrenia which is the merit badge for having spent one's life on Main Street. Indeed there was general agreement that the basic war was between Main Street and Wall Street. What was not seen so completely is that this war is the Wagnerian drama of the WASP. For a century now the best of the White Protestants have been going from the farm to the town, leaving the small city for the larger one, transferring from Shaker Heights High to Lawrenceville, from Missouri State Teacher's to Smith, from Roast Turkey to Cordon Rouge, off rectitude into wickedness, out of monogamy into *Les Liaisons Dangereuses,* from *Jane Eyre* to *Candy;* it's a long trip from the American Legion's Annual Ball to the bust-outs of Southampton. There's the unheard cry of a wounded coyote in all the minor leagues of the Junior League, in all the tacky doings of each small town, the grinding rasp of envy rubs the liver of each big frog in his small pond, no hatred like hatred for the East in the hearts of those who were left behind: the horror in the heart of social life in America is that one never knows whether one is snubbed for too much or too little, whether one was too fine or not fine enough, too graceless or too possessed of special grace, too hungry for power or not ambitious enough—the questions are burning and never answered because the Establishment of the East rarely rejects, it merely yields or ignores, it promises and forgets, it offers to attend your daughter's party and somehow does not quite show up, or comes that fraction too late which is designed to spoil the high anticipation of the night. (Or worse, leaves a fraction too early.) The WASPS who were for Goldwater were the social culls of that Eastern Society which ran the land, yes, the Goldwater WASPS were the old doctors of Pasadena with their millions in stock and their grip on the A.M.A.,

the small-town newspaper editors, the president of
the second most important bank, the wives of Texas
oil, yes the wives and family of all the prominent and
prosperous who had a fatal touch of the hick, all the
Western ladies who did the Merengue at El Morocco on
a trip to New York, and did it not quite well enough,
you could just hear the giggles in the throat of Archie
or Lightning Dick or Sad One-Eye, the Haitian and/or
Jamaican who had taught them how. Yes the memory
of those social failures is the saliva of intellectual
violence. The old Goldwater WASPS, the ones who
had been sitting in the hotel lobbies, had an insane
sting to their ideas—they were for birching America's
bare bottom where Come-you-nisms collected: white
and Negro equality; sexual excess; Jew ideas; dirty
linen, muddled thinking, lack of respect for the Constitution. The Right in America had an impacted con-
sistency of constipation to their metaphor. Small wonder they dreamed of a Republican purge. The WASPS
were full of psychic wastes they could not quit—they
had moved into the Middle West and settled the
West, they had won the country, and now they were
losing it to the immigrants who had come after and the
descendants of slaves. They had watched as their culture was adulterated, transported, converted into some
surrealist mélange of public piety *cum* rock and roll,
product of the movies and television, of the mass
media where sons of immigrants were so often king,
yes the WASPS did not understand what was going
on, they were not so ready after all to listen to those of
their ministers who would argue that America had a
heritage of sin and greed vis-à-vis the Negro, and those
sins of the blood must be paid; they were not at all
ready to listen to the argument that America's industry had been built out of the hardworking hard-used
flesh of five generations of immigrants, no, they were
Christian but they did not want to hear any more
about the rights of others, they suffered from the private fear they were not as good, not as tough, not as
brave as their great-grandfathers, they suffered from

the intolerable fear that they were not nearly so good nor so tough as those other Christians close to two thousand years ago who faced Romans, so they were now afraid of the East which had dominated the fashion and style of their life, they were ready to murder the East, the promiscuous adulterous East—in a good fast nuclear war they might allow the Russians a fair crack at New York—yes they were loaded with one hatred: the Eastern Establishment was not going to win again, this time Main Street was going to take Wall Street. So Barry had his brothers, three or four hundred of the hardest delegates in the land, and they were ready to become the lifelong enemy of any delegate who might waver to Scranton.

That was the mood. That was the inner condition of the Goldwater delegates about the time Scranton announced he was going all out for the nomination and would pry these people loose from Barry. Henry Cabot Lodge came in from Vietnam. He was, you remember, going to help. Cynics in the Establishment were quick to inform you that Lodge was actually getting the hell out before the roof fell in, but Lodge gave this message to reporters:

> . . . *One of the things that always used to please me about being in Vietnam was the thought that I might as an older man be able to do something to help our soldiers who were out risking their lives.*
>
> *Well, a couple of weeks ago I ran into this captain who was one of the battalion advisors and he said, "Are you going back to help Governor Scranton?" And I said, "No." Well, he said, "You're not?" He said, "I think you ought to."*
>
> *Well, that gave me quite a—that startled me, rather, because his attitude was: "I'm doing my duty out here, you'd better get back and do your duty pretty fast."*

Obviously, no one had ever told Henry Cabot Lodge he might not necessarily be superb. So he came in, kingpin, boy, and symbol of the Establishment, and for two weeks he worked for Scranton (although most curiously—for Lodge was back in America a week before he even made arrangements to meet with Scranton). Still, Lodge announced his readiness to be first target of the WASP Mafia. At the end of two weeks of picking up the telephone to call old friends only to have the telephone come back in the negative, Lodge looked like a man who had been handsome once. His color was a dirty wax yellow, his smile went up over the gums at the corner of his mouth and gave a hint of the skull the way ninety-year-old men look when their smile goes past the teeth. He looked like they had been beating him in the kidneys with his own liver. It was possible something had been beaten out of him forever.

Of course this was Sunday night—the first session of the convention was not ten hours off on Monday morning—and Scranton and Lodge had had a ferocious bad Sunday; the particular letter inviting Goldwater to debate Scranton before the convention had gone out earlier that day above the Governor's signature and it had gone so far as this:

> *Your managers say in effect that the delegates are little more than a flock of chickens whose necks will be wrung at will. . . . Goldwaterism has come to stand for a whole crazy-quilt collection of absurd and dangerous positions that would be soundly repudiated by the American people in November.*

Denison Kitchel, Goldwater's General Director of the National Goldwater for President Committee, issued a statement:

> *Governor Scranton's letter has been read here with amazement. It has been returned to him.*

Perhaps, upon consideration, the Governor will recognize the intemperate nature of his remarks. As it stands, they tragically reflect upon the Republican Party and upon every delegate to the convention.

Then Kitchel sent out mimeographed copies of Scranton's letter and his own reply to every Republican delegate. The Scranton mine caved in. Flooding at one end of the shaft, it was now burning at the other. Delegates do not like to be told they are a flock of chickens. It is one of those metaphors which fit like a sliver of bone up the nostril. Scranton was to repudiate his letter the following day; he accepted responsibility but disowned the letter—the language was not his—which is to say he admitted he could not run a competent organization. Nor, it developed, could he protect his own people: the name of the assistant who had actually written the letter slipped out quick enough.

Thus, one night before the convention, the letter public, Scranton may just conceivably have moved from deep depression to outright agony. The Republicans were having a Gala that night, five hundred dollars a plate for funds, the press not admitted, although many, some from the front, some from the rear, found a way in, and all the Republican luminaries were there, Eisenhower, and the Luces, Mrs. Eisenhower, Henry Cabot Lodge, Thruston Morton, George Murphy, Ray Bliss, Mrs. Goldwater, Scranton. All but Barry. In a much-announced rage about the letter, Goldwater was boycotting the Gala. Of course, it was essentially an Establishment Gala, that slowly came clear, and therefore was in degree a wake—news of the letter was passing around. The dance floor was not to be crowded this night.

Scranton came in. He walked down the center aisle between the tables looking like one of the walking wounded. People came up to greet him and he smiled wanly and sadly and a little stiffly as if he were very weary indeed, as if he had just committed hara-kiri but was still walking. When introduced, he said with wan humor, "I've read your books"—something finally splendid about Scranton.

A minute later, Scranton and Eisenhower came together. It was their first meeting in San Francisco; the General had just arrived that day, come into the Santa Fe depot after crossing the country by train. He was Scranton's last hope; he might still give momentum to the bogged-down tanks of Scranton's attack —what, after all, was the measure of magic? So Scranton must have looked for every clue in Eisenhower's greeting. There were clues running all over. Ike stood up from his table, he pumped Scranton's hand, he held his elbow, he wheeled about with him, he grinned, he smiled widely, he grinned again, his face flushed red, red as a two-week-old infant's face, his eyes twinkled, he never stopped talking, he never took his hands off Scranton, he never looked him in the eye. It was the greeting of a man who is not going to help another man.

Next day, Eisenhower dropped William Warren Scranton. He had a press conference at the Hilton in which he succeeded in saying nothing. It was obvious now he would not come out for anyone, it was also obvious he would not join the Moderates' call for a stronger civil-rights plank. "Well," he said, "he [Melvin Laird] came to see me, and the way he explained it to me, it sounded all right." Asked about an amendment the Moderates wished to put in the plank, "The authority to use America's nuclear weapons belong to the President of the United States," Eisenhower thought "this statement was perfectly all right with me because it reaffirms what the Constitution means." Still he would not fight for it. Asked how he reacted to the idea of a debate before the entire convention between Senator Goldwater and Governor Scranton, a reference directed to Scranton's now famous letter of the day before, Eisenhower said, "This, of course, would be a precedent, and I am not against precedents.

I am not particularly for them." A little earlier he had said, "I really have no feeling of my own." He didn't. He was in a private pond. He had been in one for years. Something had been dying in him for years, the proportions and magnitude of his own death no doubt, and he was going down into the cruelest of fates for an old man, he was hooked on love like an addict, not large love, but the kind of mild tolerant love which shields an old man from hatred. It was obvious that Eisenhower had a deep fear of the forces which were for Goldwater. He did not mind with full pride any longer if people felt contempt for him, but he did not want to be hated hard by anyone. So he could not declare himself, not for anything, and as he made his lapses in syntax, in word orders, in pronunciations, they took on more prominence than ever they had. At times, they were as rhythmic as a tic, or a dog scratching at a bite. He would say, "We must be objec*tive*, I mean ob*jec*tive, we must be objective . . ." and on he would go as if he were sinking very slowly and quietly into the waters of his future death which might be a year away or ten years away but was receiving him nonetheless like a marsh into which he disappeared twitch by twitch, some beating of wet wings against his fate.

> . . . *Looke, Lord, and finde both Adams met in me.*
>
> —JOHN DONNE

Now, as for Goldwater, he had dimensions. Perhaps they were no more than contradictions, but he was not an easy man to comprehend in a hurry. His wife, for example, had been at the Gala, sitting with some family and friends, but at one of the less agreeable tables on the floor, off to the side and sufficiently back of the stage so that you could not see the entertainer. It seemed a curious way for the Establishment to treat the wife of the leading contender, but I was assured by the young lady who brought me over for the introduction that Mrs. Goldwater preferred it that way. "She hates being the center of attention," I was told. Well, she turned out to be a shy attractive woman with a gentle not altogether happy but sensual face. There was something nice about her and very vulnerable. Her eyes were moist, they were luminous. It was impossible not to like her. Whereas her daughters were attractive in a different fashion. "I want the best ring in this joint, buster," I could hear them say.

Goldwater's headquarters, however, were at a remove from the ladies. Occupying the fourteenth and fifteenth floors of the Mark Hopkins, they were not easy to enter. The main elevators required a wait of forty-five minutes to go up. The alternate route was off the mezzanine through a pantry onto a service car. A half-filled twenty-gallon garbage can stood by the service-elevator door. You went squeezed up tight with high and low honchos for Goldwater, plus waiters with rolling carts working room service. Once there, the fourteenth and fifteenth floors were filthy. A political headquarters is never clean—stacks of paper, squeezed-out paper cups, typewriter carbons on the floor, jackets on wire hangers all angles on a rack—a political headquarters is like the City Room of a newspaper. But Goldwater's headquarters were filthier than most. There was a general detritus like the high-water mark on a beach. The armchairs were dusty and the sofas looked like hundred-dollar newly wed sofas dirty in a day. The air had the beat-out cigar smell of the waiting room in a large railroad station. It had nothing to do with the personnel. No one on the fourteenth or fifteenth floor had anything to do with his surroundings. You could have dropped them in Nymphenburg or a fleabag off Eighth Avenue—the rooms would come to look the same. A room was a place with a desk where the work got out.

They had something in common—professional workers for Goldwater—something not easy to define. They were not like the kids out in the street, nor did they have much in common with the old cancer-guns in the lobby; no, the worst of these workers looked like divinity students who had been expelled from the seminary for embezzling class funds and still felt they were nearest to J.C.—there was a dark blank fanaticism in their eyes. And the best of the Goldwater professionals were formidable, big rangy men, some lean, some flabby, with the hard distasteful look of topflight investigators for fire-insurance companies, field men for the F.B.I., or like bright young district attorneys, that lean flat look of the hunter, full of moral indignation and moral vacuity. But the total of all the professional Goldwater people one saw on the fourteenth and fifteenth floors was directly reminiscent of a guided tour through the F.B.I. in the Department of Justice Building in Washington, that same succession of handsome dull faces for guide, hair combed straight back or combed straight from a part, eyes lead shot, noses which offered nothing, mouths which were functional, good chins, deft moves. A succession of these men took the tourists through the halls of the F.B.I. and read aloud the signs on the exhibits for us and gave short lectures about the function of the F.B.I. (guard us from the enemy without, the enemy within, Communism and Crime—the statements offered in simple organizational prose of the sort used in pamphlets which welcome new workers to large corporations, soldiers to new commands, freshmen to high school, and magazine readers to editorials). The tourists were mainly fathers and sons. The wives were rugged, the kind who are built for dungarees and a green plaid hunting jacket, the sisters and daughters plain and skinny, no expression. They all had lead shot for eyes, the lecturers and the tourists. Most of the boys were near twelve and almost without exception had the blank private faces which belong to kids who kill their old man with a blast, old lady with a butcher knife, tie sister with telephone cord and hide out in the woods for three days. The climax of the tour was a demonstration by the F.B.I.

agent how to use a tommy gun. For ten minutes he stitched targets, using one shot at a time, bursts of three, full magazine, he did it with the mild grace of a body-worker hitting small rivets, there was solemn applause after each burst of shots.

That was a part of the Republic, and here it was at Headquarters for Goldwater. The faces in these rooms were the cream of the tourists and the run of the F.B.I.; there was a mood like the inside of a prison: enclosed air, buried urgency. But that was not altogether fair. The sense of a prison could come from the number of guards and the quality of their style. They were tough dull Pinkertons with a tendency to lean on a new visitor. One desire came off them. They would not be happy if there were no orders to follow. With orders, they were ready to put the arm on Bill Scranton, Nelson Rockefeller, or General Eisenhower (if told to). Probably they would put the arm on Johnson if he appeared and was ordered out. Naturally they were not there for that, they were there to defend Headquarters from mobs (read: niggers) and the Senator from black assassination. It made sense up to a point: Goldwater was in more danger than Scranton, at least so long as Scranton showed no sign of winning; just that day, Sunday, there had been a civil-rights anti-Goldwater march down Market Street. The heavy protection was nonetheless a fraud. No mob was getting to the fourteenth floor, nor to Goldwater's fort on the fifteenth (a separate barricade of Pinkertons guarded the twenty-odd steps), no mob was going to get all the way up with just those three elevators and a wait of forty-five units of sixty seconds each, no assassin was likely to try Headquarters when there were opportunities on the street; no, the atmosphere was created to create atmosphere, the aura at Headquarters was solemnity, debris underfoot, and grave decisions, powers put to the service of order, some conspiracy of the vault, a dedication to the necessity of taking power. That was Headquarters. One never got to see Goldwater in the place.

There was opportunity, however, to come within three feet of him later that day, once at the caucus of the Florida delegation in the Beverly Plaza, once on the street moving from hotel to hotel (Pinkertons no longer in evidence now—just cops) and again at the Clift, where he talked to the Washington delegation. There was excitement watching Barry go to work with a group, an intensity in the air, a religious devotion, as if one of the most urbane priests of America was talking at a Communion breakfast, or as if the Principal-of-the-Year was having a heart-to-heart with honor students. The Florida delegation, meeting in a dingy little downstairs banquet room, was jammed. The afternoon had turned hot for San Francisco. Eighty degrees outside, it may have been ninety in the room. Everybody was perspiring. Barry sat in the front, a spotlight on him, a silver film of perspiration adding to his patina, and the glasses, those black-framed glasses, took on that odd life of their own, that pinched severity, that uncompromising idealism which made Goldwater kin to the tight-mouthed and the lonely. Talking in a soft modest voice, he radiated at this moment the skinny boyish sincerity of a fellow who wears glasses but is determined nonetheless to have a good time. Against all odds. It was not un-reminiscent of Arthur Miller: that same mixture of vast solemnity and unspoiled boyhood, a sort of shucks and aw shit in the voice. "Well, you see," said Goldwater, talking to the Florida delegation, "if I was to trust the polls right now, I'd have to say I didn't have a chance. But why should I trust the polls? Why should any of us trust the polls? They've been wrong before. They'll be wrong again. Man is superior to the machine. The thing to remember is that America is a spiritual country, we're founded on belief in God, we may wander a little as a country, but we never get too far away. I'm ready to say the election is going to give the Democrats a heck of a surprise. Why, I'll tell you this," Goldwater said, sweating mildly, telling the folks from Florida just as keen as if he was alone with each one of them, each one of these elderly gents and real-estate dealers and plain women with silver-rimmed eyeglasses, "tell you this, I'm doing my best not to keep this idea a secret, but I think we're not only going to give the Democrats a heck of a surprise, I think we're going to win. [Applause, cheers.] In fact I wouldn't be in this if I didn't think we were going to win. [Applause.] Why, as I sometimes tell my wife, I'm too young to retire and too old to go back to work." [Laughter, loud cheers]. Goldwater was done. He smiled shyly, his glasses saying: I am a modest man, and I am severe on myself. As he made his route to the door, the delegates were touching him enthusiastically.

Back on the street—he was walking the blocks to the Hotel Clift where the Washington State delegation was having a Goldwater reception—his tail consisted of fifty or sixty excited people, some Florida delegates who didn't wish to lose sight of the man, plus a couple of cops glad to have the duty. Cars slowed down to look at him; one stopped. A good-looking woman got out and cheered. There was something in the way she did it. Just as strange Negroes scattered at random through a white audience may act in awareness of one another, so the Goldwater supporters in their thirties and forties gave off a similar confidence of holding the secret. This very good-looking woman yelled, "You go, Barry, you go, go." But there was anger and elation in her voice, as if she were declaring, "We're going to get the country back." And Goldwater smiled modestly and went on. He looked a little in fever. Small wonder. He could be President of the United States in less than half a year, he could stop a sniper's bullet he never knew when, he was more loved and hated than any man in America, and inside all this was just *him*, the man who adjusted radio knobs in the early morning in order to transmit a little better, and now conceivably adjusted a few knobs. . . .

At the Hotel Clift he talked to the Washington delegates. We were definitely back in high school. That was part of Goldwater's deal—he brought you back to the bright minted certitudes of early patriotism when you knew the U.S. was the best country on earth and there was no other. Yes, his appeal would go out to all the millions who were now starved and a little sour because some part of their life had ended in high school, and the university they had never seen. But then Barry had had but one year of college—he had indeed the mind of a powerful freshman. "I want to thank you folks from Washington for giving me this warm greeting. Of course, Washington is the name of a place I often like to get the heck out of, but I'm sure I won't confuse the two right here." (Laughter.) He was off, a short political speech. In the middle, extremism. "I don't see how anybody can be an extremist who believes in the Constitution. And for those misguided few who pretend to believe in the Constitution, but in secret don't, well they may be extremists, but I don't see any necessity to legislate against them. I just feel sorry for them." (Cheers. Applause. Happiness at the way Barry delivered anathemas.) At a certain point in the speech, he saw a woman in the audience whom he recognized, and stopped in the middle of a phrase: "Hi, honey," he sang out like a traveling salesman, which brought a titter from the delegation, for his voice had shifted too quickly, the codpiece was coming off, Rain and the Reverend Davidson. Something skinny, itchy, hard as a horselaugh, showed—he was a cannoneer with a hairy ear. Goldwater went on, the good mood continued; then at the end, speech done, he turned down a drink but said in his best gee-whizzer, "I'm sorry I have to leave because gosh I'd like to break a few with you." Laughter, and he took off head down, a little modest in the exit, a little red in the neck.

There was entertainment at the Republican Gala on Sunday night. The climax was a full marching band of bagpipers. They must have been hired for the week since one kept hearing them on the following days, and at all odd times, heard them even in my hotel room at four a.m., for a few were marching in the streets of San Francisco, sounding through the night, giving off the barbaric evocation of the Scots, all valor, wrath, firmitude, and treachery—the wild complete treachery of the Scots finding its way into the sound of the pipes. They were a warning of the fever in the heart of the WASP. There are sounds which seem to pass through all the protective gates in the ear and reach into some nerve where the eschatology is stored. Few parents have failed to hear it in the cry of their infant through the morning hours of a bad night—stubbornness, fury, waste, and the promise of revenge come out of a flesh half-created by one's own flesh; the knowledge is suddenly there that seed is existential, no paradise resides in seed, seed can be ill-inspired and go to a foul gloomy end. Some find their part of the truth in listening to jazz—it is moot if any white who had no ear for jazz can know the passion with which some whites become attached to the Negro's cause. So, too, listening to the bagpipes, you knew this was the true music of the WASPS. There was something wild and martial and bottomless in the passion, a pride which would not be exhausted, a determination which might never end, perhaps should never end, the Faustian rage of a white civilization was in those Highland wails, the cry of a race which was born to dominate and might never learn to share, and never learning, might be willing to end the game, the end of the world was in the sound of the pipes. Or at very least the danger one would come closer to the world's end. So there was a vast if all-private appeal in listening to the pipes shrill out the herald of a new crusade, something jagged, Viking, of the North in the air, a sense of breaking ice and barbaric shields, hunters loose in the land again. And this had an appeal which burrowed deep, there was excitement at the thought of

Goldwater getting the nomination, as if now finally all one's personal suicides, all the deaths of the soul accumulated by the past, all the failures, all the terrors, could find purge in a national situation where a national murder was being planned (the Third World War) and one's own suicide might be lost in a national suicide. There was that excitement, that the burden of one's soul (always equal to the burden of one's personal responsibility) might finally be lifted— what a release was there! Beauty was inspired by the prospect. For if Goldwater won, and the iron power of the iron people who had pushed him forth—as echoed in the iron of the Pinkertons on the fourteenth and fifteenth floor—now pushed forth over the nation an iron regime with totalitarianism seizing the TV in every frozen dinner, well then at last a true underground might form; and liberty at the thought of any catalyst which would bring it on. Yes, the Goldwater movement excited the depths because the apocalypse was brought more near, and like millions of other whites, I had been leading a life which was a trifle too pointless and a trifle too full of guilt and my gullet was close to nausea with the endless compromises of an empty liberal center. So I followed the four days of the convention with something more than simple apprehension. The country was taking a turn, the colors were deepening, the knives of the afternoon were out, something of the best in American life might now be going forever; or was it altogether to the opposite? and was the country starting at last to take the knots of its contradictions up from a premature midnight of nightmare into the surgical terrains of the open skin? Were we in the beginning, or turning the middle, of our worst disease? One did not know any longer, you simply did not know any longer, but something was certain: the country was now part of the daily concern. One worried about it for the first time, the way you worried about family or work, a good friend or the future, and that was the most exceptional of emotions.

II

*. . . When men are too much confined to pro-
fessional and faculty habits, and as it were in-
veterate in the recurrent employment of that
narrow circle, they are rather disabled than
qualified for whatever depends on the knowledge
of mankind, on experience in mixed affairs, on a
comprehensive, connected view of the various,
complicated, external and internal interests,
which go to the formation of that multifarious
thing called a state.*
—Burke, *Reflections on the Revolution in France*

If the details of the Republican convention of 1964
were steeped in concern, it was nonetheless not very
exciting, not technically. As a big football game, the
score might have been 76 to 0, or 76 to 3. (There
were sentimentalists who would claim that Rockefeller
kicked a field goal.) Compared however to the Republican Convention of 1940 when Wendell Willkie came
from behind to sweep the nomination on the sixth
ballot, or the 1952 convention when Eisenhower defeated Taft on the second roll call of the states, compared even to the Democratic Convention of 1960,
there were few moments in this affair, and nothing
even remotely comparable in excitement to the demonstration for Adlai Stevenson four years ago when
Eugene McCarthy put him in nomination. Yet this
convention of 1964 would remain as one of the most
important in our history; it took place with religious
exaltation for some, with dread for others, and in
sheer trauma for the majority of the Press and television who were present on the scene. For them it offered four days of anxiety as pure and deep as a child
left alone in a house. The purpose of the Press in
America has been to tinker with the machine, to ad-

just, to prepare a seat for new valves and values, to lubricate, to excuse, to justify, to serve in the maintenance of the Establishment. From I. F. Stone on the left, going far to the right of Joseph Alsop, over almost so far as David Lawrence, the essential understanding of the mass media is that the machine of the nation is a muddle which is endlessly grateful for ministrations of the intellect; so a game is played in which the Establishment always forgives the mass media for its excesses, and the mass media brings its sense of civilization (adjustment, psychoanalysis, responsibility, and the milder shores of love) to the service of the family Establishment. Virtually everything is forgiven by both sides. The contradictory remarks of politicians are forgotten, the more asinine predictions of pundits are buried with mercy. The Establishment for example would not remind Joe Alsop that in March 1964 he had written, "No serious Republican politician, even of the most Neanderthal type, any longer takes Goldwater seriously." No, the Press was not to be twitted for the limits of their technique because half their comprehension of the nation derived after all from material supplied by the Establishment; the other half came from conversations with each other. All too often the Press lives in the investigative condition of a lover who performs the act for two minutes a day and talks about it for twenty hours of the twenty-four. So a daisy chain like the *National Review* proves to be right about Goldwater's strength and the intellectual Establishment with its corporate resources is deep in error.

An explanation? Those who hold power think the devil is best contained by not mentioning his name. This procedure offers a formidable shell in which to live, but its cost is high; the housing is too ready to collapse when the devil decides to show. There has been no opportunity to study him. Just as a generation of the Left, stifled and ignored through the McCarthyism of the Fifties and the Eisenhowerism of the Fifties, caused panic everywhere when they emerged as the Beat Generation, so another generation, a generation of the Right, has been stifled, their actions reported inaccurately, their remarks distorted, their ideals (such as they are) ignored, and their personal power underestimated. The difference however is that the Beat Generation was a new flock of early Christians gathered prematurely before the bomb, an open-air asylum for the gentle and the mad, where in contrast the underground generation of the Right is a frustrated posse, a convention of hangmen who subscribe to the principle that the executioner has his rights as well. The liberal mind collapses before this notion but half of nature may be contained in the idea that the weak are happiest when death is quick. It is a notion which since the Nazis has been altogether detestable, but then the greatest intellectual damage the Nazis may have done was to take a few principles from nature and pervert them root and nerve. In the name of barbarism and a return to primitive health they accelerated the most total and surrealistic aspects of civilization. The gas chamber was a full albino descendant of the industrial revolution.

But that is a digression. To return to the as yet milder political currents of the Left and the Right in America, one could say the Beat Generation was a modest revolution, suicidal in the center of its passion. At its most militant it wished for immolation rather than power, it desired only to be left free enough to consume itself. Yet in the mid-Fifties liberals reacted with a profound terror, contumely, and ridicule to its manifestations as if their own collective suicide (the private terror of the liberal spirit is invariably suicide, not murder) was to be found in the gesture of the Beat. What then the panic of the liberal Establishment before a revolution of the Right whose personal nightmare might well be their inability to contain their most murderous impulse, a movement of the Right whose ghost is that unlaid blood and breath of Nazism which has hovered these twenty years like a succubus over the washed-out tissues of civilization. Consider but one evidence of the fear: that part of the Press called Periodicals sat in a section of the gallery to the left of the speakers in the Cow Palace. There were one hundred writers in this Periodical section of the gallery and six passes to get down to the floor where one could talk to delegates and in turn be looked at by them. Of those six passes, one or two were always available. Which meant that the majority of writers did not try to get down to the floor very often. Sitting next to one another the writers were content to observe—there were killers on the floor.

There were. It was a convention murderous in mood. The mood of this convention spoke of a new kind of society. Chimeras of fascism hung like fogbank. And high enthusiasm. Some of the delegates were very happy. *"Viva,"* would shout a part of the gallery. *"Olé,"* would come the answer. There was an éclat, a bull roar, a mystical communion in the sound even as *Sieg Heil* used to offer its mystical communion. *Viva-Olé.* Live-Yay! Live-Yay! It was the new chic of the mindless. The American mind had gone from Hawthorne and Emerson to the Frug, the Bounce, and Walking the Dog, from *The Flowering of New England* to the cerebrality of professional football in which a quarterback must have not only heart, courage, strength and grace but a mind like an IBM computer. It marks the turn we have taken from the Renaissance. There too was the ideal of a hero with heart, courage, strength, and grace, but he was expected to possess the mind of a passionate artist. Now the best heroes were—in the sense of the Renaissance— mindless: Y. A. Tittle, John Glenn, Tracy, Smiling Jack; the passionate artists were out on the hot rods, the twist band was whipping the lovers, patriotism was a football game, a Fascism would come in (if it came) on Live-Yay! Let's live-yay! The hype had made fifty million musical-comedy minds; now the hype could do anything; it could set high-school students to roar *Viva-Olé,* and they would roar it while victims of a new totalitarianism would be whisked away to a new kind of camp—hey, honey, do you twist, they would yell into the buses.

> *When men of rank sacrifice all ideas of dignity to an ambition without a distinct object, and work low instruments and for low ends, the whole composition becomes low and base.*
> —BURKE, *Reflections on the Revolution in France*

First major event of the convention was Eisenhower's appearance at the Cow Palace to give a speech on Tuesday afternoon. The arena was well-chosen for a convention. Built in the Thirties when indoor sports stadiums did not yet look like children's nurseries, the Cow Palace offered echoes—good welterweights and middleweights had fought here, there was iron in the air. And the Republicans had installed the speaker's platform at one end of the oval; the delegates sat therefore in a file which was considerably longer than it was wide, the speaker was thus installed at the handle of the sword. (Whereas the Democrats in 1960 had put the speaker in the middle of the oval.) But this was the party after all of Republican fathers rather than Democratic mothers. If there were any delegates to miss the psychic effect of this decision, a huge banner raised behind the speaker confronted them with the legend: "Of the people, By the people, For the people." "Of the people" was almost invisible; "By the people" was somewhat more clear; "For the people" was loud and strong. This was a party not much "of the people" but very much "for the people," it presumed to know what was good for them.

And for fact, that had always been Ike's poor lone strength as a speaker, he knew what was good for you. He dipped into his speech, "here with great pride because I am a Republican," "my deep dedication to Republicanism"—he had not been outward bound for five minutes before the gallery was yawning. Ike had always been a bore, but there had been fascination in the boredom when he was President—this, after all, was *the* man. Now he was just another hog wrassler of rhetoric; he pinned a few phrases in his neat determined little voice, and a few phrases pinned him back. Ike usually fought a speech to a draw. It was hard to listen. All suspense had ended at Monday morning's press conference. Ike would not come out in support of Scranton. So the mind of the Press drifted out with the mind of the gallery. If Ike said a few strong words about the Civil Rights Bill—"Republicans in Congress to their great credit voted far more overwhelmingly than did our opponents to pass the Civil Rights Bill"—it meant nothing. The Moderates tried to whoop it up, the Goldwater delegations looked on in ranked masses of silence. Ike went on. He gave the sort of speech which takes four or five columns in the New York *Times* and serves to clot the aisles of history. He was still, as he had been when he was President, a cross between a boy and an old retainer. The boy talked, earnest, innocent, a high-school valedictorian debating the affirmative of, Resolved: Capitalism is the Most Democratic System on Earth; and the old retainer quavered into the voice, the old retainer could no longer live without love.

Ike had bored many a crowd in his time. He had never bored one completely—he had always known how to get some token from a mob. Ever since 1952, he had been giving little pieces of his soul to draw demonstrations from the mob. You could always tell the moment. His voice shifted. Whenever he was ready to please the crowd, he would warn them by beginning to speak with a brisk little anger. Now it came, now he said it. ". . . Let us particularly scorn the *divisive* efforts of those outside our family, including sensation-seeking columnists and commentators [beginning of a wild demonstration] because," said Ike, his voice showing a glint of full spite, "I assure you that these are people who couldn't care less about the good of our party." He was right, of course. That was not why he said it, however; he said it to repay the Press for what they had said about him these last three weeks; the sensation they had been seeking was—so far as he was concerned—to arouse needles of fury in an old man's body—he said what he said for revenge. Mainly he said it to please the Goldwater crowd, there was the hint of that in his voice. The Goldwater delegations and the gallery went into the first large demonstration of the convention. Trumpets sounded, heralds of a new crusade: cockroaches, columnists, and Communists to be exterminated. There were reports in the papers next day that delegates shook their fists at newspapermen on the floor, and at the television men with their microphones. The mass media is of course equipped for no such war. Some of the men from the mass media looked like moon men: they wore red helmets and staggered under the load of a portable camera which must have weighed fifty pounds and was packed on their back; others of the commentators had portable mikes and hats with antennae. To the delegates they must have looked like insects grown to the size of a man. Word whipped in to the delegations from the all-call telephone in the office trailer of the Goldwater command post back of the Cow Palace. Cut the demonstration, was the word from F. Clifton White. The demonstration subsided. But the Press did not, the rest of the mass media did not. They remain in a state of agitation: if Ike was ready to accuse, anyone could serve as hangman. Anyone would. Anyone they knew.

Much later that Tuesday, after the full reading of the full platform, came a debate between the Moderates and the Conservatives. Success in politics comes from putting one's seat to a chair and sitting through dull wrangles in order to be present after midnight when the clubhouse vote is cast. Playboys do not go far in these circumstances, nor adventurers; the mediocre recognized early that a society was evolving which would enable them to employ the very vice which hitherto had made life intolerable—mediocrity itself.

So the cowardly took their place in power. They had the superior ability to breathe in hours of boredom.

Politics was now open however to the disease of the bored—magic. Magic can sweep you away. Once a decade, once every two decades, like a big wind which eludes the weather charts and seems to arise from the caverns of the ocean itself, so does a hurricane sweep a convention. It happened with Wendell Willkie in 1940; it flickered on the horizon with Stevenson in '60; it was Scranton's hope to work a real debate on the last session before the balloting. If he could win even once on some small point, rumors of magic could arise. The Moderates had forced therefore a floor fight to propose a few amendments to the Republican platform of '64. One: that only the President have the authority to use America's nuclear weapons. Two: repudiate the John Birch Society. Three: introduce a language of approval for the Civil Rights Act. The chances of success were small at best: only an extraordinary assault on the emotions of the Goldwater delegations could sway them to vote yes for the amendments.

The Moderates however went to battle moderately. Their speakers were impressive (as such a quality is measured in the *Times*). They were Christian Herter, Hugh Scott, Clifford Case, George Romney, Lindsay, Javits, Rockefeller. They were not, however, lively speakers, not this night. Lindsay and Javits were presentable in professional groups; devoted to detailed matters, they spoke with reason; Case spoke like a shy high-school teacher; Christian Herter was reminiscent of Mr. Chips; Hugh Scott owned no fire. Carlino (Majority Leader in the New York Assembly) sounded like a successful restaurant owner. And Governor Romney of Michigan had his own special amendments, he was a moderation of the moderates. As he spoke, he looked like a handsome version of Boris Karloff, all honesty, big-jawed, soft-eyed, eighty days at sea on a cockeyed passion. He spoke in a loud strong voice yet one sensed a yaw at the center of his brain which left his cerebations as lost as Karloff's lost little voice. No, the only excitement had come at the beginning. Rockefeller was not a man who would normally inspire warmth. He had a strong decent face and something tough as the rubber in a handball to his makeup, but his eyes had been punched out a long time ago—they had the distant lunar glow of the small sad eyes you see in a caged chimpanzee or gorilla. Even when hearty he gave an impression the private man was remote as an astronaut on a lost orbit. But Rockefeller had his ten minutes at the podium and as he talked of suffering "at first-hand" in the California primary from the methods of "extremist elements," threatening letters unsigned, bomb threats, "threats of personal violence," telephone calls, "smear and hate literature," "strong-arm and goon tactics," the gallery erupted, and the boos and jeers came down. Rockefeller could have been Leo Durocher walking out to the plate at Ebbets Field to protest an umpire's decision after Leo had moved from the Dodgers to the Giants. Again the all-call in the Goldwater trailer outside the Cow Palace was busy, again the delegations were told to be silent, and obeyed. But the gallery would not stop, and Thruston Morton, the Chairman, came forward like one of the sweepers in *Camino Real* to tell Kilroy his time was up. Rockefeller had his moment. "You quiet them," he said to Morton. "That's your job. I want my time to speak." And there was a conception of Rockefeller finally— he had few ideas and none of them were his own, he had a personality which was never in high focus (in the sense that Bobby Kennedy and Jimmy Hoffa are always in high focus) but he had an odd courage which was profound—he could take strength from defying a mob. Three hundred thousand years ago, a million years ago, some gorilla must have stood up to an enraged tribe and bellowed back and got away alive and human society was begun. So Rocky finally had his political moment which was precisely right for him.

But the other Moderates did not. There was in their collective voice a suggestion of apology: let-us-at-least-be-heard. Speakers who were opposed to the amendments sounded as effective, sometimes more. Ford from Michigan spoke after Rockefeller, and had better arguments. It was not, he suggested, the purpose of a party which believed in free speech to look for formulas to repress opinion. He was right, even if he might not be so ready to protect Communists as Reactionaries. And Senator Dominick of Colorado made a bright speech employing an editorial from *The New York Times* of 1765 which rebuked Patrick Henry for extreme ideas. Delegates and gallery whooped it up. Next day Dominick confessed. He was only "spoofing." He had known: there was no *New York Times* in 1765. Nor was there any editorial. An old debater's trick. If there are no good facts, make them up. Be quick to write your own statistics. There was some umbilical tie between the Right Wing and the psychopathic liar.

More speakers came on. After four or five speakers for each side, a vote would come. Each time the amendment was voted down. Eight hundred and ninety-so-many to four hundred-and-a-few, went the votes. Hours went by, three hours of debate. After a while, the Moderates came collectively to seem like a club fighter in still another loser. A vacuum hung over empty cries for civil rights. One wondered why a Negro delegate loyal to the Party for thirty years had not been asked by the Moderates to make a speech where he could say: *You are sending me home to my people a mockery and a shame. My people have been saying for thirty years that the Republican Party has no love for the colored man, and I have argued back. Tonight you tell me I was wrong. You are denying me the meaning of my life.*

Such a speech (and there were Negro delegates to give it) might not have turned the vote, doubtless it would not have turned the vote, but it was the Moderates' sole chance for an explosion which could loose some petrified emotion, some magic. They did not take it. Probably they did not take it because they did not care that much if they lost. By now, it might be better to lose decisively than come nearer to winning and divide the party more. So they accepted their loser's share of the purse, which is that they could go back East and say: I campaigned at the convention for civil rights. Tomorrow was nominating day. The last chance in a hundred had been lost.

> *The Bleat, the Bark, Bellow & Roar—*
> *Are Waves that Beat on Heaven's Shore.*
> —WILLIAM BLAKE, *Auguries of Innocence*

Everett Dirksen gave the nominating speech for Goldwater, Dirksen from Illinois, the Silver Fox of the Senate, the Minority Leader, the man who had done the most, many would claim, to pass the Civil Rights Bill, for it was his coalition with Hubert Humphrey on cloture which had carried the day. "I guess Dirksen finally got religion," Humphrey said, and Dirksen, making his final speech for the bill, declared, "There is no force so powerful as an idea whose time has come." It was said that when Goldwater voted against the bill, Dirksen would not speak to him. Two weeks later, Dirksen agreed to nominate Goldwater. "He's got it won, that's all," Dirksen said of Goldwater, "this thing has gone too far."

This day, nominating day, any orator could have set fire to the Cow Palace. The gallery and Goldwater delegations were as tense and impatient as a platoon of Marines going down to Tijuana after three weeks in the field. But this day Dirksen had no silver voice. He made a speech which contained such nuggets as, "In an age of do-gooders, he was a good doer." Dirksen was an old organist who would play all the squeaks in all the stops, rustle over all the dead bones of all the dead mice in all the pipes. He naturally made a large point that Barry Goldwater was "the grandson of the peddler." This brought no pleasure to the crowd. Main Street was taking Wall Street; Newport Beach, California, would replace Newport; and General Goldwater, Air Force Reserve, possessed sufficient cachet to negotiate the move; but not the grandson of the peddler. Dirksen however went on and on, making a sound like the whir of the air conditioning in a two-mile tunnel.

When he was done, they blew Dirksen down, the high screams of New Year's Eve went off, a din of screamers, rattles, and toots, a clash of bands, a dazzle of posters in phosphorescent yellow and orange and gold, the mad prance of the state standards, wild triumphant pokes and jiggles, war spears, crusader's lances, an animal growl of joy, rebel cries, eyes burning, a mad nut in each square jaw, *Viva-Olé, Viva-Olé,* bugle blasts and rallying cries, the call of heralds, and a fall from the rafters of a long golden rain, pieces of gold foil one inch square, hundreds of thousands of such pieces in an endless gentle shimmer of descent. They had put a spot on the fall—it was as if sunlight had entered every drop of a fine sweet rain. I ran into Mike Wallace on the floor. "The guy who thought of this was a genius," said Mike. And the sounds of the band went up to meet the rain. There was an unmistakable air of beauty, as if a rainbow had come to a field of war, or Goths around a fire saw visions in a cave. The heart of the beast had loosed a primitive call. Civilization was worn thin in the center and to the Left the black man raised his primitive cry; now to the far Right were the maniacal blue eyes of the other primitive. The jungles and the forests were readying for war. For a moment, beauty was there—it is always there as tribes meet and clans gather for war. It was certain beyond certainty now that America was off on a ride which would end—was it God or the Devil knew where.

But the ride did not begin for another seven hours and seven nominations. Knowland seconded Goldwater's nomination; and Clare Boothe Luce, Charlie

Halleck, Senator Tower. Then Keating nominated Rockefeller, a twenty-two minute demonstration, decent in size but predictably hollow. More seconding speeches. Next came Scranton's turn. Dr. Milton Eisenhower, Ike's younger brother, did the nominating. It was good, it was clear, but there was not much excitement any more. One knew why the older Eisenhower had wanted the younger Eisenhower to be President. One also knew why he had not come very near—he gave a hint of Woodrow Wilson. Then the demonstration for Scranton. It was respectable, it let loose a half hour of music, it had fervor, the Scranton supporters died pure, an enjoyable demonstration. But the music was softer. Instead of *Viva-Olé* and the bugle blasts and rallying cries of the crusaders, one now heard "Boys and Girls Together," or "Hail, Hail, the Gang's All Here." And the Scranton posters did not have the deep yellow and deep orange of the phalanxes who had jammed the gorge for Goldwater; no, they bore blue and red letters on white, or even black on white, a gray photograph of Scranton on a white background with letters in black—the sign had been designed by Brooks Brothers, you may bet. Even some of the lapel buttons for Scranton revealed a camp of understatement, since they were five inches in diameter, yet Scranton's name was in letters one-eighth of an inch high. It made one think of *The New Yorker* and the blank ordered harmoniums of her aisles and text.

Now went the nominations hour after hour like the time between four in the morning and breakfast at a marathon dance. Here came the nominating speeches, and the pumped-up state demonstrations on the floor which spoke of plump elderly tourists doing the hula in Hawaii. Then would come a team of seconding speeches, the weepers and the wringers, the proud of nose and the knotty of nose, the kickers and the thumpers, the ministerial bores and the rabbinical drones, the self-satisfied, the glad-to-be-there, the self-anointed, the unctuous, the tooth suckers, the quaverers.

Fong was nominated, and Margaret Chase Smith, first woman ever to be nominated for President. Now she had a lock on the footnotes in the history books. Romney was nominated, and Judd, defeated Congressman Walter H. Judd of Minnesota, given a grand-old-man-of-the-party nominating speech. The band played "Glory, Glory, Hallelujah." Just after World War II, early in 1946, Judd had been one of the first to talk of war with Russia. Last came Lodge who scratched himself. The nominations were done. The balloting could begin. They cleared the floor of the Press.

We had been there off and on for seven hours, circling the delegations, talking where we could, a secondary sea of locusts. All through the seven hours of this afternoon and evening, there was the California delegation. They could not be ignored. They sat in the front rows off the center aisle just beneath the speaker on the podium. They wore yellow luminescent Goldwater shirts, the sort of sleeveless high-colored shirts which highway workers wear to be phosphorescent at night. On the floor there were a thousand sights and fifty conversations those seven hours, but there was nothing like the California delegation. In California Rockefeller had lost to Goldwater by less than three percent of the vote, and, losing, had lost all the delegates. California had eighty-six delegates—all eighty-six by the rules of the victory were for Goldwater. So there were eighty-six yellow shirts right down front. Winning California, the Right had also won the plums of the convention, the distribution of tickets in the gallery, central placement on the floor, the allegiance of the Cow Palace cops. They had won the right to have their eighty-six faces at the center of the convention.

Most of the California delegation looked like fat state troopers or prison guards or well-established ranchers. A few were thin and looked like Robert

Mitchum playing the mad reverend in *Night of the Hunter*. One or two were skinny as Okies, and looked like the kind of skinny wild-eyed gas-station attendant who works in a small town, and gets his picture in the paper because he has just committed murder with a jack handle. Yes, the skinny men in the California delegation leered out wildly. They looked like they were sitting on a body—the corpse of Jew Eastern Negritudes—and when the show was over, they were gonna eat it. That was it—half the faces in the California delegation looked like geeks. They had had it and now they were ready to put fire to the big tent.

There was one man who stood out as their leader—he had the face to be a leader of such men. Of course he looked not at all like a robber baron, the pride of Pinkerton, and a political boss all in one, no, nor was he in the least like an amalgam of Wallace Beery and fat Hermann Goering, no he was just Bill Knowland, ex-Senator William F. Knowland, Lord of the China Lobby, and honcho number one for Barry in Northern and Southern Cal.

So began the balloting. In twenty minutes there was another demonstration. The California standard, a white silk flag with a beast, some mongrel of bear and wild boar, danced in the air as if carried by a knight on a horse. The chairman for South Carolina intoned, "We are humbly grateful that we can do this for America. South Carolina casts sixteen votes for Senator Barry Goldwater." Barry was in. Four years of work was over. Final score: 883 for Goldwater. Scranton, 214, Rockefeller had 114, Romney 41. Smith received 27, Judd 22, Lodge 2, and Fong had 5.

When the voting was done, when the deliriums were down, an ooh of pleasure came up from the crowd, like the ooh for an acrobat. For Scranton accompanied by his wife was walking down the ramp to the podium, down the high ramp which led from the end-arena exits to the speaker's stand. It was a walk of a hundred feet or more, and Scranton came down this ramp with a slow measured deferential step, like a boy carrying a ceremonial bowl.

He made a clear speech in a young rather vibrant voice. He was doing the thing he was best at. He was making a gesture his elders would approve. He called on Republicans "not to desert our party but to strengthen it."

They cheered him modestly and many may have thought of his comments about Goldwater. On different days through June and July he had said: "dangerously impulsive," "spreading havoc across the national landscape," "a cruel misunderstanding of how the American economy works," "injurious to innumerable candidates," "chaos and uproar," "talking off the top of his head." "Hypocrisy . . ." says our friend Burke, "delights in the most sublime speculations; for never intending to go beyond speculation, it costs nothing to have it magnificent." "I ask . . ." Scranton said. He asked his delegates to make Goldwater's nomination unanimous.

Anywhere but in politics the speed with which the position had been shifted would be sign of a monumental instability. But politics was the place where finally nobody meant what they said—it was a world of nightmare; psychopaths roved. The profound and searing conflicts of politicians were like the quarrels between the girls in a brothel—they would tear each other's hair one night, do a trick together the next. They had no memory. They had no principles but for one—you do not quit the house. You may kill each other but you do not quit the house.

One could imagine the end of an imaginary nightmare: some time in the future, the Iron Ham (for such had become the fond nickname attached to President Barry Goldwater) would be told, thinking back on it all, that Billy-boy Scranton should be removed for some of the things he had said, and old Eisenhower, our General Emeritus, would find it in himself to say at a press conference on TV that while removal could not in itself be condoned, that is for high political figures, still it was bad, of course, policy, for people to have gotten away with insulting the President even if it was in the past and in the guise of free speech which as we all know can be abused. They would shave Scranton's head. Like a monk would he take the walk. And Old Ike would walk with him, and tell Willy S. a joke at the end, and have his picture taken shaking hands. Then, back to the White House for a two-shot drinking beer with Barry, the Iron Ham. After it was over, Barry would go back to the people who had put the ring in his nose.

> . . . *They should not think it amongst their rights to cut off the entail, or commit waste on the inheritance, by destroying at their pleasure the whole original fabric of their society; hazarding to leave to those who come after them a ruin instead of a habitation.*
> —Burke, *Reflections on the Revolution in France*

> *Goldwater: There have been several suggestions made. I don't think we would use any of them. But defoliation of the forests by low-yield atomic weapons could well be done. When you remove the foliage, you remove the cover.*

Driving away from the Cow Palace after the nomination, I could hear Goldwater on the car radio. He was celebrating. He was considerably more agreeable than Dick Nixon celebrating—no all-I-am-I-owe-to-my-mother-and-father-my-country-and-church; no, Goldwater was off instead on one of his mild rather tangy excursions, "I feel very humble," he said, and you could feel the itch in the long johns and the hair in the nose, a traveling salesman in an upper berth, belt of bourbon down the hatch—as Mrs. Goldwater entered the room, he cried out, "Hi, honey," and added just a touch mean and small-town, "You didn't cry very much tonight."

"No," said Mrs. Goldwater, "wait till tomorrow."

The questioning went back and forth. He was all voice and very little mind, you could tell he had once been so bright as to invent and market a novelty item called Antsy Pants, men's white shorts with red ants embroidered all over them. But he had a voice! It made up for the mind. Lyndon Johnson's hambone-grits-and-turnip-greens was going to play heavy to this; Goldwater on radio was sweet and manly, clean as Dad in the show of new shows, One Man's Dad. They asked him, *Senator, you said that you would not wage a personal campaign against the President.* Yes, said Goldwater. *Well, sir,* said the interviewer now, *today you called President Johnson the biggest faker in the U.S.* Butters of ecstasy in the interviewers mouth. *It's going to be a hard-hitting campaign, I assume then?* "Oh," said Goldwater, "I think you'll find some brick-bats flying around."

The dialogue went on: *Could you tick off just a few of the major issues you think will be in the campaign against the Democrats?* "I think," said Goldwater, "law and dis—the abuse of law and order in this country, the total disregard for it, the mounting crime rate is going to be another issue—at least I'm going to make it one, because I think the responsibility for this has to start someplace and it should start at the Federal level with the Federal courts enforcing the law.

"I noticed one tonight in the evening paper, for example—a young girl in New York who used a knife to attack a rapist is now getting the worst of the deal and the rapist is probably going to get the Congressional Medal of Honor and sent off scot-free," said Goldwater, neglecting to tell us that the girl had had her indictment dismissed, and the alleged rapist was already up on a charge of attempted rape. Goldwater now said in the sort of voice Daddy employs when he is ready to use the strap, "That kind of business has to stop in this country and, as the President, I'm going to do all I can to see that women can go out in the streets of this country without being scared stiff." Yes, he would. He was a Conservative and he was for States' Rights. It was just that he wasn't for *local* rights.

> *By this wise prejudice we are taught to look with horror on those children of their country, who are prompt rashly to hack that aged parent in pieces, and put him into the kettle of magicians, in hopes that by their poisonous weeds, and wild incantations, they may regenerate the paternal constitution, and renovate their father's life.*
> —BURKE, *Reflections on the Revolution in France*

Next day was the last day of the convention. Bill Miller was nominated for Vice-President. He was not a very handsome man nor did his manner seem particularly agreeable, but then the thought obtruded itself that the President of the United States was now in a more dramatic statistical relation to violent death than a matador. So a candidate would not necessarily look for too appealing a Vice-President—it might encourage notions of succession in the mind of an assassin. One would look instead for deterrents. William Miller was a deterrent.

III

A little later on the last day, Nixon made the speech of introduction for Goldwater. In the months ahead, when the bull in Barry swelled too wild and he gave promise of talking again of Negro assailants getting Medals of Honor, they would send in Nixon to calm him down. The Eastern Establishment, hydra head, was not dead after all; they still had Nixon. He was the steer to soothe the bull. Poor Barry. He had tried to lose Nixon in Cleveland, he had said, "He's sounding more like Harold Stassen every day." Nixon however was as easy to lose as a plain wife without prospects is easy to divorce.

"My good friend and great Republican, Dick Nixon . . ." was how Goldwater began his historic acceptance speech. It had come after a rich demonstration of happiness from the delegates. A boxcar of small balloons was opened in the rafters as Goldwater came down the ramp with his wife, his sons, his daughters. The balloons tumbled in thousands to the floor where (fifty balloons being put out each second by lighted cigarettes) a sound like machine-gun fire popped its way through the cheers. Fourth of July was here once more. He looked good, did Goldwater. Looking up at him from a position just beneath the speaker's stand, not twenty feet away, it was undeniable that Barry looked as handsome as a man who had just won the five-hundred-mile race in Indianapolis, had gone home to dress, and was now attending a party in his honor. He was even, protect the mark, elegant.

Then he began his speech. Today, the voice for large public gatherings had dignity. It was not a great voice, as Churchill's voice was great; there were no majesties nor storms of complexity, no war of style between manner and the obligation to say truth; but it was a balanced manly voice which would get votes. His speech was good in its beginning:

> *Now my fellow Americans, the tide has been running against freedom. Our people have followed false prophets. . . . We must, and we shall, set the tide running again in the cause of freedom. . . . Every breath and every heartbeat has but a single resolve, and that is freedom. . . . Tonight there is violence in our streets, corruption in our highest offices, aimlessness among our youth, anxiety among our elderly . . . despair among the many who look beyond material success toward the inner meaning of their lives.*

As the speech went on, the mind went out again on a calculation that this candidate could win. He was humbug—H. L. Hunt's idea of freedom would not be very close to the idea of freedom in the minds of the children who were for Barry, no, nor William Knowland's idea either, no, nor the Pinkertons, the hawkshaw *geist* of the F.B.I., nor the fourteenth and fifteenth floors. Goldwater was a demagogue—he permitted his supporters to sell a drink called Gold Water, twenty-five cents a can for orange concentrate and warm soda—let no one say it went down like piss—he was a demagogue. He was also sincere. That was the damnable difficulty. Half-Jew and blue-eyed—if you belonged in the breed, you knew it was manic-depressive for sure: a man who designed his own electronic flagpole to raise Old Glory at dawn, pull her down at dusk—he had an instinct for the heart of the disease— he knew how to bring balm to the mad, or at least to half the mad; Goldwater would have much to learn about Negroes. But one thing was certain: he could win. He would be breadwinner, husband and rogue to the underprivileged of the psyche, he would strike a spark in many dry souls for he offered release to frustrations deeper than politics. Therefore, he could beat Lyndon Johnson, he could beat him out of a variety of cause, out of natural flood or hurricane, in an epidemic of blacklash, or by an epidemic of guilt—how many union workers fed to the nose with exhortations that Johnson was good for take-home pay might rise and say to themselves, "I've been happy with less." Indeed I knew Goldwater could win because something in me leaped at the thought; a part of me, a devil, wished to take that choice. For if Goldwater were President, a new opposition would form, an underground—the time for secret armies might be near again. And when in sanity I thought, Lord, give us twenty more years of Lyndon Johnson, nausea rose in some cellar of the throat, my stomach was not strong enough to bear such security; and if true for me, true for others, true perhaps for half or more of a nation's vote. Yet what of totalitarianism? What of war? But what of war? And the answer came back that one might be better a little nearer to death than the soul dying each night in the plastic encirclements of the new architecture and the new city, yes better, if death had dimension and one could know the face of the enemy and leave a curse. What blessing to know the face of the enemy by the end of the second third of the twentieth century.

And what of the Negro if Goldwater won? What of all the small-town Southern sheriffs who wished to wipe their hands in the black man's hair? And a fury, a white fury, burst out of the mind and said, "No white sheriff is necessarily so very much worse than the worst Negro," no, the mad light of the black hoodlum might be getting equal geek to geek to the worst of the California delegation. Then came a memory of James Baldwin and Diana Sands on a show called *Night Line* where television viewers could make a telephone call to the guests. Baldwin had received a call from a liberal which went, "I'd like to help, and I'm asking you how." "Don't ask me, baby," said Baldwin, "ask yourself." "You don't understand," said the liberal, "I know something about these matters, but it's getting confusing for me. I'm asking you in all sincerity where you think my help could be best offered." "Well, baby," said Baldwin, "that's *your* problem." And Diana Sands, pinky extended in total delicate black-lady disgust, put the receiver back in the cradle. "You see," said Baldwin, talking to Les Crane, the master of ceremonies, "I remember what an old Negro woman told me once down South. She said, 'What the white man will someday learn is that there is no remission of sin.' That I never forgot," said Jimmy, "because you see it's perfectly possible the white will not be forgiven, not for a single cut or whipping or lynch mob or rape of a black woman," his voice now as soft and reminiscent of the wind as some African man of witchcraft. And I had to throttle an impulse to pick up the phone and call Baldwin, and say, "You get *this,* baby. There's a shit storm coming like nothing you ever knew. So ask yourself if what you desire is for the white to kill every black so that there be total remission of guilt in your black soul." And the mind went out still again.

The country was in disease, it was conceivably so ill that a butcher could operate with dirty hands and have magic sufficient to do less harm than the hospital with its wonder drugs and the new pestilence. (As the oil goes out, the earth turns cold, an arid used-up space, a ground for jumping off Texas to the used-up pits of the moon.) Still, you could not keep Americans from madness; our poetry was there, our symbolic logic: $AuH_2O + GOP + 64 = $ Victory! color of orange juice, Go, Go, Goldwater. Mrs. Goldwater's maiden name was Johnson, a portent of triumph to Barry? *Viva-Olé*. Eager to slay.

The country was in disease. It had been in disease for a long time. There was nothing in our growth which was organic. We had never solved our depression, we had merely gone to war, and going to war had never won it, not in our own minds, not as men, no, we had won it but as mothers, sources of supply; we did not know that we were equal to the Russians. We had won a war but we had not really won it, not in the secret of our sleep. So we had not really had a prosperity, we had had fever. *Viva-Olé*. We had grown rich because of one fact with two opposite interpretations: there had been a cold war. It was a cold war which had come because Communism was indeed a real threat to freedom, or it had come because capitalism would never survive without an economy geared to war; or was it both—who could know? who could really know? The center of our motive was the riddle wrapped in the enigma—was the country extraordinary or accursed? No, we had not even found our Communist threat. We had had a secret police organization and an invisible government large enough by now to occupy the moon, we had hunted Communists from the top of the Time-Life Building to the bottom of the Collier mine; we had not found that many, not that many, and had looked like Keystone cops. We had even had a Negro Revolution in which we did not believe. We had had it, yes we had had it, because (in the penury of our motive) we could not afford to lose votes in Africa and India, South America and Japan, Vietnam, the Philippines, name any impoverished place: we were running in a world election against the collective image of the Russ, and so we had to give the black man his civil rights or Africa was so much nearer to Marx. But there had not been much like love in the civil rights. Just Dirksen. So we were never too authentic. No.

We had had a hero. He was a young good-looking man with a beautiful wife, and he had won the biggest poker game we ever played, the only real one—we had lived for a week ready to die in a nuclear war. Whether we liked it or not. But he had won. It was our one true victory in all these years, our moment; so the young man began to inspire a subtle kind of love. His strength had proved stronger than we knew. Suddenly he was dead, and we were in grief. But then came a trial which was worse. For the assassin, or the man who had been arrested but was not the assassin—we would never know, not really—was killed before our sight. In the middle of the funeral came an explosion on the porch. Now, we were going mad. It took more to make a nation go mad than any separate man, but we had taken miles too much. Certainties had shattered. Now the voice of our national nerves (our arts, our events) was in a new state. Morality had wed itself to surrealism, there were cockroaches in all the purple transistors, we were distractable. We had an art of the absurd; we had moral surrealism. Our best art was *Dr. Strangelove* and *Naked Lunch, Catch-22; Candy* was our heroine; Jack Ruby our aging juvenile; Andy Warhol, Rembrandt; our national love was a corpse in Arlington; and heavyweight champion turned out to be Cassius Clay; New York was the World's Fair plus the Harlem bomb —it would take a genius to explain they were the same—and Jimmy Baldwin said, "That's *your* problem," on the Les Crane show at one A.M. Even the reverends were salty as the sea.

Yes, our country was fearful, half mad, inauthentic. It needed a purge. It had a liberal Establishment obeisant to committees, foundations, and science—the liberal did not understand that the center of science was as nihilistic as a psychopath's sense of God. We were a liberal Establishment, a prosperous land—we had a Roman consul among us—the much underrated and much disliked Lyndon Johnson was become a power in the land and doubtless a power upon the land; civilization had found its newest helmsman in the restraints, wisdom, and corruption of a major politician, of an organization boss to whom all Mafias, legit and illegit, all syndicates, unions, guilds, corporations and institutions, cadres of conspiracy and gents for health, Medicare, welfare, the preservation of antibiotics, and the proliferation of the Pentagon could bend their knee. The Establishment (the Democratic Establishment and the reeling columns of the Republican Establishment, falling back upon the center in the thundering confusion of Barry Goldwater's breakthrough) had a new leader, a mighty Caesar had arisen, Lyndon Johnson was his name, all hail, Caesar. Caesar gave promise to unify the land. But at what a cost. For if the ideology were liberal, the methodology was total—to this political church would come Adlai Stevenson and Frank Sinatra, the President of U.S. Steel and the President of the Steel Worker's Union, there would be photographs of Johnson forty feet high in Atlantic City—Big Bubber Lyndon—and parties in which minority groups in native costume would have their folk dance: could one see the ghost of Joe Stalin smiling on his pipe?

Yes, if we all worked to beat Barry, and got behind Lyndon and pushed, radicals and moderate Republicans, Negroes and Southern liberals, college professors and Cosa Nostra, café society and Beatniks-for-Johnson, were we all then going down a liberal superhighway into the deepest swamp of them all? For

Johnson was intelligent enough to run a total land, he had vast competence, no vision, and the heart to hold huge power, he had the vanity of a Renaissance prince or a modern dictator, whereas Barry might secretly be happier with his own show daily on radio. If Goldwater were elected, he could not control the country without moving to the center; moving to the center he would lose a part of the Right, satisfy no one, and be obliged to drift still further Left, or moving back to the Right would open schisms across the land which could not be closed. Goldwater elected, America would stand revealed, its latent treacheries would pop forth like boils; Johnson elected, the drift would go on, the San Francisco Hiltons would deploy among us. Under Goldwater, the odds were certainly greater that nuclear war would come, but under Johnson we could move from the threat of total war to war itself with nothing to prevent it; the anti-Goldwater forces which might keep the country too divided to go to war would now be contained within Johnson. Goldwater promised to lead the nation across the edge of a precipice, Johnson would walk us through the woods, perchance to quicksand itself. Goldwater would open us to the perils of our madness, Johnson would continue our trip into the plague. Goldwater could accelerate the Negro Revolution to violence and disaster—Johnson might yet be obliged to betray it from within. And what a job could be done! Who in such a pass should receive the blessing of a vote—the man who inspired the deepest fear, or the man who encouraged us to live in a lard of guilt cold as the most mediocre of our satisfied needs?

Still, the more Goldwater talked, the less impressive became his voice. When he went on too long, his voice grew barren. One could never vote for him, one could not vote for a man who made a career by crying Communist—that was too easy: half the pigs, bullies, and cowards of the twentieth century had made their fortune on that fear. I had a moment of rage at the swindle. I was tired of hearing about Barry Goldwater's high fine courage. Yesterday, on the floor, talking to a young delegate from Indiana, I had said, "Did it ever occur to you that Fidel Castro might have more courage than Barry Goldwater?"

"Yes, but Castro is a criminal mentality," said the boy.

I had cut off the argument. I was too close to losing my temper. Would the best of the young in every hick town, washed by the brainwater of the high school and the Legion, come to join this conservative crusade because Goldwater made an appeal to freedom, to courage, to change? What a swindle was in the making, what an extinction of the best in Conservative thought. They were so righteous, these Republicans. Goldwater might end with more warfare, security, and statism than any Democrat had ever dared; as a conservative, he would fail altogether (doubtless!) but certain he was to do one thing: he would march into Cuba. That was too much. One could live with a country which was mad, one could even come to love her (for there was agony beneath the madness), but you could not share your life with a nation which was powerful, a coward, and righteously pleased because a foe one-hundredth our size had been destroyed. So one got up to leave at this—we would certainly be strong enough to march into Cuba.

Then Goldwater uttered his most historic words: "Extremism in the defense of liberty is no vice. . . . Moderation in the pursuit of justice is no virtue," and I sat down and took out my notebook and wrote in his words, since I did not know how famous they would become. And thought: Dad, you're too much. You're really too much. You're too hip, baby. I have spent my life seeking to get four-letter words into U.S. magazines, and now you are ready to help me.

And as I left the arena, there was a fire engine and the cry-of a siren and the police with a gaunt grim look for the end of the week. There had been a fire burning, some small fire.

On the way out, outside the Cow Palace, a wet fog

was drifting, and out beyond the exits, demonstrators from CORE were making a march. They had been out there every day of the convention: Monday, Tuesday, Wednesday, and Thursday now, each day had demonstrated, carrying their placards, marching in a circle two abreast, singing "We Shall Overcome," shouting, "Goldwater Must Go," marching round and round like early Christians in the corrals waiting to be sent to the arena, while about them, five, six, ten deep, was a crowd of the Republican curious, some with troubled faces, some with faces troubled by no more than appetite, hounds staring at the meat, these white girls and Negro boys walking side by side, the girls pale, no lipstick, nunlike, disdainful, wearing denim shirts and dungarees; the Negroes tall and sometimes handsome, not without dignity, bearded almost all, the wild Negro girl in the center screaming savage taunts at the watching crowd, rude as Cassius Clay with a high-yaller mouth, and the crowd dreaming of an arena where lions could be set on these cohabiting blacks and whites, and the blacks and whites in the marching circle with their disdainful faces. Yes, kill us, says the expression on the face of the nunlike girl with no lipstick, you will kill us but you will never digest us: I despise you all. And some of the old WASPS are troubled in their Christian heart, for the girl is one of theirs, no fat plain Jewess with a poor nose is this one, she is part of the West, and so their sense of crisis opens and they know like me that America has come to a point from which she will never return. The wars are coming and the deep revolutions of the soul.

The Democratic Convention of 1964.

One extraordinary error in the last piece. It assumed Goldwater would do well. He proved too dogged, however, to be a demagogue, and his campaign was singu-

larly inept—the real possibility of what he had to offer America would not appear until Vietnam. In the meantime, one had been to the Democratic Convention. It took place in Atlantic City, which is perhaps the filthiest city in America, its window sills as greasy as its alleys, over a stretch of sultry days which spoke of future hurricane, and Hubert Humphrey was the symbol, appearing everywhere, smiling, smiling with the used-up, spirit-sucked face of an actor who has been smiling for twenty years.

The Mafia was there on the fringe, minor-league Mafia, with beehive head-dresses on the hustlers from Newark, and small-beer hoods, and the Democratic Establishment everywhere, blank, blank as the smile in a dull woman's eye. And Lyndon Johnson's two pictures flank and flank to the podium, two pictures going forty feet up. On the floor were factions. They had little to do with one another. They were too far apart in their beginnings, CIO and Southern manse, but they were gotten together for the convention, and between speeches there was as much enthusiasm on the floor of Convention Hall as can be found in a large railroad station on a summer afternoon.

My Hope for America: *A Review of a Book by Lyndon Johnson*

IN 20 years it may be taken for granted that 1964 was the year in which a major party nominated a major pretender to conservatism. It was a loss, and it was conceivably a horror, for 1964 was also a year in which a real conservative still had a great deal to say to the nation. He could have demonstrated with no vast difficulty that America was under the yoke of a monstrous building boom whose architecture gave promise of being the ugliest in the history of man, that our labor unions had watered the value of labor until physical work had become as parasitical as white-collar work, and that our medicine had been over-burdened beyond repair by a proliferation of wonder drugs whose side effects (with the notable exception of thalidomide) were still largely unknown—hence a delayed mass poisoning might yet be the fruit of this research. Our fruits, our vegetables, our cattle, had lost the opportunity to feed on native soil and organic food; the balance of nature, the fisheries, the economy of marine life, and the insect economies were being disrupted to the root by marinas and insecticides; our old neighborhoods and old homes were being—one could swear it—systematically demolished, and our educational system was glutted by a host of intellectual canapés: art appreciation, domestic economy, sexual efficiency, the modern novel, and so forth.

A real conservative could also have pointed out that the Civil Rights Act, no matter how imperfect and conceivably unconstitutional, was an act to be voted for, since finally there was a matter more important than the protection of property rights—it was spiritual rights: the Negro was entitled to his spiritual rights even if there were hard niggling costs to the rights of the Constitution. Finally, a great conservative could have noted that the health of Communism was its misery, that like all top-heavy structures its greatest danger was in its growth. Prosperity was Communism's poison, but attack from capitalism was its transfusion of blood. So the time was open for a great debate. Should we go back to isolationism? Did we not already possess enough nuclear Doomsdays to protect ourselves, was it not perhaps time to recognize that the industrialization of the backward nations was a thankless venture which wise men would avoid? Might it not be best to let the Communists have Asia and Africa after all? Would they not strangle on the meal? Yes, America was perhaps ready to listen to the sophistications of a conservative, if such a man was there to appear in 1964.

But what a conservative came down the pike! Marooned in a hopeless traffic with hate groups and bigots, Southern bullies and oil pirates, offering a program of sinister hints that a Federal police force would protect the young ladies of our land on their walk through our streets at night; reasoning with all the homely assurance of a filthy sock that he would protect the past by destroying the present (as in those remarks about scorching the foliage in Vietnam in order to keep the guerrillas from concealing themselves); wasting the substance of his campaign in pointless technical arguments with the Pentagon; and boring reconciliations and new feuds with the stricken Moderates of his party—the alleged conservative candidate was perhaps no more than a demagogue of the Right with a manly Christian air, a sweet voice, eyeglasses, and total innocence of a sense of contradiction, a spirit so naturally conservative that on the grounds of his home he raised the American flag with an electronic flagpole. Up at dawn, down at dusk, commanded the photoelectric cells in the mast. Well, one couldn't vote for such a man. He pressed the wrong buttons.

The mandate would go therefore to Lyndon Johnson. So most of America had seemed to decide by the eve of election. But it was nonetheless a vote heavy with gloom, and stricken with a sense of possible bad consequence, for there was much about Johnson which appealed not at all, and some of the evidence was intimate. He had written a book. That is intimate evidence. *My Hope for America*, he had called it. Now, of course, a book written by a high official must not be judged by average standards, or one would be forced to say, for example, that Jack Kennedy was not a very good writer and that Bobby Kennedy, at last reading, wrote a dead stick's prose—his style almost as bad as J. Edgar Hoover's. But even at its worst, the prose style of Jack Kennedy (and his ghost writers) is to the prose style of L.B.J. (and *his* ghost writers) as de Tocqueville is to Ayn Rand. It is even not impossible that *My Hope for America* is the worst book ever written by any political leader anywhere.

The private personality of L.B.J., as reported by the authority of the best gossip, is different from his public presence. He is, one is told, not too unlike Broderick Crawford in *All the King's Men,* roaring, smarting, bellowing, stabbing fingers on advisers' chests, hugging his daughters, enjoying his food, mean and unforgiving, vindictive, generous, ebullient, vain, suddenly depressed, then roguish, then overbearing, suddenly modest again only to bellow once more. It is somewhat like the description of an early Renaissance prince, and if one looks hard at the photograph of the President on the cover of *My Hope for America,* a leader of *condottieri* stands forth—hard, greedy, exceptionally intelligent eyes whose cynicism is spiked by a fierce pride, a big fleshy inquisitive (and acquisitive) nose, thin curved mouth (a boss mouth) and a slab of round hard jaw, deep dimple on the upper lip, deep dimple on the chin. It is not a bad face altogether, it is sufficiently worldly to inspire a kind of confidence that while no age of high ideals is close at hand, yet no martyrs are to be tortured, for there is small profit in that.

It is a face and a concealed personality which could even, considering the Republican alternative, inspire a touch of happiness, if it were not for the public image—that boundless sea of overweening piety which collects here in this slim volume, this cove of Presidential prose whose waters are so brackish that a spoonful is enough to sicken the mind for hours. *My Hope for America* is an abominable, damnable book, and what makes it doubly awful is that nearly all of its ideas are blessed. It is in fact difficult to disagree with almost any one of them.

Who can argue on the side of poverty, or against justice, or against the idea of a Great Society? Let Barry Goldwater argue, not I. No, the ideals in this book are double-barreled, double-ringed, a double end of the cornucopia. More for the poor, more for the rich; more for peace, more for war; dedicatedly opposed to Communism, cautiously conciliatory; out to raise the income of poor nations, out to squash the economy of Cuba; all out for the Negro, all violence to be checked in city streets; all for the Democratic party, all for a party which includes Democrats *and* Republicans. There is even, and it is the achievement of this book, a curious sense of happiness running through its paragraphs. It it that happiness which is found at the end of the vision. It is as if the dreams of Rousseau and Condorcet and Bakunin and Herzen and Marx and Lenin and Trotsky and John Dewey and the Webbs and Keynes and Roosevelt, Dreiser, and Darrow—name any of a hundred, any of that long stream of political engineers who dreamed of changing a material world by material means to make all men free and equal—had come down at the end to Little Ol' Lyndon, and hot damn, he had said, discovering Progressive religion in 1964, that's the ticket, that's the liver-eating ticket! And he was off to bring it off. And happy as a clam. That's the happiness which comes off this book. It is like a dream of heaven in a terminal ward.

For beneath this odd disembodied happiness is a prose more sinister than the most pious of Lyndon Johnson's misrepresentations of his own personality; it is a prose which stirs half-heard cries of the death by suffocation of Western Civilization, it is a prose almost so bad and so deadening as the Georgian catechisms Josef Stalin used to hammer out: "Why is the Communist Party the party of the Soviet people? The Communist Party is the party of the Soviet people because . . ." It was enough at the time, reading Stalin, to keep from becoming a Communist. Now, reading Lyndon!—the horror is that one must still vote for him. But what a book is *My Hope for America*.

Examine it: 127 pages, a little more than 200 words to a page, most of the pages half pages or blank pages so that in bulk there are 17,000 words collected in 13 short chapters; they have titles like this—"President of All the People," "A President's Faith and Vision," "Building the Atlantic Partnership, "This Developing World," "Creative Federalism." Each page of each chapter is divided into paragraphs. Page 8 has 12 paragraphs; the average page has four or five with a generous space between each paragraph. This is not because the remarks have the resonant echo of Pascal's *Pensées,* rather—one idea does not lead to another. So the space must be there. It is useful for burying whichever infinitesimal part of the brain died in the gas of the preceding phrase.

Yet every altruistic idea and every well-tuned moderation which Lyndon Johnson's political experience has put together over the years is somehow worked into the organum of his credo. It is impossible to disagree with a single of its humanistic desires ("We know that we can learn from the culture, the arts, and the traditions of other countries"); it is equally impossible to feel the least pleasure at the thought these goods may yet come to be—just so bad and disheartening is the style of this book:

> *Reality rarely matches dream. But only dreams give nobility to purpose. This is the star I hope to follow—which I know most of you have seen, and which I first glimpsed many years ago in the Texas night.*

> *When the helpless call for help—the hearing must hear, the seeing must see, and the able must act.*

> *It is an America where every man has an equal chance for the well-being that is essential to the enjoyment of the freedom that we brag about.*

> *The Gulf of Tonkin may be distant Asian waters, but none can be detached about what happened there.*

High-school students will be writing essays on these paragraphs. One's stomach turns over. It is certain that if Barry Goldwater had written the same book, everyone would be agreed his style was a menace. Still, what is quoted up to here is still English, English more or less. It is in the depth of the real prose articulated by Johnson and his corps of ghost writers that the heart of the darkness resides. For Johnson is not a writer and has no wish to be. He is a communications engineer. He uses words in interlocking aggregates which fence in thoughts like cattle. At bottom, the style consists of nothing but connectives and aggregate words—that is, political phrases five words long which are one aggregate word and so should be hyphenated. Example:

> *And it is one-of-the-great-tasks-of-Presidential-leadership to make our people aware that they share-a-fundamental-unity-of-interest-and-purpose-and-belief.*

The essence of totalitarian prose is that it does not define, it does not deliver. It oppresses. It obstructs from above. It is profoundly contemptuous of the minds who will receive the message. So it does its best to dull this consciousness with sentences which are nothing but bricked-in power structures. Or alternately a totalitarian prose slobbers upon an audience a sentimentality so debauched that admiration for shamelessness is inspired. But then, sentimentality is the emotional promiscuity of those who have no sentiment:

> *When I was a child, one of my first memories was hearing the powder go off on an anvil on Armistice Day. I remember the terror that flowed from the Lusitania. I remember seeing boys come marching home, and the welcome we gave them at our little schoolhouse. When Pearl Harbor was attacked . . .*

There is one expanding horror in American life. It is that our long odyssey toward liberty, democracy and freedom-for-all may be achieved in such a way that utopia remains forever closed, and we live in freedom and hell, debased of style, not individual from one another, void of courage, our fear rationalized away. We will all have enough money and we will all have a vote. The money will buy appliances made of plastic, and the money will buy books just as bad as *My Hope for America* or *The Conscience of a Conservative.*

The dream of democracy—that the average man possesses riches within himself worthy of a lord—will evolve into some anomalous electronic shape of human, half genius, half lout, and the liberation of existence will not take place. Only the buildings will continue to be built—bigger housing for all, slum clearance, urban renewal, Edward Durrell Stone, until we will look as if indeed we lost a war, as if we had been bombed to the ground, and built ourselves up again just so quickly and cheaply as the barracks could be slapped together.

"In the next forty years," writes Johnson, "we must rebuild the entire urban United States." But who will do it? Whose vision will prevail? Which head of horror may condemn generations not yet born to look at faceless buildings and roofless roofs, the totalitarianism stealing in from without, from the formless forms and imprisoned air of a new society which had lost the clue a democracy could become equable only if it became great, that finally the world would continue to exist only by an act of courage and a search for style. Democracy flowers with style; without it, there is a rot of wet weeds. Which is why we love the memory so of F.D.R. and J.F.K. For they offered high style to the poor. And that is worth more than a housing project. That is the war against poverty.

Still Lyndon Johnson must be given a vote. Because *My Hope for America* contains one good sentence, one more than Barry Goldwater could claim. This sentence reads: ". . . the wall between rich and poor is a wall of glass through which all can see." It inspires a corollary which is almost as good—the space between hypocrisy and honest manner may not forever insulate the powerful from the poor.

The Argument of an Elector

THE NEXT TWO PIECES are written by an occasional voter. If he stood in line on Election Day for Henry Wallace in 1948, and John F. Kennedy in 1960, he did not vote at all in the years between. The act of giving assent to people whose politics were essentially similar seemed to him part of a tremendous swindle.

Perhaps it was. One reason the plague may have set its roots so deep was that all extremes in American politics decamped or absconded after the Second World War. The liberal Left fell into the Center with a whimper, the Right discovered itself to be respectable so long as it left anti-Semitism and/or rabid Jim Crow to its own fringe and contented itself with hunting Communists in exchange for accepting the foreign policy of the Center. In truth, there seemed little to vote about between 1948 and 1960. Adlai Stevenson may have been somewhat more agreeable than Dwight D. Eisenhower, but in those days I had a formula— it is still, I think, accurate—that the Republicans plotted war, but the Democrats were the only ones who could go to war; if it was the Democrats who looked generally to make peace, it was, in fact, the Republicans who were able to arrange the peace. The cause was not mysterious. The Republicans put forth war policies for their millions of patriots which only the Democrats could carry out, since only the Democrats could bring the liberals and the labor unions along. On the other hand, one had to be Republican to make peace without being seriously accused of Communist sympathy. Thus, Truman undertook the Korean War, and Eisenhower ended it.

The other part of the formula read: do not, however, vote for a man or a party who is uncongenial, even if an objective superiority is obvious—as, for example, the Republicans' superior ability to make peace. There was obviously an ambiguity present in the hard Marxist front of one's ideas, some notion that the personality of the candidate was not separate from the history he would make. That *soft* idea arrived at its climax with Kennedy. For it was obvious something odd had occurred in American politics: for once, the image and the politics diverged critically. Jack Kennedy was a moderate liberal in program but a romantic figure in image—so all variety of ferment grew out of his image. Jack Kennedy may not have been as skillful a politician as Lyndon Johnson, but he had one hundred times as much effect on the styles and modes of American life, on the desires of Americans, on what they finally demanded from life; so Jack Kennedy had a revolutionary effect on American life. A new political principle was at loose—where a difference in issues was not simple to measure, then the candidate whose personality was least predictable and platitudinous, or ideally most brilliant, complex and intriguing, was the man who was going to bring the most political good to the voting populace, because he was going to enrich the emotional complexity of their lives. It was a way of saying that in a time of no real political differences, a real contrast of personality was going to make a political difference.

That this new principle is still but one principle among others may be demonstrated by the next two pieces. The first, about the senatorial campaign between Bobby Kennedy and Kenneth Keating, is a pure application of the principle; but the second, about the New York Mayoralty campaign, engages the idea in more complex fashion. John Lindsay was running against Abe Beame—it was obviously going to be more interesting to live with Lindsay every day than Beame—about equal to the difference between Kennedy and Johnson. But William F. Buckley was also in the race, and it is possible no one in political life had a personality so glittering as Buckley's. If he had been elected, New York would have had a robber bridegroom for mayor.

But there was no question of voting for him, not even temptation. For his local politics were absurd—he was not serious about the city, or at least there was no suggestion for a moment that he understood New York* or cared to—he was more eager to go to war with China. So politics came before image. And that left one with the job of writing about John Lindsay, a difficult matter for it is hard to convince New Yorkers to vote for a man you admire—it is necessary to get into the bedrock of the admiration, and this, here, in this case, meant that you had to write about New York and what it might be like to campaign for six months in its junkyards and canyons.

A Vote for Bobby K.

WHEN THERE first began to be talk, back last winter, of Bobby Kennedy going in against Kenneth Keating, I had the reaction of a prize-fight manager who has seen better days: Put down no bets, they're a couple of bums. Keating never did a thing to me. He had a face like the plastic dough children play with. Smells like a bottle of moistened saccharine, sticks to the fingers, fails to hold its shape. I disliked the rhetoric with which he strutted into discussions of Cuba; the righteousness was enough to make you throw up. For righteous politicians, like bullies, have their greatest test of character when they've got you on the

*Having since read Buckley's book, *The Unmaking of a Mayor*, I am forced to admit Buckley understood more than a little about New York.

ground—can they keep from kicking you in the ear? At his best, Keating seemed a passable if unctuous assistant to a hard worker like Javits—at his worst he was errand boy for Rockefeller plus every special interest there to be discovered. So Keating lit the kind of fire in my political heart which a turkey gobbler would light on the table if you developed the suspicion he was still alive. If one had to vote for Keating, there was no vote. The choice was left with Bobby. Bobby!—whom everybody I know called Raul Castro. Bobby!—the Irish equivalent of Roy Cohn on the good old McCarthy team; Bobby!—with the face of a Widmark gunsel, that prep-school arrogance which makes good manual laborers think of smashing a fist through a wall; Bobby! who wrote books called *The Enemy Within*, about Come-You-Nism and crooked unions, Bobby who wrote in a style so bad that (to repeat from something just written) he had a dead stick's prose; Bobby, who had always had it break the right way for him; Bobby, who played the game down the center, so had no sense at all of how it felt to be outside, try to get in. Who could vote for Bobby?

But we've had a couple of months of the campaign, and a liberal hogshead of much ado about almost no difference. Since each of the candidates was considerably farther to the right even a few years ago, their protestations of liberalism now, about which Hentoff, I. F. Stone, and Arthur Schlesinger have given us copious documentation back and forth, are not finally convincing, or even important to the vote. If Keating and Kennedy were both cons up before a parole board and were debating who had prayed his way back closer to Jesus, and each was buttressed in his arguments by impossible-to-follow allegations, and by disputes over microscopic facts delivered by lawyers altogether skillful at working the grit from a detail, one would have a natural suspicion that when a con claims he is close to Jesus it is to get parole—which con is actually the closest would have little to do with allegations, facts, or details. Or, in this case, issues. It would take a constitutional lawyer to decide on the issues whether Keating or Kennedy is now more liberal. When it comes to being more liberal in this hour, in this election, you could not get a short curled hair between them. They're so liberal you don't have to vote, not for liberalism—you got a liberal either way. Of course, if the country turns right, you got a conservative either way. Have you? Well, you know you have with Ken Keating. He doesn't have a face like plastic dough for nothing. But we are with Bobby. Here the difference begins to appear. I don't know. I wouldn't pretend to say Bobby Kennedy is not capable of marching at the front of a Right Wing movement. But the Right is not likely to suffer from a lack of leaders. Goldwater may be no more than the cork out of the bottle. The appeal of the Right, since it is emotional, will attract demagogues. I think Bobby Kennedy may be the only liberal about, early or late, who could be a popular general in a defense against the future powers of the Right Wing. For there's no one else around. The Democratic Party is bankrupt, bankrupt of charisma; the Right Wing has just begun. Anyone who was at the Democratic Convention in Atlantic City must confess—if they can afford to—that the mood was equal to a yellow jaundice ward on the banks of a swamp.

By this logic, it comes to this: we are in the absence of real and immediate political issues. So we must vote for one candidate because he is a neutron, or must vote for the other because he is an active principle who will grow and change and become—odds are —a powerful leader of the Left or the Right. Posed that way, I take the second alternative. I vote for the active principle. To vote for a man who is neuter is to vote for the plague. I would rather vote for a man on the assumption he is a hero and have him turn into a monster than vote for a man who can never be a hero. For follow it through: a hero, even a failed-hero, or a hero-as-monster, is more likely to create other heroes, by his example or by opposition to him, than a man who gains power and has never been anything at all. A forceful political structure with a great number of particular heroes is a way to describe the Renaissance; a powerful political structure governed by faceless men is a way to describe the Mafia. The vote goes then to Bobby Kennedy. He has finally a face.

Say one thing more. Few vote by logic alone. Sentiment enters. I have affection for Bobby Kennedy. I think something came into him with the death of his brother. I think Bobby Kennedy has come a pilgrim's distance from that punk who used to play Junior D. A. for Joe McCarthy and grabbed headlines by riding Jimmy Hoffa's back. Something compassionate, something witty, has come into the face. Something of sinew. So I think. I could be wrong, but I'd rather go this way and be wrong, than vote the other way trying to stop a possibility with a nonentity. When the issues at stake are small, it is natural to vote for the man who has the more arresting personality, as once before, when issues were small, America elected Jack Kennedy. Of course, if you remember, Jack Kennedy was not then enormously popular in New York. He had a dubious liberal record and seemed unpredictable. New York voted for him but did not like him. In New York we prefer to vote to stop things. So New Yorkers know nonentity. They know durance sufficiently vile to have endured for twelve years a nonentity for Mayor and a nonentity, these last six years, for Senator. My vote goes therefore to establishing a new face in the Senate. Is that not half the welfare of a liberal society—to have something new to discuss at the dinner table? Consider: six more years of Ken Keating with Brussels sprouts or six with Bobby K. and some red snapper.

Lindsay and the City

I WAS TALKING to a woman at a party the other night, and she said Abe Beame was an old machine politican and so she was going to vote for him because he would know how to run the machine. And I said New York is not a machine but a malignancy.

Well, I repeat the story not only to take a bow for having the last word with a lady, but because I've brooded on the remark and think it has something to do with why John Lindsay may not be our next Mayor. He has been running day in, day out, about as hard as a man can run these last six months and yet there seems a quicksand beneath the effort—as votes are won, others slip away—I know whenever I say I am going to vote for him, I hear the same bad news: he has been a disappointment, say some, his personality has failed to come alive, so has his campaign. The campaign and the man are long and dull, I am told, and ill-tempered; there have been no real issues, or at least no ability to find and dramatize the real issues, Lindsay has somehow allowed a fine beginning to dissipate itself. And I think then of that campaign he has run and the extraordinary difficulty of it, for Lindsay has been running against the malignancy and how do you dramatize that? You cannot dramatize a condition which is concealed by the organism itself because it is too terrifying to contemplate: the separate organs accommodate one another no longer but must grow each of them at their own best speed. Cooperation impossible, only separate growth remains. That is malignancy.

New York is ill beyond belief. There are forces in the city, Left, Right and Center, which are out of control. They cannot collaborate with other forces, they cannot, in fact, *exist* with other forces—their only logic is to grow by themselves. There is a Right

Wing in New York whose only ultimate satisfaction will come from deporting every Negro to Jersey unless he has been taught to say Yessir all over again; there is a militant black Left who swear Whitey must eat the turd before peace is here, and there is the Mob and the machine in the center, all the highways and housing projects gutting the city of its last purchase on beauty in order to manufacture new money for themselves. The action in the center is the worst of all for it is mined into the vaults of all the banks in town and all the concrete blocks and the cement mixers, into the cops (Bill Buckley's noble hard-working much-abused cops) and it is the secret sweat in the pores of every bureaucrat in this thicket-ridden legal-istically-swindled city, this jungle of ordinances and metastatic deals which has polluted the air, leaked away the water, defaced the architecture, and made our subways as famous in Asia as the Georgia chain gangs.

There is something else to make it worse. For each malignancy begins with an intolerable and just need which cannot be satisfied and cannot be forgotten. The paranoia of the Right develops because they want—or believe they want—quiet houses on quiet streets, and healthy food, and decent air, and a life lived by principle; since everything in the scheme of things works to deny them, so everything in the scheme of things seems to point to a conspiracy which springs violence loose at randon, and puts poisons in food, and looks to rebuild and so destroy old neigh-borhoods, and shatters every principle into chaos and active contradiction. Whereas the need of the Center is for power, but its power came originally out of loyalties. Every mob guy and machine politician was gutting the city with one hand and feeding a lot of particular families with the other. So there are still memories of favors and good nights of drinking in bars and the old days in the old neighborhood and legends of men who were real men. The machine is a method which used to be able to work, for it was the closest thing to a culture for the poor, and the poor still need it, they need a personal touch in the big anonymous void of the city, a sense of myth and connection, a league of the hot guys and the hard guys, a hope to satisfy some greed. Many of the poor need the machine with a passion, for if they lose it, they are lost in the city, they are adrift in the void; so they have to keep coming out for the machine. But the machine can't take care of them properly any more, for the machine knows it has nothing to offer to the Left and to the Right but placation, and that is equal to just letting the malignancies grow—so the machine sees that the city is not going to go on for-ever. It starts to grow too, it accelerates the rate at which it devours, it starts to bulldoze wholesale and to squeeze money from the juice of concrete, and from union jurisdictions and courts and clubs and covenants and realtors on the fix until the entire city gives promise it soon will look like a convention of prisons.

And on the Left, in that Harlem where the blood of eight generations has come to a boil, there are men who live their life for a cause—they are trying to save their people from going mad, and they have a sense at times that the pursuit of their life is in itself mad, for eight generations boil in the blood, and the blood goes over, it is kept on the boil by events which take place eight hundred miles and a thousand south of here, and so more and more of the kids in Harlem want not justice but revenge and threaten to become implacable and grow not on liberty but power and so must demand more and more and more before they have yet anything at all.

That is another aspect of the horror—violence, sick-ness, greed and rage, Right, Center and Left, and all of it with origins in passion and loyalty, in idealism, principle, all the ingredients for building the new world and the great city.

But of course there is no great city. Just the ma-lignancy and Lindsay in a situation where he must get his money from the Republican machine and his votes from the Right and the Left. On the Right is Bill Buckley, all bless, and on the Left is Adam Clayton Powell, an undisputed genius. Any man who can still run Harlem in any way at all is an undisputed genius, but it is part of Powell's peculiarly private luck to tie himself up always with the worst candidate in town, now known lately as Honest Abe D. (D. for Dog—I'm no Dog) Beame.

That's a pretty combination for any candidate. And Buckley accuses Lindsay of being in league with Adam Clayton Powell, in a debate, nowhere else, and Lindsay answers, Why, no, Mr. Powell has given his support to Mr. Beame, and Buckley is silent on that. Bill is not one of the major debaters in America for nothing—a week later he is making the same accusation and they are cheering his words in Queens. Debating, you see, is a highly difficult but very low art since it depends upon being scrupulously dishonest. You fix facts with fancy and throw the suspicion of fancy on the other man's facts. Nobody in America is better at this than William B., just as no one I suspect is more majestically unsuited for here becoming Mayor since it is possible Old Bill has never been in a subway in his life. To be fair it must also be said that no one could have been more majestically suited for spoiling Lindsay's campaign. Buckley's personality is the highest Camp we are ever going to find in a Mayoralty. No other actor on earth can project simultaneous hints that he is in the act of playing Commodore of the Yacht Club, Joseph Goebbels, Robert Mitchum, Maverick, Savonarola, the nice prep-school kid next door, and the snows of yesteryear. If he didn't talk about politics—if he was just the most Camp gun ever to walk into *Gunsmoke* I'd give up Saturday nights to watch him. But he does talk about politics time to time, and his program for New York is to drop an atom bomb posthaste on the atom bomb of the Chinese.

A man like that cannot be kept from getting an enormous minority vote. The aged put rouge on their cheeks, and in a dying city, theatre is life, Camp is all. Camp is going to defeat John Lindsay, for Camp is the iridescence of the malignant and cancer cells are bizarre but beautiful under a microscope—they look like a shopping center in the night. Of course Buckley's votes will not come from people who even know the word "Camp," no, his sort of votes come from the kind of girls who want to work at Bell Telephone; but if Lindsay loses, Camp will still have defeated him—a secret admiration for Buckley's high Camp has been cutting into the righteous wrath of all us Wagner-aged citizens—we are finally apathetic about the great dump in which we live, we laugh at Buckley, we laugh with him, we say let the city burn, let it burn, and Lindsay goes wrong, a little solemn, a little empty, too earnest much.

Well, fellow voters, call on the Lord, Jack Kennedy was that way in '60, swear it. Tall, slightly blank, slightly dull as a speaker, full of facts, no fire, and a bemused slightly out-of-it look. Which comes I think from the schizophrenic recognition that one is a man trying to contend with the relations between miracles (for how else can politics appear at the top?) and that the means of acquiring the power to go out and save the world (for that is the secret glory and ambition of a major politician) can be obtained only by talking about all the things which have nothing to do with miracles, or society, or even with people, but are instead statistics and programs and situation papers and debater's tricks and well-timed name-calling and allegations and shaking hands so slimy a clam would throw up, and worst of all saying the same thing day in, day out, week after week, month after month until your soul begins to die, because repetition, kids, kills the soul, and even as it is dying and the manner gets empty and the rhetoric more flat, one is grappling out there in those great celestial regions at the empty back of the brain, wrestling with the wonder of how do you create a miracle, how do you give Harlem what it begins to need, and keep your own Republicans from going mad, and get the money to do it, and clean the slime and the concrete, and get the water back and get the fire out of the air and the fumes and clear out the sense of the city dying in its own corruption like a monster eating himself to death in a dungeon, and with it all, being out every day, out to capture the same votes and having to make the same speeches.

The last time I saw Lindsay was in June. He was in great form, his color was great, vitality came off him— huge enthusiasm. He looked like a man of twenty-eight. He won every vote in the house. That was in June. Now he's empty, people say. He looks much older in photographs. I do not wonder. The wonder is that he is not half dead.

But just as he was leaving that afternoon in June, he said with a big grin like a sailor in a boxing ring, "Mailer, you know you have to be a little insane to run for Mayor of this town." Yes, you do, I think, and yes John Lindsay may be a little insane to have tried, but by God I write this to say I hope he wins, John Lindsay, because I think he's okay, in fact I think he's a great guy, and it would be a miracle if this town had a man for mayor who was okay. Ill-tempered the campaign may have been, empty and dull to some, and with no real issue but malignancy, but cheers to you, John Lindsay, and honors to your run.

On to Vietnam

LYNDON JOHNSON is a triumph of spirit, wholly scientific. He carries polls on his hip, takes a look at society with the worries of a big-time contractor, constructs jobs, and with his pal McNamara is off to war as a statistician. He can tell you that yesterday we knocked off 94 gooks. Science is, of course, the only true religion Americans still have left: like all religions it is worshiped abjectly by those who know it least.

Beautiful women, literary people, social planners, editorial writers, presidents, politicians, and a sprinkling of illiterates do not know that science is most exact in those regions where it has progressed into the secrets of the universe about as far as the precision and exactitude of English spelling have advanced us into the secret lore of meaning. Which is to say: a distance. But not a great distance. Where science is exact, it is vastly insignificant: where it is significant, it is open-ended, not certain, prey to reasoning by analogy, torn by debate, sustained by darkest mystery, and when all is said, about as scientific as literary criticism. Be it understood between us that science possesses no secure idea of what are electricity, time, space, and the structure of the atom. Yet science has come together with love-of-America to form the latest amalgam in the guaranteed most awful religion of them all: love-of-America plugged in to some intellectual supermachine.

For one hundred years, love-of-America (as a secret primitive religion—a shy girl whose still waters run damnably Fatherland deep) has been running around with one stout dull thunder or another. The beaux have names like capitalism, conformity, medicine, corporate spirit, mass communication, Red-hunting or science. Science is the latest and comes in as the word made flesh, as the Sacred Name which punishes and preserves all us people, the brave lad who lifts rockets off their base, and even tomorrow will take out your old used liver and replace it with a new eight-year-old's liver. The new liver is available because the boy died of some mysterious new disease they can name but cannot cure. However, the research assistants who researched this operation have declared authoritatively that this specific mysterious disease does not affect the liver. Of course these are the research assistants who did the work on possible side effects of thalidomide before there were side effects and declared the drug harmless. Of course research assistants are like Hollywood producers. The more failures, the more jobs.

Two pieces follow about this most scientific war. The first was a speech written for Vietnam Day, May 25, 1965, in Berkeley, California, and printed later in *The Realist* (with a prefatory note to explain that four or five paragraphs in the speech had been taken, in slightly altered form, from the book review of *My Hope for America,* and from the piece on the Republican Convention of 1964). The second article on Vietnam is a reply to a Symposium in *Partisan Review* and is furnished with the editor's statement from which it departed.

Both pieces say the same thing, yet emphases are different, tone is very different, and the second goes further than the first.

A Speech at Berkeley on Vietnam Day

YEARS AGO in Austin, Texas, not far from the L.B.J. Ranch, even less far from the radio station owned by Lady Bird Johnson, at a time when our President was still Vice-President, I read a few lines I had written about Lyndon Johnson to an audience at the University of Texas:

> *Johnson had compromised too many contradictions, and now the contradictions were in his face: when he smiled, the corners of his mouth squeezed gloom; when he was pious, his eyes twinkled irony; when he spoke in a righteous tone, he looked corrupt; when he jested, the ham in his jowls looked to quiver. He was not convincing.*

That Texas audience laughed as if I were William Faulkner talking about the Snopes family.

Years later, getting ready to write about Johnson again, I endeavored to come closer:

The private personality of L.B.J., as reported by the authority of best gossip, is different from his public presence. In private, one is told, he is not too unlike Broderick Crawford in All the King's Men, *roaring, smarting, bellowing, stabbing fingers on advisers' chests, hugging his daughters, enjoying his food, belching, burping, mean and unforgiving, vindictive, generous, ebullient, vain, suddenly depressed, then roguish, then overbearing, suddenly modest again only to bellow and fart once more.*

I was trying to convince myself to vote for him. I had already decided Goldwater had all the homely assurance of a filthy sock. My vote nonetheless was heavy with gloom, stricken with a sense of bad consequence. There was much about Johnson which appealed not at all, and some of the evidence was intimate.

He had written a book. *My Hope for America,* he called it. Now, a book written by a high official must not be judged by average standards or one would be forced to say, for example, that Jack Kennedy was not a very good writer and Bobby Kennedy, at last reading, wrote a dead stick's prose. But even at its worst, the prose style of Jack Kennedy (and his ghost writers) is to the prose style of L.B.J. (and *his* ghost writers) as de Tocqueville is to Ayn Rand. Reviewing Johnson's book for the *Herald Tribune,* I said:

> *It is even not impossible that* My Hope for America *is the worst book ever written by any political leader anywhere . . . a boundless sea of overweening piety . . . an abominable damnable book . . . a prose which stirs half-heard cries of death by suffocation.*

I went on to say that Johnson was not a writer but a communications engineer.

The essence of totalitarian prose is that it does not define, it does not deliver. It oppresses. It obstructs from above. It is profoundly contemptuous of the minds who will receive the message. So it does its best to dull this consciousness with sentences which are nothing but bricked-in power structures.

It was obvious *My Hope for America* was part of the expanding horror of American life. It would be used to brainwash high-school kids. Like all horror, it stayed in the memory. For it offered a surrealistic clue to Lyndon Johnson's real secret vision of a Great Society: jobs for all, everybody with an interesting job, the farmers taken care of—their subsidy checks written by computers—every industrial worker with his own psychoanalyst, every student who was able to pass the aptitude tests able to stay in school forever, Medicare, antibiotics in every glass of drinking water, tranquilizers added to the television dinners, birth-control pills in the booze.

The President was willing to go even further. One could conceive of him making a speech: "Let us reason together. Freedom is indivisible. Marijuana might be just such a freedom. But there are those who argue with justice that marijuana is passed from mouth to mouth. That is, by common consent, unsanitary. Therefore I propose Congress draw up a law requiring marijuana to be marketed solely in suppositories."

There would be a recreation program for all American children—mass calisthenics in air-conditioned stadiums with a glassed-over dome. The majors would have eighty-two baseball teams in each league and the additional teams would take their names from the new housing complexes built around shopping centers —the teams would be called Bypass 60, Ramp 6, Belt 1, Lower Alternate Freeway 4, the Coral Gate Arms.

The colleges would look like factories, the housing projects would keep looking like prisons, the corporation office buildings would be indistinguishable from the colleges, and not even an airline hostess would know where the airport ended and the motel bedroom began.

The sexual revolution would push on. Ladies' magazines would wonder whether the orgy had become a vital solution to suburban life. If there would be statisticians to point out that the modern orgy grouping showed an average of eight people and one erection, still State Department intellectuals could point out on their orientation tours through the universities of America that the Sexual Revolution was just begun, and ways would be found to increase vitality.

Camp would have moved on to the Happy Hunting Ground of old art movement. A new art movement would be in. It would be called Shit. Its test would be: is this object, happening, work, event or production more resonant than it was yesterday? Movies about the Strategic Air Command with Jimmy Stewart, Hubert Humphrey speeches, old Lawrence Welk records, news photographs of Mayor Wagner, Senate testimony by Robert McNamara, interviews with J. Edgar Hoover—these would be the artifacts of the new art movement—Camp was out and Shit was in.

Well, the President contemplating this perspective could not be altogether happy. "The Great Society is a dud," was his lament. "I don't even have an issue with which to slow down the Nigras and their Rights."

The President believed very much in image. He believed the history which made the headlines each day was more real to the people than the events themselves. It was not the Negro movement that possessed the real importance, it was the Movement's ability to get space in the papers. That ability was equaled only by the President's ability to attach himself to the image of civil rights. But his ability to control the image, even put it down where necessary, was hampered by one fact. In the Great Society there was no movement, program, plan or ideal which was even remotely as dramatic as the civil-rights movement. So the civil-rights movement was going to crowd everything else out of the newspapers. There was going to be no way to control the Negro Movement, and no way to convince the Negro Movement that their victory was due to his particular attentions. You can never convince a movement of your power unless you can send them back after you have called them forth. So the President needed another issue. Then it came to the President.

Hot damn. Vietnam.

Vietnam, that little old country which had been under his nose all these years. Things were getting too quiet in Vietnam. If there was one thing hotter than Harlem in the summer, it was air raids on rice paddies and napalm on red gooks. Now he had a game. When the war got too good, and everybody was giving too much space to that, he could always tell the Nigras it was good time to be marching on the White House; when they got a little too serious he could bring back Vietnam. He could even make all those Barry Goldwater rednecks and state troopers happy—that was a happy nation, when everybody had something going for them. The Nigras had their civil rights and the rednecks could be killing gooks. Yes, thought the President, his friends and associates were correct in their estimate of him as a genius. Hot damn. Vietnam. The President felt like the only stud in a whorehouse on a houseboat.

Ladies and gentlemen, you will notice that up to this point, I have offered little in the way of closely reasoned quiet argument. I did observe for myself that in the discussions about Vietnam which took place last Saturday in Washington, and were seen by many of us on television, there was an abundance of rational arguments advanced for our escalation in Vietnam and an equal abundance of equally rational arguments against our involvement there.

Well, so far you have received no rational arguments from me today and you are not likely to receive many more as we go on. I believe our present situation in Vietnam is so irrational that any attempt to deal with it logically is illogical in the way surrealism is illogical, and rational political discussion of Adolf Hitler's motives was illogical and then obscene. Bombing a country at the same time you are offering it aid is as morally repulsive as beating up a kid in an alley and stopping to ask for a kiss. Reading the papers these days is a nightmare of unrequited love. If one's country lives like a woman in some part of the unconscious dream life of each of us, if beneath all our criticisms and detestations of America's vulgarity, misuse of power, and sheer pompous stupidity there has been still some optimistic love affair with the secret potentialities of this nation, some buried unvoiced faith that the nature of America was finally good, and not evil, well, that faith has taken a pistol whipping in the last months. The romance seems not even tragic or doomed, but dirty and misplaced.

Still, let me assume there is some point in trying to be reasonable about Vietnam even if it is only to discover that there is no logic in the situation. But let me at least make one straightforward attempt to understand what transpires there. I will, however, insist that the logic we employ runs close to the vein of theological argument, for we must try to speak rationally about a mystery.

Since any interpretation which seeks to justify our role in Vietnam on legal grounds is criminal—since we have no legal justification to be in the country; we are in fact there (as many of you doubtless know already) in violation of the Treaty of the Geneva Conference of 1954 which we were pledged not to obstruct—the only positive argument for our presence is that while we are illegally in Vietnam we are there at least to fight Communism.

Well, that is a large question. It is part of a large mystery. We may leave the largest parts of it for last. What may properly concern us first are the arguments and complexes of argument which revolve around the domino theory. Vietnam, says this much discussed theory, is a domino, supporting all the other dominoes of Southeast Asia. This is, of course, argument with the aid of metaphor, argument by image. But metaphors have curious mechanics. There is much dispute about their properties. Edgar Snow, for example, would argue that the dominoes of Southeast Asia are already falling. Insofar as they are dominoes, Indonesia has fallen, and Cambodia. Both nations recognize the Viet Cong as the legitimate government of South Vietnam. Burma gives guarantees to China not to give bases to any U.S. forces. India and Pakistan oppose a U.S. invasion of North Vietnam. Japan makes known its desire not to fight, de Gaulle excludes French aid, no NATO power promises support for a wider war.

The suspicion must begin that we are not protecting a position of connected bastions so much as we are trying to conceal the fact that the bastions are just about gone—they are not dominoes, but sand castles, and a tide of nationalism is on the way in. It is curious foreign policy to use metaphors in defense of a war; when the metaphors are critically imprecise, it is a swindle.

It is worse than that. The escalation in February began immediately after the Viet Cong attacked our air base near Pleiku, and killed seven American soldiers. In retaliation for this attack, or using the attack as our pretext for an offensive we had already planned, the Air Force proceeded—for the first time—to bomb areas over the Seventeenth Parallel in North Vietnam. It is, if we are to use metaphors, it is as if you and I have a small street fight on a city block. You catch me by surprise, you win, and I choose to come back with my gang and stick a plastic bomb on your house. Your maid loses a hand in the explosion; your friend, paying a visit, is blown to bits. I send flowers to the funeral, and a card offering my services as a fire-insurance adjuster. Is it possible the ideology of the Communists is being opposed by the spirit of the Cosa Nostra?

Let me list another difficulty to fighting Communism in Vietnam. It is that the communism of the Viet Cong is attached to the local nationalism. With the exception of a few dedicated career soldiers, however, the average American in Vietnam is not much interested in the future of Asia. The freedom-loving spirit of our experts in Saigon has about as much real comprehension of the life of the Asian peasant as the President of the Hilton Hotels Incorporated is on talking terms with his dishwashers at the Hilton Istanbul.

For those of us here, for close to 200,000,000 Americans, Vietnam is faceless. How many Americans have ever visited that country? Who can say which language is spoken there, or what industries might exist, or even what the country looks like? We do not care. We are not interested in the Vietnamese. If we were to fight a war with the inhabitants of the planet of Mars there would be more emotional participation by the people of America than there is even now for our share of the war in Vietnam. Until recently, until February of this year, South Vietnam could have fallen and most of us would not have known nor cared particularly if the territory acquired by the Viet Cong were as big as Brooklyn or as big as the state of Texas. Never in our history has so portentous a war been accelerated in a place which means so little to Americans. Therefore we must admit that we confront a mystery. Which is: why are we already thus involved in a combat which is potentially huge, yet empty of emotional meaning?

The only answer which makes sense is that we are in this war to drive matters to a military climax, we are escalating the war in Vietnam, we are bombing North Vietnam, as the first steps in a sequence which is aimed to destroy the nuclear plant of China. But, if escalation carries up to the summits and abysses of such a moment, then the odds are large that an atomic war will also be upon us. Civilization as we know it would be gone. It is possible all life as we know it would be gone. So we are back to the mystery. Only now it is worse. It asks us to explain why all life would be destroyed for a war in a country we do not care about.

The ill of civilization is that it is removed from nature—disproportions thrive everywhere. The war in Vietnam is just such a monstrous disproportion. We are present at a mystery. All monstrous disproportion conceals a mystery or an insanity. If a man suffering from a fever decides to cure it by walking through fire, we must say he has either a secret motive or is insane.

Perhaps President Johnson has a secret motive.

I do not speak of the desire to bomb the atomic works of China as his secret motive. That desire is, for one thing, public—William Buckley was writing in *National Review* about his desire for such an act a month before the first big February air raids on North Vietnam were begun. Indeed, a large part of the Pentagon has been obsessed with similar desires since 1946. For twenty years Congressmen have been standing up in Congress to read speeches written by War Department officials which exhort America to destroy the Soviet Union by atom bomb before the Soviet Union becomes too strong. That desire has never ceased. *We are a conservative property-loving nation obsessed with the passion to destroy other nations' property.*

So one would not speak of the impulse to bomb the nuclear industry of China as a secret motive. That is a public motive. It is merely not overpublicized. Not yet. If President Johnson has a secret motive, it would have to be then of another sort. Most strong motives are finally psychological—money or power is required to satisfy some imbalance in ourselves.

So President Johnson's motive in escalating the war in Vietnam may be psychic in its nature. This assumes of course that the prime mover in the new war in Vietnam is precisely the President, it assumes that Vietnam is not the unhappy expression of vast inevitable historic forces too large for any man; no, to the contrary this premise supposes flat-out that there was a choice in Vietnam, and one man, balanced at the fulcrum of power between the Pentagon on one side and his liberal support on the other, decided to accelerate the war.

So it is a thesis which would say that the mystery of Vietnam revolves around the mystery of Lyndon Johnson's personality.

To ferret one's way into the recesses of that mysterious and explosive personality is an activity which would give pause to many. It gives pause to me. He is after all a very intelligent man. He is doubtless more intelligent than you or me. He is certainly most intelligent about getting his way. He is also a complex man, and his sides are many. The only side of him which is evident to all is that he is famished for popularity.

At the Democratic Convention in Atlantic City in 1964, not one picture of the President was hung behind the speaker's rostrum, but two. They were each forty feet high. So said his public relations. These photographs, however, looked like they were eighty feet high, high as an eight-story motel. They dominated every moment of the Convention. They spoke of an ego which had the voracity of a beast.

At that convention, there were other clues to the mystery of the President's personality. It was apparent he had vast affection for the powers of television, an affection so huge it shrank from any pretext that he might have equally large affection for his delegates. They were left marooned for the most part behind two huge television towers.

Perhaps a fifth of the delegates were seated in front of those towers. The rest were installed behind. From nearly every position behind the television towers, it was not possible to have a direct view of the speaker on the rostrum. One had to watch him on television. Delegates began to fight for a seat which gave them a good view rather than a poor view of the television set.

The Republican Convention in San Francisco which nominated Barry Goldwater had been not quite so orderly as a rodeo. The Democratic Convention was cancerous—the electronic machines were more crucial than the men.

It was evident that the Establishment was in the service of a most subtle and modern tyrant, an Emperor, to whom all Mafias, legit and illegit, all syndicates, unions, guilds, corporations and institutions . . . could bend their knee. The Establishment had a new leader, a mighty Caesar had arisen, Lyndon Johnson was his name, all hail, Caesar.

Caesar gave promise to unify the land. But at what a cost. For if the ideology were liberal, the methodology was total—to this political church would come Adlai Stevenson and Frank Sinatra, the President of U.S. Steel and the President of the Steel Worker's Union, the CIO and the C.I.A., Martin Luther King and the Pentagon.

Even before the election, a question was there. If we all worked to beat Barry, and got behind Lyndon and pushed, radicals and moderate Republicans, Negroes and Southern liberals, college professors and Cosa Nostra, café society and Beatniks-for-Johnson, were we all then going down a liberal superhighway into the deepest swamp of them all?

For Johnson was intelligent enough to run a total land, he had vast competence, no vision, and the heart to hold huge power, he had the vanity of a modern dictator. Under Johnson we could move from the threat of total war to war itself with nothing to prevent it; the anti-Goldwater forces which might keep the country too divided to go to war would now be contained within Johnson.

That was a final description of the Democratic Convention, and still it missed the point. Because the final unhappy point was that Barry Goldwater had established Johnson's power with such total perfection that the man elected had come closer to total control of America than any President before him. What could increase the fear is that Johnson might not be a whole man so much as he was alienated, a modern man, a member in a most curious sense of a minority group.

Lyndon Baines Johnson a member of a minority group? It is an extraordinary forcing of category. It is obvious some other notion is intended than a description of a Negro, a Jew, a Mexican, a Nisei, or a Puerto Rican. Will it make sense if we say Lyndon Johnson is alienated? Alienated from what? you may ask.

But one must speak first of alienation, that intellectual category which would take you through many a turn of the mind in its attempt to explain that particular corrosive sensation so many of us feel in the chest and the gut so much of the time, that sense of the body growing empty within, of the psyche pierced by a wound whose dimensions keep opening, that unendurable conviction that one is hollow, displaced, without a single identity at one's center. I quote Eric Josephson:

> It [alienation] has been used to refer to an extraordinary variety of psychosocial disorders, including loss of self, anxiety states, anomie, despair, depersonalization, rootlessness, apathy, social disorganization, loneliness, atomization, powerlessness, meaninglessness, isolation, pessimism and the loss of belief or values. Among the groups . . . described as alienated . . . are women, industrial workers, white-collar workers, migrant workers, artists, suicides, mentally disturbed, addicts, the aged, the young generation as a whole, juvenile delinquents in particular, voters, nonvoters, consumers, audiences of mass media, sex deviates, victims of prejudice and discrimination, the prejudiced, bureaucrats, political radicals, the physically handicapped, immigrants, exiles, vagabonds and recluses.

What a huge and comprehensive list. Is anything to be gained by adding to it the name of Lyndon Johnson? You may still ask—what is he alienated from? The

Asian peasant? The dishwasher at the Istanbul Hilton? Of course not. You cannot be alienated unless you wish to participate. Lyndon Johnson does not wish to share a bowl of rice with an Asian peasant.

How then is he alienated, and from what? And I say to you in no disrespect and much uneasiness that it is possible he is alienated from his own clear sanity, that his mind has become a consortium of monstrous disproportions of pictures of himself in duplicate forty feet high, eighty feet high. Lyndon Johnson is not alienated from power, he is the most powerful man in the United States, but he is alienated from judgment, he is close to an imbalance which at worst could tip the world from orbit.

The legitimate fear we can feel is vast. Because there was a time when Lyndon Johnson could have gotten out of Vietnam very quietly—the image had been prepared for our departure—we heard of nothing but the corruption of the South Vietnam government and the professional cowardice of the South Vietnamese generals. We read how a Viet Cong army of 40,000 soldiers was whipping a government army of 400,000. We were told in our own newspapers how the Viet Cong armed themselves with American weapons brought to them by deserters or captured in battle with government troops; we knew it was an empty war for our side, Lyndon Johnson made no attempt to hide that from us. He may even have encouraged the press in this direction for a time. Abruptly, he dropped escalation into our daily life.

There is fear we must feel. It was not the action of a rational man, but a man driven by need, a gambler who fears that once he stops, once he pulls out of the game, his heart will rupture from tension. You see, Lyndon Johnson is a member of a minority group and so he must have action. But now let me explain. A member of a minority group is—if we are to speak existentially—not a man who is a member of a category, a Negro or a Jew, but rather a man who feels his existence in a particular way. It is in the very form or context of his existence to live with two opposed notions of himself.

What characterizes a member of a minority group is that he is forced to see himself as both exceptional and insignificant, marvelous and awful, good and evil. So far as he listens to the world outside he is in danger of going insane. The only way he may relieve the unendurable tension which surrounds any sense of his own identity is to define his nature by his own acts; discover his courage or cowardice by actions which engage his courage; discover his judgment by judging; his loyalty by being tested; his originality by creating. A Negro or a Texan, a President or a housewife, is by this definition a member of a minority group if he contains two opposed notions of himself at the same time. What characterizes the sensation of being a member of a minority group is that one's emotions are forever locked in the chains of ambivalence—the expression of an emotion forever releasing its opposite—the ego in perpetual transit from the tower to the dungeon and back again. By this definition nearly everyone in America is a member of a minority group, alienated from the self by a double sense of identity and so at the mercy of a self which demands action and more action to define the most rudimentary borders of identity. It is a demand which will either kill a brave man or force him to grow, but when a coward is put in need of such action he tears the wings off flies.

The great fear that lies upon America is not that Lyndon Johnson is privately close to insanity so much as that he is the expression of the near insanity of most of us, and his need for action is America's need for action; not brave action, but action; any kind of action; any move to get the motors going. A future death of the spirit lies close and heavy upon American life, a cancerous emptiness at the center which calls for a circus.

The country is in disease. It has been in disease for a

long time. There has been nothing in our growth which was organic. We never solved our depression, we merely went to war back in 1941, and going to war never won it, not in our own minds, not as men, no, we won it but as sources of supply; we still do not know that we are equal to the Russians. We won a war but we did not really win it, not in the secret of our sleep.

So we have not really had a prosperity, we have had fever. We have grown rich because of one fact with two opposite interpretations: There has been a cold war. It has been a cold war which came because Communism was indeed a real threat to our freedom, or a cold war which came because capitalism could not survive without an economy geared to war; or is it both—who can know? Who can really know?

The center of our motive is an enigma—is this country extraordinary or accursed? And when we think of Communism, we have to wonder if we are accursed. For we have not even found our Communist threat. We have had a secret police organization and an invisible government large enough by now to occupy the moon, we have hunted Communists from the top of the Time-Life Building to the bottom of the Collier mine, we have not found that many, not that many, and we have looked like Keystone Cops.

We have even had a Negro Revolution in which we did not believe. We have had it, yes we have had it, because (in the true penury of our motive) we could not afford to lose votes in Africa and India, South America and Japan, Vietnam, the Philippines, name any impoverished place: we have been running in a world election against the collective image of the Russ, and so we have had to give the black man his civil rights or Africa was so much nearer to Marx. But there has not been much like love in the civil rights. We have never been too authentic. No.

We have had a hero. He was a young good-looking man with a beautiful wife, and he won the biggest poker game we ever played, the only real one—we lived for a week ready to die in a nuclear war. Whether we liked it or not. But he won. It was our one true victory in all these years, our moment; so the young man began to inspire a subtle kind of love. His strength proved stronger than we knew. Suddenly he was dead, and we were in grief.

But then came a trial which was worse. For the assassin, or the man who had been arrested but was not the assassin—we will never know, not really—was killed before our sight. In the middle of the funeral came an explosion on the porch. Now, we were going mad. It took more to make a nation go mad than any separate man, but we had taken miles too much. Certainties had shattered.

Our country was fearful, half-mad, inauthentic—it needed a war or it needed a purge. Bile was stirring in the pits of the national conscience and little to oppose it but a lard of guilt cold as the most mediocre of our needs. We took formal public steps toward a great society, that great society of computers and pills, of job aptitudes and bad architecture, of psychoanalysis, superhighways, astronauts, vaccinations, and a Peace Corps, that great society where nothing but frozen corn would be sold in the smallest towns of Iowa, where censorship would disappear but every image would be manipulated from birth to death.

Something in the buried animal of modern life grew bestial at the thought of this Great Society—the most advanced technological nation of the civilized world was the one now closest to blood, to shedding the blood and burning the flesh of Asian peasants it had never seen. The Pentagon had been kept on a leash for close to twenty years. Presidents so mediocre in their talents as Truman and Eisenhower had kept the military from dominating the nation.

But Johnson did not.

Out of the pusillanimities or the madnesses of his secret sleep he came to a decision to listen to the advice of his military machine, that congeries of Joint Forces, War Department and C.I.A. which had among other noteworthy achievements planned the Bay of Pigs. It was now planning its escalation in Vietnam. And Johnson was in accord. The body of a consummate politician took recognition as it slept that the nation was in disease and its only cure—out where the drums were beating and the fires would not cease—was to introduce us to the first anxieties of a war whose end might be limitless. Miserable nation cursed with a computer for its commander-in-chief, a computer with an ego so vain it could not bear the memory of his predecessor and the power he had had for a week when the world was on the edge of nuclear war.

Yet, there still remains the largest question of them all. It is the question of fighting Communism. Look, you may say, is it not possible that with all our diseases admitted, we are still less malignant than the Communists, we are the defense of civilization and they, not us, are the barbarians who would destroy it? If that is true, then—as some of you may argue—the logic must be faced, the Chinese must be stopped, we must bomb their bomb. And I would argue in return that neither capitalism nor Communism is the defense of civilization but that they are rather each—in their own way—malignancies upon the spirit of honest adventure and open inquiry which developed across the centuries from primitive man to the Renaissance, and that therefore there is no man alive who can say at this point which system will perpetrate the greater harm upon mankind.

But this I do know: existence alters the nature of essence. An unjust war, an unnatural war, an obscene war brutalizes what is best in a nation and encourages every horror to rise from its sewer.

The Communists could capture every nation on earth but our own and we would still be safe if our intention were clean. Yes. For in the vertiginous terrors of nuclear warfare rests one rock ledge of safety—in future no great power can ever be destroyed without destroying every other power which would attack it. As a corollary no philosophy of government can occupy nine-tenths of the globe without being altered to its roots. The health of Communism, its secret necessity, is an enemy external to itself; war is indeed the health of the totalitarian state, and peace is its disease. Communism would split and rupture and war upon itself if ever it occupied most of the world, for then it would have to solve the problems of most of the world and those problems are not soluble in the rigidity of a system. Like all top-heavy structures the greatest danger to Communism lies in its growth. Prosperity is its poison, for without a sense of crisis, Communism cannot discipline its future generations. Attack from capitalism is Communism's transfusion of blood. So our war against Communism, most particularly our war against Communism in Asia, is the death of our future. I am going to quote Senator Wayne Morse:

> We shall win one military victory after another; we shall destroy cities, industrial installations, and nuclear installations; we shall kill by the millions. . . . That course of action will lay a foundation of hatred on the part of the colored races of the world against the American people. In due time, those installations will be rebuilt . . . on the foundation of intense hatred by Asians for the people of the United States. That hatred will even be inherited by generations of American boys and girls fifty, seventy-five, one hundred, yes, two hundred years from now.

I say: end the cold war. Pull back our boundaries to what we can defend and to what wishes to be defended. Let Communism come to those countries it will come to. Let us not use up our substance trying to hold onto nations which are poor, underdeveloped, and bound to us only by the depths of their hatred for us. We cannot equal the effort the Communists make in such places. We are not dedicated in that direction. We were not born to do that. We have had our frontier already. We cannot be excited to our core, our historic core, by the efforts of new underdeveloped nations to expand their frontiers.

Let the Communists flounder in the countries they acquire. The more countries they hold, the less supportable will become the contradictions of their ideology, the more bitter will grow the divisions in their internal interest, and the more enormous their desire to avoid a war which could only destroy the economies they will have developed at such vast labor and such vast waste. Let it be their waste, not ours. Our mission may be not to raise the level of minimum subsistence in the world so much as it may be to show the first features and promise of that incalculable renaissance men may someday enter.

I have one set of remarks more to make. They concern practical suggestions. I have been visionary in my demands. For it is visionary in 1965 to ask of America that it return to isolationism. No, this country wishes to have an empire. The grimmest truth may be that half of America at least must be not unwilling to have a war in Vietnam. Otherwise Lyndon Johnson could not have made his move, since Lyndon Johnson never in his life has dreamed of moving against a majority.

Let us then insist on this—it is equally visionary, but it is at least visionary in a military way and we are talking to militarists—let us say that if we are going to have a war with the Viet Cong, let it be a war of foot soldier against foot soldier. If we wish to take a strange country away from strangers, let us at least be strong enough and brave enough to defeat them on the ground. Our Marines, some would say, are the best soldiers in the world. The counter-argument is that native guerrillas can defeat any force of a major power man to man.

Let us, then, fight on fair grounds. Let us say to Lyndon Johnson, to Monstrous McNamara, and to the generals on the scene—fight like men, go in man to man against the Viet Cong. But first, call off the Air Force. They prove nothing except that America is coterminous with the Mafia. Let us win man to man or lose man to man, but let us cease pulverizing people whose faces we have never seen.

But of course we will not cease. Nor will we ever fight man to man against poor peasants. Their vision of existence might be more ferocious and more determined than our own. No, we would rather go on as the most advanced monsters of civilization pulverizing instinct with our detonations, our State Department experts in their little bow ties, and our bombs.

Only, listen, Lyndon Johnson, you have gone too far this time. You are a bully with an Air Force, and since you will not call off your Air Force, there are young people who will persecute you back. It is a little thing, but it will hound you into nightmares and endless corridors of nights without sleep, it will hound you. For listen—this is only one of the thousand things they will do. They will print up little pictures of you, Lyndon Johnson, the size of postcards, the size of stamps, and some will glue these pictures to walls and posters and telephone booths and billboards—I do not advise it, I would tell these students not to do it to you, but they will. They will find places to put these pictures. They will want to paste your picture, Lyndon Johnson, on a postcard, and send it to you. Some will send it to your advisers. Some will send these pictures to men and women at other schools. These pictures will be sent everywhere. These pictures will be pasted up everywhere, upside down.

Silently, without a word, the photograph of you, Lyndon Johnson, will start appearing everywhere, upside down. Your head will speak out—even to the peasant in Asia—it will say that not all Americans are unaware of your monstrous vanity, overweening piety, and doubtful motive. It will tell them that we trust our President so little, and think so little of him that we see his picture everywhere upside down.

You, Lyndon Johnson, will see those pictures up everywhere upside down, four inches high and forty feet high; you, Lyndon Baines Johnson, will be coming up for air everywhere upside down. Everywhere, upside down. Everywhere. Everywhere.

And those little pictures will tell the world what we think of you and your war in Vietnam. Everywhere, upside down. Everywhere, everywhere.

A Happy Solution to Vietnam: From a Partisan Review Symposium

Statement by the EDITORS of Partisan Review

We do not think that the present or past policies of the United States in Vietnam are good ones, and we lament the increasing and often self-defeating military involvements which those policies require. We have not heard of any alternative policy, however, which would actually lead to a negotiated peace in Vietnam or promote the interests of the people of Southeast Asia. This is not to say that the critics of American actions in Vietnam are therefore required to propose a specific policy. But it is not unfair to ask that their criticism be based on more than the apolitical assumption that power politics, the Cold War, and Communists are merely American inventions. Most of the criticism of Administration policy at the teach-ins and in the various petitions we have been asked to sign has simply taken for granted that everything would be fine if only the Yanks would go home. It is not clear whether these critics think Asia will not go Communist if American troops are withdrawn or whether they don't care. Nor is it clear whether they really care what happens to the people of Southeast Asia so long as America gets out.

The creation of a world in which free societies can exist should be the goal of any international policy. Our policies in Vietnam do not promote that end, even though it is claimed that they are justified because the United States is preventing a Communist take-over. Nor do the policies of North Vietnam, Communist China or the Viet Cong, however they are explained. As for our policies in the Dominican Republic, they cannot be justified even on the grounds that the United States is preventing a Communist coup. They are a disastrous violation of any democratic principle, a violation likely to alienate the people of South America, especially the youth, or even drive them into an alliance with precisely those Communist forces our government claims to be combatting.

The fiasco in the Dominican Republic illustrates, we think, what is basically wrong with our policies. So long as we are not able to understand the political and economic problems of rapidly changing countries, and to support democratic revolutionary groups, we are bound to find ourselves in a false dilemma, always having to decide at the last minute whether to intervene, as though that were the only solution. Military action can be a substitute for political foresight only if we propose to police the whole world, and to imagine that we can do that is to lack even hindsight.

Obviously the time has come for some new thinking. And some of it has to be about what's happening in different parts of the world, regardless of what the United States does or fails to do.

ELEANOR CLARK	STEVEN MARCUS
MARTIN DUBERMAN	WILLIAM PHILIPS
IRVING HOWE	NORMAN PODHORETZ
ALFRED KAZIN	RICHARD POIRIER
BERNARD MALAMUD	RICHARD SCHLATTER

Mailer's Reply

Three cheers, lads. Your words read like they were written in milk and milk of magnesia. Still, your committee didn't close shop until close after this extraordinary remark: "The time has come for new thinking." Cha cha cha.

We will do our best to serve. First let it be established—as is done nowhere in the statement—that the editors support the war in Vietnam. For after all somber dubiety, and every reservation, we are left back at the beginning—"we have not heard of any alternative policy which would actually lead to a negotiated peace in Vietnam . . ." But to provide alternative policy, people's front must remind you how the war in Vietnam goes on. The following statistics are furnished by Ho Chi Minh. No, indeed they are not. They are from a statement by Robert McNamara before the Senate Subcommittee on Department of Defense Appropriations and appeared August 5 in the *Times*.

> *We now estimate the hard core of Viet Cong strength at some 70,000 men. . . . In addition, they have some 90,000 to 100,000 irregulars and some 30,000 in their political cadres, i.e., tax collectors, propagandists, etc. We have also identified at least three battalions of the regular North Vietnamese Army, and there are probably considerably more.*

At least three battalions! That is to say, at most 3,000 North Vietnamese. If the battalions are understrength the figure may be half the size. But, continue with McNamara:

> *At the same time the government of South Vietnam has found it increasingly difficult to make a commensurate increase in the size of its own forces, which now stand at about 545,000 men, including the regional and local defense forces but excluding the national police.*
> *Clearly, the time has come when the people of*

South Vietnam need more help from us and other nations if they are to retain their freedom and independence.

We have already responded to that need with some 75,000 United States military personnel, including some combat units. This number will be raised to 125,000 almost immediately. . . . But, more help will be needed in the months ahead . . . to back up the hard-pressed army of South Vietnam.

"Responded to that need." McNamara is the best thing to come along since Elmer Gantry. Let me give a little more. From a news conference, two months earlier, June 16. "In 1964 alone . . . about 10,000 men were brought from North Vietnam to fight in South Vietnam." Whereas in 1965 we will only bring in 100,000 Americans.

Well, McNamara is on record (again June 5) about ratios:

The South Vietnamese regular and paramilitary forces facing the Viet Cong total something in excess of 500,000 men. And they're facing, as I mentioned, about 165,000 guerrillas, a ratio something on the order of 4 to 1 [sic]. That's considerably less than is recognized as required to effectively deal with guerrillas.

The Pentagon's argument is that a government army must outnumber guerrillas in the ratio of ten to one if they are to hold the countryside and administer it well. But in South Vietnam, it happens to be the Viet Cong which holds most of the countryside and proceeds each year with its 30,000 political troops, its "tax collectors," to occupy and *govern* more land than the year before, against an army—depending on how you count—from three to eight times its own size. Only an army fighting a war in which the agricultural population is near to unanimous behind them (or near to unanimous *against* the South Vietnamese) can do thus well. Can you conceive of another explanation?

Now, our entrance in force will shift this imbalance. It will certainly prolong the war: It will also shift the moral center of America. I quote a piece by Charles Mohr, *New York Times*, August 9.

> *The attempts by public information officers to deemphasize the importance of civilian deaths and the burning of village huts at the hands of United States marines have not been duplicated by senior Marine Corps officers here. . . .*
>
> *General Walt quickly conceded last week that on one military operation his troops had killed three children and a woman. He expressed deep regret. The marines have also conceded that at least 51 huts were burned on another operation.*
>
> *A Vietnamese observer who discussed the incident shook his head and said, "The 10-year-old children who witnessed their village being burned are the ones who at 15 will take up rifles for the Viet Cong and fight to the death."*

If World War II was like *Catch-22*, this war will be like *Naked Lunch*. Lazy Dogs, and bombing raids from Guam. Marines with flame throwers. Jungle gotch in the gonorrhea and South Vietnamese girls doing the Frug. South Vietnamese fighter pilots "dressed in black flying suits and lavender scarves" (*The New York Times*).

Add a little to this: let us recognize that we are in a war commanded by a President whose deepest and tenderest emotion seems to be directed toward his own boils and rash. Public life, he forever reminds us, is cruel to public figures. There is a catch in his voice as he makes such remarks. He is happier with the balm of paid prose. Remember Jack Valenti's words last June?

> *. . . The new President sat there, like a large*

gray stone mountain, untouched by fear or frenzy, from whom everyone began to draw strength. And suddenly, as though the darkness of the cave confided its fears to the trail of light growing larger as it banished the night, the nation's breath, held tightly in its breast, began to ease, and across the land the people began to move again. The President, thank the Good Lord, has extra glands . . .

Well, we are literary politicians—we know what to deduce from such a style. It is of course possible that Johnson is no more Machiavellian than any major gent. But it is also possible there are disproportions to the man. Should one think of Macbeth or Uriah Heep? Valenti's prose opens the drawer to some fine horrors.

Besides, our present policy in Vietnam which the editors gloomily, glumly, *inevitably* (they are liberals after all) proceed to defend, is in fact a policy which is the antithesis of the previous policy. The previous policy, the policy in effect just before escalation, was the unstated policy to lose quietly in Vietnam, and get out. There were better countries to defend. It was a practical policy which might in practice have worked or not worked, but the new policy, the policy of escalation, is a radical policy; it is a policy of the radical right, right out of the naked-lunching heart of the WASP in his fevers. For no one can know, not even Johnson himself, if escalation is our best defense against Communism, a burning of orphans to save future orphans, or if the war is the first open expression of a totalitarian Leviathan which will yet dominate everything still not nailed down in American life: art, civil rights, student rebellions, public criticism in mass media. We may be living in the shadow of the biggest hype of them all, our last con game: red-neck dynamics; liberal rhetoric. There is the ineradicable suspicion that liberal rhetoric was conceived by Satan to kiss the behind of something unspeakable.

Recapitulate: we have an accelerating war whose justification by the Establishment is that there is final and historic honor in fighting an unpopular war if the cause is grave and just. That is one possibility. I cannot say with certainty that this cannot be so. But, in turn, who of you can say with greater certainty that the President is not insomniac in his vanities; and that the nation is not insane with Christ, Pop art, Fiberglass, moonshots, race riots, and Hilton Hotel architecture?

The editors ask for a counterpolicy. I offer it. It is to get out of Asia. A Communist bureaucrat is not likely to do any more harm or destroy any more spirit than a wheeler-dealer, a platoon sergeant, or a corporation executive overseas. We have our malignancies, Communism has theirs. Whether capitalism or Communism will finally prove more monstrous is out of my capacity, or yours, to guess, but it is perhaps evident to both of us that Communism cannot grow without exploding its own form. If Marx's vision conceivably left room for some minds to remain fertile, Stalin fixed a process of petrifying thought until post-Marxian thought is now an ideology which cannot change remotely so fast as reality and so must be insulated from reality by war. War is the health of Communist ideology, whereas peace and the abrupt *strifeless* acquisition of backward countries is a nightmare to ideology. For backward lands which are not used up by war have wealths of primitive lore with which to mine the foundations of ideology.

Consider: a quiet end to the war in Vietnam by the agency of a quiet victory of the Viet Cong might have given the world one more backward Red nation with still one more tenacious home-grown stubborn little Communist party at odds with China and in intrigue with Russia, thereby dividing world Communism somewhat further. Now, grace of escalation, we have the likelihood that any future alignment between Russia and China will be a little more on China's terms; and for China vis-à-vis North Vietnam (which countries formerly shared the distaste of England and Ireland for one another) we have accelerated a collaboration.

Of course all those Washington Pistols, all those keepers of the chalice, will talk about India falling if we "get out." And there will be tears in Joe Alsop's eyes. Of course. And I, of course, don't know. Maybe if Vietnam falls, so, too, falls India. So to what? Do we really want India? Do we desire it? Do we desire deeply to die of indigestion? Might it not be simpler if the Communists die of the same disease? But, in fact, might they not hesitate? For, the more Communism grows at a vertiginous rate, the more it must suffer from vertigo. It is like America. So, Communism might even come to recognize that Communism in possession of three-quarters of the world cannot have any world. The world is now balanced on too much. So Communism might even retreat before the terror of ideology being lost in the jungles and grasslands. What if Communism is not an unstoppable force—but is rather (since we can only approach comprehension of these matters by metaphor) a giant with a specific neurosis that it will awake one morning on the compulsion to eat its own limbs. I say: throw Asia open to Communism. The meal will not be taken. If it is, we will even live to see the Communists destroy themselves. It is certain we cannot destroy them. We, like them, can only eat upon ourselves—this is after all a century for perverts and Reds.

But, believe me not. Take the alternative: might against might. Our troops against theirs—no, of course we are not serious. Even Barry Goldwater knows that we can't defeat the Communists militarily, not even with atom bombs. How could we occupy what was left? The cost of rebuilding it. The boredom for America's young couples—obliged to live out their early married years in rebuilt cities in Siberia and Mongolia. All the ration stamps. All the ghosts of 900,000,000 atomized corpses. No, we don't really want to defeat Communism militarily. But we do want to stand up man to man, stick to stick. If we cannot stop Communism by the force of our armies, we could of course pitch in to help create a world society of military and bureaucratic behemoths who will nibble at one another forever in small dribbled-out land wars while totalitarian tissues fill up with the waters of political edema, yes, just as our good prophet and saint, George Orwell, was dying to remind us.

Look to the other side. To absolute isolation. If all the world were Communist but America, America would be militarily in no poor position. We could still fight the rest of the world if we chose to. That is the paradoxical nature of nuclear war. But it is doubtful if Communism would then have the impetus to fight anything. Can anyone—even Dwight—conceive of Communism remaining unruptured in its cast-concrete heart on a diet of English lords, French intellectuals, Italian lovers, African drums, Zen, Yoga, pot, the New Wave, Pop art, Camp—the prospect invites occupation. "Come on in, honey, this hustler's got enough diseases to keep you dripping all your days."

That, of course, is not programmatic, I would assure you. The world will never go to the Communists because they will never get through Asia, Africa and South America. They will bog down in the cultural swamps of our imperial wastes; their minds will rupture in the new pressures on their cast-iron formulations. For Communism contends with an impossibility: one cannot bring a modern economy to a backward country in a hurry, bulldozing through a wealth of primitive lore, without manufacturing a horde of mass men. And mass man is equal to the plague. Nihilistic, he is addicted to modern communications. Shakespeare, comic books, motors, electronics, jazz, plastic, fucking, frozen food, are all equal grit to his Disposeall. He consumes whatever culture is before him and is the secret enemy of any government which presumes to rule him. His secret allegiance is always to the enemy. So let the Communists rather than the

Americans do the manufacturing of mass men in backward lands, in order that the secret allegiance of those new mass men be exactly to us.

For there is one way in which the West is superior to the Communists, and without that superiority, mass man cannot live. Mass man is an insatiable man, a malignancy of directionless greed at the mercy of his secret addiction—which is art. No population ever on earth has loved art so much as mass man, for that is the only hope of his deliverance: that he may encounter some great art before he is dead. Only great art can penetrate into the tomb of the modern soul and bring a moment of cease to the backed-up murders of the modern heart. Here, on this violent spit, friends, is the place we are ahead in the Cold War. For our artists are better, our writers are better, our jazz musicians are better, our painters go further, our vision is more fierce, it explores more. It is relentless we almost dare to think. It may even prevail if we do not burn too many women and children fighting for Christ. Oh, Christ, what assholes be Americans.

Yet it may be too easy to end on this fine proud and strenuous moral note. For the sweet bloody truth is not so neat. If the Lord of the Snopes went to war in Vietnam because finally he didn't have the moral courage to try to solve an impossible mix of Camp, red-neck, civil rights, street violence, playboy pornography and all the glut which bugs our works, if Lyndon Johnson finally decided in his fine brain that only a war was going to get America off the pot (we were that mercilessly screwed to the john by fifty years of smelling our national armpit every time the truth rose up to kiss us) well, what he didn't realize was that the war in Vietnam was not going to serve as cloaca for our worst emotions but instead was going to up the ante and give us more Camp, more red-neck, more violence in the streets, more teen-age junkies, more polite society gone ape, more of everything else Lyndon was trying to ship overseas.

Still, with it all, confess it, Mailer, the country is now in good humor. A wild good humor—it has been the wildest summer in years from Watts to Easthampton; it has been wild. The truth is, maybe we need a war. It may be the last of the tonics. From Lydia Pinkham to Vietnam in sixty years, or bust. We're the greatest country ever lived for speeding up the time. So, let's do it right. Let's cease all serious war, kids. Let's leave Asia to the Asians. Let us, instead, have wars which are like happenings. Let us have them every summer. Let us buy a track of land in the Amazon, two hundred million acres will do, and throw in Marines and Seabees and Air Force, Scuba divers for the river bottom, motorcyclists for the mud-races, carrier pilots landing on bounce-all decks in typhoons, invite them all, the Chinks and the Aussies, the Frogs and the Gooks and the Wogs, the Wops and the Russkies, the Yugos, the Israelis, the Hindoos, the Pakistanis. We'll have war games with real bullets and real flame throwers, real hot-wire correspondents on the spot, TV with phone-in audience participation, amateur war-movie film contests for the soldiers, discotheques, Playboy Clubs, pictures of the corpses for pay TV, you know what I mean—let's get the hair on the toast for breakfast. So a write-in campaign (all of us) to King Corporation Exec Mr. Pres; let us tell him to get the boys back home by Christmas, back from Vietnam and up the Amazon for summer. Yours—readers—till the next happening.

Unless Vietnam is the happening. Could that be? Could that really be? Little old Vietnam just a happening? Cause if it is, Daddy Warbucks, couldn't we have the happening just with the Marines and skip all that indiscriminate roast tit and naked lunch, all those bombed-out civilian ovaries, Mr. J., Mr. L.B.J., Boss Man of Show Biz—I salute you in your White House Oval; I mean America will shoot all over the shithouse wall if this jazz goes on, Jim.

Farewell to Vietnam

As IS EVIDENT by now, the only explanation I can find for the war is that we are sinking into the swamps of a plague and the massacre of strange people seems to relieve this plague. If one were to take the patients in a hospital, give them guns and let them shoot on pedestrians down from hospital windows you may be sure you would find a few miraculous cures. So the national mood is bound to prosper from the war in Vietnam. For a time. Let us go back to our hospital patients. Some of them we see stripped to the waist, crying with joy as they fire off their machine-gun blast. All the light of the Lord is in their eye again. But not all can fire at once, and some on the sidelines throw up in sheer excitement, others are forced to eat from nervousness, others diddle in the slop, and *zap!* there went the first—the nice old man about to die has just bit the jugular of the nice old lady, and some are beginning to slide in the blood. And some are beginning to slide like snakes. Sellah, sellah—is it better to be a foul old Cannibal or a Christian dying of nausea?

Have you read these paperbacks from

CATCH-22 Joseph Heller 95c

SEVEN PILLARS OF WISDOM T. E. Lawrence 95c

THE LEANING TOWER and Other Stories Katherine Anne Porter 50c

IDIOTS FIRST Bernard Malamud 75c

THE NATURAL Bernard Malamud 75c

THE DEVIL'S ADVOCATE Morris L. West 60c

THE SHOES OF THE FISHERMAN Morris L. West 75c

THE GUNS OF AUGUST Barbara Tuchman 95c

THE ZIMMERMAN TELEGRAM Barbara Tuchman 60c

THE FEMININE MYSTIQUE Betty Friedan 95c

THE CAINE MUTINY Herman Wouk 95c

THE CITY BOY Herman Wouk 75c

BRIDESHEAD REVISITED Evelyn Waugh 75c

THE LOVED ONE Evelyn Waugh 50c

MOSQUITOES William Faulkner 60c

THE LIE Alberto Moravia 95c

THE EMBEZZLER Louis Auchincloss 75c

GO TELL IT ON THE MOUNTAIN James Baldwin 60c

THE FIRE NEXT TIME James Baldwin 50c

THE WHITE NILE Alan Moorehead 75c

THE BLUE NILE Alan Moorehead 60c

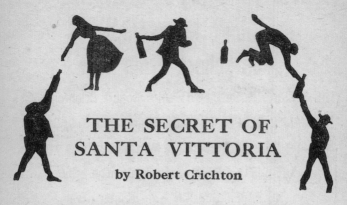

THE SECRET OF
SANTA VITTORIA

by Robert Crichton

THE NATION'S #1 BESTSELLER

From time immemorial the Italian hill town of Santa Vittoria had existed as a world unto itself, hostile to strangers, wholly involved in growing and making the fat black wine that was its glory and its lifeblood. As the Allied armies approached, the Germans sent an occupying force to claim the town's great treasure—one million bottles of wine. At this moment a leader emerged—the clownish wine merchant Bombolini. Behind him the town united, forgetting ancient feuds, lovers' rivalries, the division between aristocrat and peasant, pooling its energies and resources to outwit the invader.

"This brilliant novel should be celebrated with a fanfare of trumpets, with festivals in the streets." —*The New York Times*

"Crichton tells his story with grace, pace, warmth, and a wonderful free-reeling wit that skips among the vineyards like an inebriated billygoat." —*Time Magazine*

95¢

Don't Miss These Bestsellers From Dell

THE SECRET OF SANTA VITTORIA Robert Crichton   95c

GAMES PEOPLE PLAY Eric Berne M.D. $1.25

THE FIXER Bernard Malamud   95c

THE DIRTY DOZEN E. M. Nathanson   95c

THE PAPER DRAGON Evan Hunter   95c

TAI-PAN James Clavell   95c

THERE IS A RIVER: THE STORY OF EDGAR CAYCE
Thomas Sugrue   95c

I, A WOMAN Siv Holm   75c

A DANDY IN ASPIC Derek Marlowe   75c

AN ODOR OF SANCTITY Frank Yerby   95c

THE DOCTORS Martin L. Gross $1.25

PEDLOCK & SONS Stephen Longstreet   95c

THE MENORAH MEN Lionel Davidson   75c

CAPABLE OF HONOR Allen Drury $1.25

BILLION DOLLAR BRAIN Len Deighton   75c